RISE UP!
HOW YOU CAN JOIN THE FIGHT
AGAINST WHITE SUPREMACY

CRYSTAL M. FLEMING

Henry Holt and Company, *Publishers since 1866*

Henry Holt® is a registered trademark of Macmillan Publishing Group, LLC

120 Broadway, New York, NY 10271

mackids.com

Library of Congress Cataloging-in-Publication Data

Names: Fleming, Crystal Marie, 1981– author.

Title: Rise up! : how you can join the fight against racism / Crystal Fleming.

Other titles: How you can join the fight against racism

Description: First edition. | New York : Henry Holt and Company, 2020. | Includes
bibliographical references and index. | Audience: Ages 12 + | Summary: "An overview
of the roots and legacies of racial bias and white supremacy in the United States."—
Provided by publisher.

Identifiers: LCCN 2020007640 | ISBN 9781250226389 (hardcover)

Subjects: LCSH: Racism—United States—History—Juvenile literature. | United States—
Race relations—History—Juvenile literature.

Classification: LCC E184.A1 F5763 2020 | DDC 305.800973—dc23

LC record available at https://lccn.loc.gov/2020007640

Our books may be purchased in bulk for promotional, educational, or business use.
Please contact your local bookseller or the Macmillan Corporate and
Premium Sales Department at (800) 221-7945 ext. 5442 or by email at
MacmillanSpecialMarkets@macmillan.com.

First edition, 2021 / Designed by Liz Dresner

Printed in the United States of America

ISBN 978-1-250-22638-9 (hardcover)

1 3 5 7 9 10 8 6 4 2

CONTENTS

A NOTE ON LANGUAGE

Before we dive in, here's a heads-up about some of the decisions I've made about racial and ethnic terminology in this book. All labels referring to racial and ethnic identities have been capitalized throughout the text. This includes terms like "Native American," "Asian American," "African American," "Hispanic" and "European." For clarity and consistency, the words "Black" and "White" are capitalized when referring to people or groups, even in cases when the words were lowercase in quoted references.[1] The nouns "blackness" and "whiteness" as well as the phrases "white supremacy" and "white supremacist" appear in lowercase. In keeping with guidance from the Native American Journalists Association, the word "Indigenous" is also capitalized throughout when referring to the identities of individuals and groups.[2] I use the words "Hispanic," "Latino," and "Latinx" interchangeably—the latter to signal inclusion for people who prefer a gender neutral or non-binary term.[3] I first learned that the preferred styling of the words "antisemitism" and "antisemitic" are the lowercase, non-hyphenated forms from science writer Erin Biba. The Associated Press issued the same guidance in 2021 and I've followed suit throughout this book.[4]

Finally, because this is a book about racism, I occasionally refer to racist terms such as the *N-word* (a hateful epithet weaponized against Black people) and the *R-word* (a hateful epithet weaponized against Indigenous people). If you don't know what these harmful words mean, all the better. But if you want an explanation, you can learn more by checking out this endnote.[5]

INTRODUCTION

What is racism? Where did it come from? Why does it still exist? And what can we do about it? These are the kinds of questions that may have led you to this book. These are also the kinds of questions that have inspired me as an educator, researcher, and sociologist. Over the course of my career I have spent years studying racism, and the struggle against racism in this country and in Europe as well.

Before we jump in, let me properly introduce myself! I'm Dr. Crystal Marie Fleming, and throughout this book I'll be your personal guide in unpacking the history and ongoing realities of racism. I was born in Chattanooga, Tennessee, and I'm now a professor and social scientist living in New York. And, even though I'm African American and have spent many years studying issues of race, I did *not* know much about racism as a young person. In fact, it wasn't until I attended college that I really began to understand what racism means and how it operates.

My amazing mother worked hard to make sure I believed I could do anything I set my mind to. For Mom, this meant shielding me from racist beliefs. But it also meant that I grew up almost entirely unaware that racism and other kinds of injustice shaped the world around us—and our experience of it.

I still remember the first time I consciously realized I was "Black." I was in the second or third grade in elementary school. I had recently been admitted to the "Gifted and Talented" track because of my high achievement scores. One day, the teacher—a young White woman—called on me to read a passage from a book. When I finished reading, the teacher told the class that she liked how David, another kid in the class, and I pronounced the word "aunt." We both said it like "unt" instead of "ant" like most of the other students. I looked at David and then looked at myself and realized that we both had brown skin. That was the first time I really thought about the fact that we were the only Black students in the class. And luckily, that realization was accompanied by a compliment, as the teacher told everyone that our way of saying "aunt" was correct.

Looking back on that moment, I remember feeling happy about having something in common with David. But I didn't know enough about racism at the time to question why there were only two of us in the Gifted and Talented track.

I also remember reading about slavery and the American Civil War in middle school and thinking that it was such a sad history—without realizing that I myself was a descendant of slaves. At no time do I remember being taught to draw connections between past and present racism. Nor did I learn about the ways in which our society today is still structured by racial injustice. As far as I knew, racial oppression was mainly a thing of the past.

In fact, the first person to teach me about racism was not a Black person—but rather, a White man. In college, I took a sociology class taught by Dr. Ira Silver—one of my favorite professors. The class addressed many forms of inequality, including racism. For the first time, I began to learn about injustice and realize how my own life—and the lives of my family and community members—had been shaped by racism and other forms of oppression. I came to understand that being African American meant having to deal with and overcome systemic barriers that had long been invisible to me. I also began to realize that economic inequality and poverty were intertwined with racial injustice.

The class was a huge revelation for me and ultimately changed my life. Learning about inequality as well as activism for social justice sparked my thirst for knowledge and made me decide to become a sociologist. And, as I began to study these issues, my mom started to share with me her own reflections on experiencing and overcoming racism.

It is my hope that you, too, will be changed by reading this book. My goal is to share with you some of the knowledge I've acquired about the history and sociology of racism, while also equipping you with tools for standing up against racism and making the world a better place.

As we prepare to dig into this vast and important topic, I want you to begin to think about these questions:

- *How would you describe your racial or ethnic identity?*
- *Do you remember the first time you learned about race?*
- *Have you ever discussed race or racism with your family members?*

- *What, if anything, have you learned about racism at school?*

If you're anything like I was as a kid, you may not have given much thought to these questions before. Or, perhaps you've directly experienced or observed racism and you're looking to learn even more. Either way, take this opportunity to consider your answers to these questions—knowing that they may change over time.

UNDERSTANDING THE MEANING AND ORIGIN OF RACISM

Since this book explores the origin and consequences of racism, it's important that we clearly understand what the word means. Racism has two basic elements that we need to address—**racist ideas** and **racist practices**.[1] The first part of racism, racist ideas, is the *belief* that human beings are divided into superior and inferior racial groups. According to racist ideology, these racial groups or races are thought to represent biological and cultural differences that are *permanent* and can't be changed. A major theme we'll explore throughout this book is the fact that racist ideas have distorted our cultural practices, media representations, and even our laws for hundreds of years.

Social scientists have shown that racist thinking doesn't just involve the use of racial labels—it involves *ranking* human groups according to race and creating a hierarchy in which some racial groups are said to be superior or inferior. In other words, if you just describe someone as Black, that doesn't necessarily mean that you are expressing a racist idea. You might just be using a social label that reflects their cultural identity. But if you describe Black people as a group that will always be inferior (or superior) to others because of their biology or culture, then you *would* be expressing a racist belief.

When I teach classes about race, some of my students admit that they used to think that racial labels like Black, White, Asian, and Latino have always been used by human beings. But these labels are *social constructions*. This means that they were created by human beings in a specific place and time.

What we know for sure is that racial labels were invented in Europe during a time of philosophical and intellectual change called the *Enlightenment*. The Enlightenment, which took place from the 1600s through the 1700s, was a period of intense debate and intellectual activity in which educated Europeans (usually wealthy men) began to establish their vision of science as well as notions of individual freedom, liberty, and equality—ideas with which we are still familiar today. It was also during this era that European nations sought to expand their reach by attempting to conquer people living in other parts of the globe, including the Americas and Africa.

One of the ironies of the Enlightenment is the fact that even as Europeans were writing about principles of equality, they were also creating ways of dividing and ranking human beings into groups that they described as civilized and other groups they defined as primitive. It was in this context that Europeans began to invent racial categories and labels, as well as ideas about racial superiority and inferiority. And these same racist ideas were used to argue that (superior) Europeans *should* dominate non-European groups.

As explained above, racist ideas are just *one* aspect of racism. The second element of racism involves *social behaviors and practices* that give advantages and disadvantages to people depending on the racial label that is forced on them. This means that racism is not just about the way we see the world, ourselves, and each other—it's also about the actions we take, and the actions others take, that create an unequal playing field. In other words, racism involves unfair discrimination and produces a racial hierarchy.

These two components—racist beliefs and practices—create *systemic racism*. This is very important, because some people mistakenly think that racism is only about prejudice or bias against other groups. But racism is more than just having prejudiced ideas—it's a *system of power* that creates opportunities and wealth for people who are viewed as racially superior while creating poverty, hardships, and suffering for people who are viewed as racially inferior.

Another term we should consider is *structural racism*.[2] This refers to the notion that racist ideas and practices in different social institutions—like the family, education, or judicial system—combine to create long-lasting and deeply embedded inequalities.

Take, for example, the case of Black people and people of color in the South Bronx—an impoverished area of New York City. Children and youth living in this neighborhood are exposed to environmental toxins from an early age due to the impact of residential segregation and racist housing policies. As a result of pollution from nearby factories, trucks, and highways, people in the South Bronx struggle with asthma at a much higher rate than most other neighborhoods in the United States.[3] Studies suggest that the combination of environmental racism and racism in housing also has negative consequences for health and educational inequalities. According to Claudia Persico, a policy researcher, "even short-term exposure to pollution causes test scores to drop."[4]

Educational inequalities, in turn, are also linked to difficulties in finding good jobs as well as higher rates of arrest and imprisonment for Black people and people of color. As you can see from this one example, the forces of systemic racism in different spheres of society—including neighborhoods to schools and policing—are linked. Whether we think of racism as a "system" or a "structure," the bottom line is that our culture, laws, and policies create widespread advantages and disadvantages for members of different racial groups.

At this point, you might be wondering where racism comes from and how long it has existed as a system of power. To understand how racism came to be, we have to time travel back in history. Although it may seem that concepts like race and racism have been around forever, they're actually a pretty recent development.

For thousands and thousands of years, humans were mainly defined on the basis of *ethnicity*, not race. Ethnicity is best understood as a social identity rooted in a shared cultural heritage, nationality, religion, or ancestry. Unlike race, ethnicity reflects the way we see ourselves and is sometimes easier to shift or change—as when, for example, a person converts from one religion to another. By contrast, racial categories are imposed on us based on how others view our appearance. This means that although we may have a racial identity (for example, I identify as Black), that identity is largely shaped by the racial ideas, categories, and representations that already exist in society.[5]

Long before the invention of race and racism in Europe during the Enlightenment, violence and oppression were often directed against ethnic groups—especially ethnic minorities. At times, Europeans were also dominated by other ethnic groups, like the rulers of the Ottoman Empire.

Religion was frequently used to justify ruling over ethnic outsiders. For example, throughout history it was common for Christians to view people from other religions as "heathens" who should be dominated, enslaved, or forced to convert. Similarly, Islamic kingdoms and rulers often turned to their religious doctrine to justify enslaving people who were not Muslim. Religion, culture, and language have frequently been used to draw boundaries between insiders and outsiders, between oppressors and the oppressed, and for most of human history, ethnic identities were the major distinctions humans used to define themselves.

Things started to change in the medieval period when Europeans increasingly began to treat a religious minority—Jews—as a *racial* group instead of an ethnic group.[6] Although European Jews had been persecuted and targeted with violence as a result of their ethnicity for centuries, they could usually survive anti-Jewish oppression by converting to the religion of the majority group (for example, Christianity).

However, in the 1400s and early 1500s, European countries like Portugal and Spain imposed "blood purity laws" that excluded people with Jewish or North African ancestry from being full citizens. Little by little, the Spanish and Portuguese began defining Jews as a group that was permanently inferior and even subhuman rather than a group that could be assimilated through religious conversion. Over time, even converting to Christianity wasn't enough to protect Jews from prejudice and violence. Ultimately, the rulers of Spain forced all Jews to leave the country in 1492—the very same year that Columbus began his voyage to America.

The persecution of Jews as a permanently inferior biological or cultural group is what scholars call *antisemitism*. The emergence of antisemitic beliefs and practices in Europe planted the seeds for modern racism during the Enlightenment. This is because, unlike the ethnic forms of oppression that came earlier in history, racism as we know it today defines people as members of permanent, unchangeable racial groups that are culturally or biologically ranked. When Jews were labeled as having "impure blood" in medieval Europe, we can detect the early signs of the racist thinking that would more clearly emerge later and take on its most insidious form when Hitler rose to power in Nazi Germany. Although modern racism has many targets—including Indigenous people, people of African descent, and other groups treated as "racial inferiors"—many historians argue that the *racialization* of Jews occurred first.

Young survivors of the Holocaust in Auschwitz (1945)
[USHMM/State Archives of the Russian Federation]

So, to recap: Racism as a system of power is a fairly new invention. Humans have been around for hundreds of thousands of years, but it was not until the last few centuries that we began to see a shift from ethnic identities and oppression to *racialized identities and oppression*. This shift first took place in Europe, but racist ideas and practices have now spread throughout the globe. Racial labels and racist ideas were created during the Enlightenment era in order for Europeans to claim that their ruling over, exploiting, or excluding minority groups was justified.

THE FOUR "LEGS" OF WHITE SUPREMACY

Now that we've covered the core concept of racism, let's get more specific and consider the meaning of white supremacy. We'll examine this concept in more detail in Chapter 2, but for now, I want to provide a brief overview of what white supremacy is and how it came into existence.

White supremacy is the specific kind of racist system that we in the Western world are living with today. It's a system in which people who are socially labeled as White receive benefits, privileges, and power. To understand how white supremacy was built, let's use the simple analogy of a table. As you know, most tables have four legs. White supremacy also has four "legs," upon which it was established. These legs include *colonization*, *Indigenous genocide*, *capitalism*, and *transatlantic slavery*.[7]

Earlier, I mentioned the fact that Europeans began to invent racial labels and racist ideas around the same time period during which they began to travel beyond Europe and rule over people living in the Americas, Africa, and other parts of the world. The word for this process of expansion and domination is *colonization*. In addition to utilizing colonialism to establish white supremacy, Europeans engaged in *genocide* against Indigenous people, the second pillar of white supremacy. This means that they perpetrated mass murders against Native peoples in order to take their land and resources. They also justified their violence by portraying Native peoples as inferior and barbaric. Here again, we see that the purpose of racist ideas is to gather power and wealth at the expense of others.

As European colonizers began to take land and resources from other groups, including Indigenous people, they also established a new economic system—*capitalism*. This is the third leg of white supremacy. All societies have ways of organizing their economy, and in a capitalist system the people who own land, raw materials, and buildings and factories hold power over workers. The important thing to bear in mind is that the colonies established by Europeans needed workers to do all of the hard labor required to fulfill the needs of the population. Someone had to work the fields to grow food and other agricultural products. Someone had to build the railroads and construct new buildings. And Europeans could not (and would not) do that work on their own!

Because of their desperate need for labor and their desire for resources, Europeans began to enslave and oppress many different kinds of people—including poor people (even some poor Europeans), Indigenous people, and, eventually, Africans and their descendants.[8] Although slavery is an ancient practice that has existed all over the world, *transatlantic slavery* was uniquely justified on the basis of racist ideas. As we will learn in Chapter 4, the ideology of white supremacy was used to violently impose slavery upon people of African descent while Europeans created their colonial empires.

At first, Europeans used religious ideas to justify slavery.[9] People who were not Christian were labeled heathens who deserved to be in bondage. But over time, European colonizers increasingly used the idea of race to claim that it was okay to enslave Indigenous people and Africans. The idea of race provided a convenient excuse for enslaving darker-skinned people and benefiting from their free labor, while creating economic and political opportunities for people labeled White.[10]

Diagram of a slave ship
[Lilly Library of Rare Books and Manuscripts, Indiana University]

THE DISCOMFORT OF LEARNING ABOUT RACISM

Okay, we've covered a lot of ground, so I want to take a moment now to check in with you and ask how you might be feeling. Have you noticed any feelings of discomfort while reading this chapter? If so, don't worry—it's perfectly normal to feel uncomfortable addressing racism.

For young people of color, racism can be a very difficult topic for all kinds of reasons. Learning that some people view members of your group as inferior can be quite painful and confusing. Unfortunately, some Black and Brown kids even worry that they actually *are* inferior—or are even to blame for mistreatment, which, of course, is not the case. You might also feel angry or upset learning about the violence that has been directed against people who look like you. These days, there are also many disturbing videos from cell phones and body cam footage that show racially marginalized people being killed by police officers. These images—as well as direct experience with racial violence—can create anxiety and fear for Black youth in particular.

Finally, racism is a challenging topic for young people of color for another important reason—many are personally harmed by racist taunts, bullying, and slurs, and are disadvantaged by racist policies. For young people of color, racism is not ancient history or just something that happens to someone else—it can also be your lived experience or that of your friends and family. If you are a Black or Brown person reading this book, I want to acknowledge that learning about these issues isn't easy. I also want you to know that the racist ideas we are going to examine are *always* wrong and that they do *not* reflect your true value as a person. As you make your way through these chapters, my hope is that you will gain a better understanding of how racism works so that you can detect and disrupt it in your own life. I also want you to feel inspired and empowered by the stories of Black and Brown activists and ordinary people who have rejected racist ideas and bravely challenged racism for generations.

Racism can bring up uncomfortable feelings for young White people, too. As you learn about the history of white supremacy, you might feel angry or upset by the racist ideas and acts of injustice that were enacted by Europeans and their descendants. Or, you might worry that others will assume you are a "racist" just based on the color of your skin. At times, you might feel confused about what it means to be White. If any of this applies to you, what I want you to know is that there is a long, honorable tradition of White antiracism in this country and other parts of the world. This means that even as Europeans were creating modern racism and constructing the legs of white supremacy, there were also Europeans and people who were labeled White who fought against racism and stood in solidarity with people of color.

Finally, some of you reading this book might identify as multi-racial or "mixed." You might also experience a range of confusing and uncomfortable feelings as well—and that's totally okay! At times, you might wonder where you fit in the history of race and racism, as well as the struggle against it. Or, you might feel like you don't quite belong in any of the racial or ethnic labels we'll explore in these chapters. The truth is, no human being is actually "racially pure"—at the end of the day, we are all mixed and have a common origin in Africa.

If you identify as multiracial, I want you to know that your lived experiences at the borders of racial and ethnic categories are very important, and mixed-race people have played an important role in antiracist movements as well.

The purpose of this book is to empower all youth, regardless of your background, to rise up and join the fight against racism. As we go along, we will discover that young people have always played an important role in the struggle for justice, from Frederick Douglass, who escaped from slavery as a young man and became an influential abolitionist, to members of the International Indigenous Youth Council who are currently working to protect Native American communities. But changing our society for the better requires looking at painful histories, confronting injustice, and committing to a vision of humanity that embraces our differences. Sometimes we will feel sad and discouraged when addressing racism. Even after researching and teaching about these topics for many years, I still experience feelings of disappointment, anger, and sadness when learning about or experiencing racial violence. You might feel that way, too, as you read this book.

But learning about racism can also make us feel other emotions. We can feel inspired by the courage of abolitionists, civil rights activists, and others who have stood in solidarity with people of color against white supremacy. We can feel encouraged by the fact that throughout history, there have always been people, including young people, who advocated love, compassion, and empathy for others despite our differences. We can feel grateful for all of the activists, educators, politicians, religious leaders, and ordinary people who struggled against injustice in their day so that we could live in a world with less violence and harm. But most of all, I want you to feel hopeful, because the future depends on the changes that teens like you will bring about.

Indigenous Peoples March
[JohnHHarrington]

I am filled with hope each time I see my students begin to connect the dots and understand the meaning of racism for the very first time in their lives. Many of them had to wait until college to learn about race and racial oppression because, like me, they weren't taught about these issues in high school, middle school, or elementary school. By reading this book, you have an amazing opportunity to get a huge head start on creating positive change. In many ways, this is the book I wish I'd had when I was a kid.

CREATING ANTIRACIST CHANGE

You've probably heard the saying that "knowledge is power." Well, the truth is that knowledge is only power when it's put into action. In the very last chapter of the book, I suggest five concrete steps you can take to dismantle systemic racism. If you want to get a head start on thinking about antiracist change, let's take a sneak peek at a few things we all can do to promote a more just and inclusive society.

THE FIVE STEPS

1. Make a lifelong commitment to antiracism.

This step is all about getting into the right frame of mind. As you will see throughout this book, the racial hierarchy we are still living with was deliberately constructed and maintained over hundreds of years. Those of us who want to build a better world have to be ready and willing to hang in there for the long haul and make a lifelong commitment to standing up for what's right.

2. Build relationships across racial and ethnic lines.

Racism thrives on division and separation. Antiracism involves breaking down barriers and building solidarity across racial and ethnic communities. In the chapters to come, we will see examples of people from different racial and ethnic groups working together to end white supremacy. Creating meaningful and authentic friendships with a diverse range of people can help challenge stereotypes, expose us to new perspectives and cultures, and strengthen our commitment to racial justice.

But it's not enough to just have friends from a variety of racial and ethnic backgrounds—we also need to make sure that our relationships are *antiracist*. A common misconception is the belief that having a friend or a close relationship with someone of a different race or ethnicity proves that you're not racist. Building antiracist connections with others involves being honest about the impact of racism on our lives, discussing difficult subjects, and admitting our mistakes if we say or do something that is harmful or offensive.

3. Speak up against racist ideas, images, and behavior.
Protest! Protest! Protest! That's a common thread that unites antiracists. There are lots of ways—big and small—to speak up against racist ideas, images, and behavior in our everyday lives. For far too long, our culture has brushed racial injustice under the rug. But in each of the following chapters, we will see examples of Black and Brown people who refused to remain silent about racial injustice and inequality. White folks, too, have a role to play in challenging racist beliefs and discriminatory treatment. So, one important thing we can all do is get in the habit of using our voice to support people and communities targeted by racial violence.

4. Support intersectional justice.
Intersectionality is a word that we'll encounter toward the

end of the book, but I want to go ahead and bring it to your attention now. Supporting intersectional justice means being aware that the fight against racism is also connected to the struggle against sexism, transphobia, homophobia, ableism, poverty, and other forms of oppression. Later on, I'll explain how Black women and women of color have been on the forefront of developing tools for recognizing and resisting multiple forms of inequality.

5. Get political.

The word "politics" carries a wide variety of meanings and includes everything from civic engagement and getting involved in your local community to voting, learning more about the political system—and even running for office! The important thing to understand is that antiracism requires getting politically active in some way, shape, or form. In order to open up your political imagination, I recommend studying the work of grassroots organizers like Mariame Kaba, an educator and activist who believes that true justice involves creating a radically new society without prisons, policing, and punishment. The political vision she embraces is called *abolition*. Rather than merely advocating for "reforms," Kaba and other abolitionists call for "the creation of new institutions that actually work to keep us safe and are not fundamentally oppressive."[11]

As you read the following pages, you can reflect on these five steps—both in terms of the impact you can make as well as the progress that's already been made as a result of the hard work of antiracist activists past and present. My hope is that this book will not only teach you a lot about racism, but also inspire you to use your growing knowledge to make a positive difference. Together, we can—we must!—rise up and build a more just and inclusive society. But first, we have to figure out how to *unlearn* racism even as we learn about it. And, that's the topic of our next chapter.

ONE

(UN)LEARNING RACISM

Racial prejudice is not something we're born with—it has to be taught and learned. And, if we're going to rise up and change our society for the better, we also need to think about how to unlearn racism in our everyday lives. Throughout this chapter, we're going to explore how living in a racist society exposes all of us to racist ideas—and consider how we can begin the lifelong work of seeing all human beings as truly equal.

When we are born, we don't know any words at all—much less words related to race. And since we cannot know about race as newborns, we cannot discriminate against people on the basis of their race. But as we grow, observe, and interact with the people in our lives, we go through a process called *socialization*. Socialization is a word for the ways in which the people and institutions around us influence our behavior and beliefs. Human beings are *social creatures*, which means that we grow and develop in community with others.

Families provide our first communities, and we learn a lot about how we should or should not behave from what our parents and other family members teach us. Our families also pass on ideas and beliefs, including racial beliefs about ourselves and other people. Even babies are very observant and can tell when the people around them approve or disapprove of others. If our family members show hostility to people of a different race, we'll pick up on those messages. Many studies have shown that although we aren't born knowing about race, we certainly learn about it very early. Research suggests that even *toddlers* show evidence of racial bias.[1] They weren't *born* that way but *become* that way as a result of socialization.

But it's also true that our parents and authority figures can teach us the importance of seeing beyond race and acknowledging our equality. In the last chapter, I shared with you a little bit about my family. Although my mom didn't specifically talk to me about racism, she did teach me to respect people regardless of their racial or ethnic background. She always had positive stories to share with me about her connections to people across racial lines. For example, she told me that, when she was young and in school, her White teachers in our hometown of Chattanooga, Tennessee, would sometimes invite her to their homes for dinner with their families. Watching my mom interact with people at her job, at our church, and in our neighborhood taught me the value of seeing others as equals no matter the color of their skin.

I was lucky to never hear racist remarks or jokes in our household when I was a child. It wasn't until I was much older that I realized that many children do not have the same experience. In fact, it is likely that millions of people across the country hear or make racist jokes and disrespectful comments about racial groups on a daily basis. When young people observe adults and other authority figures saying negative things about racial groups, they learn to make generalizations—also known as *stereotypes*—and look down on people on the basis of their racial identity. This is one example of how we absorb racial prejudice through our socialization.

Learning about race also happens through the subtle messages we receive from media—the television shows, cartoons, video games, movies, and YouTube clips that we consume. We're going to explore the role of the media in fostering racism later on in the book, but for now I just want to point out that the images we see carry a great deal of influence over the way we perceive ourselves and others. Images in films and cartoons teach us how to view groups of people.

Kirk Alyn as Superman (1948) [Wikimedia Commons]

To take just one example, many of the "heroes" on television and in movies like *Superman, Wonder Woman*, or *Captain America* have traditionally been played by White actors. As a result, most White children grow up seeing other White people portrayed as strong, inspiring figures with magical powers. But Black children and children of color don't have as many opportunities to see heroes who look like them.

When I was growing up, my favorite TV show was *Star Trek: The Next Generation*—I was what you'd call a certified Trekkie.* You have to be a *really* serious nerd to watch *Star Trek*. The most important character on the show was Jean-Luc Picard, captain of the Starship *Enterprise*—a really cool, kind, and clever White man with a British accent who traveled around in a spaceship with his crew exploring the universe. There were certainly Black and Brown characters on the show, including Geordi La Forge—a lieutenant commander who was played by an African American actor named LeVar Burton—and Guinan, a mysterious woman with psychic abilities played by Whoopi Goldberg, a popular African American actress.

As a kid, I didn't give much thought to the fact that Captain Picard was a White man or that Geordi and Guinan were Black. Their race didn't matter to me. I enjoyed seeing the crew of the Starship *Enterprise* encounter alien life across the cosmos, carry out scientific experiments, and utilize jaw-dropping technology like teleporting across great distances. But reflecting back on the show as an adult, I began to realize that *Star Trek: The Next Generation*, like most television shows, centered on the actions of its White characters. People of color were almost always shown in a subordinate position. Without realizing it, I absorbed the idea that White men like Jean-Luc Picard should be the heroes and leaders, while Black and Brown people should take on the roles of helpers and assistants.

----

*A Trekkie is a person who REALLY likes *Star Trek*.

We continue to see these patterns in popular culture and media today. For example, the Hollywood films *Exodus: Gods and Kings* (2014) as well as *Gods of Egypt* (2016) both feature a nearly all-White cast of European-descended actors, despite the fact that both films are set in Egypt—an African nation! As of this writing, Marvel still hasn't produced a movie with an Asian lead actor—though one is currently in the works. And, it wasn't until 2019 that a Black woman—Regina King—was finally featured as the star superhero of a television series for her role as Angela Abar in HBO's *The Watchmen*.[2]

Even the cartoons we watch carry hidden and not so hidden messages that reinforce racist beliefs. One spring, I was teaching a college class about racism in the media when a student in the lecture hall pointed out that the popular cartoon *Tom & Jerry* (you know the one—with the cat and the mouse) actually had a "Black Mammy" character—a racist and sexist portrayal of African American women that dates back to slavery.

Aunt Jemima Mammy figure [*Ladies' Home Journal*, January 1951]

During slavery, White Americans created images of African American women that were demeaning and disrespectful, often attempting to portray them as subservient, unattractive, and with exaggerated figures. Throughout U.S. history, the image of the "Mammy" has represented a very negative, false, and hurtful portrayal of African American women that was used to dehumanize Black women and girls. According to sociologist Patricia Hill Collins, images like the "Mammy" have been used by Whites to "control" and dominate Black women. When African American women are represented as subservient in film and other media, people learn that it is socially acceptable to demean and disrespect them in real life.

As a young girl, I don't remember seeing *any* Black women at all featured in *Tom & Jerry*. So, you can imagine my surprise when the student in my class raised their hand and told me about the Mammy character. How could there have been a Mammy if I didn't remember seeing her? I was so astounded that I actually stopped my lecture to pull up a video of the cartoon to see if it was true. And, unfortunately, the student was right. In fact, some video providers like Amazon Prime actually include a warning label on old episodes of *Tom & Jerry* to acknowledge their racist content.[3] The truth is that we are all exposed to subtle racial messages and images even when we don't realize it!

In addition to the media, schools are another type of social institution that have a great deal of influence over how we see the world. Think about the classes you've taken up until this point in your life. Do you have a favorite teacher—someone who has made a big impact on you? Teachers are important authority figures, and they play a big role in our socialization. The lessons they share with us in the classroom include ideas about racial history and social groups. Like everyone else, teachers are also social animals, so they, too, have been influenced by their own upbringing and experiences. As a result, educators bring their own prior beliefs about race into the classroom and pass on their ideas about racial groups to their students—often unintentionally.

Sometimes we learn race and racism from other kids. When I was in elementary school, the racist term "African Booty Scratcher" was often used as an insult on the playground. It's a dehumanizing and false representation of Africans meant to depict them as an inferior, uncivilized group. But when I was a child, I had no idea that African Booty Scratcher was a racist insult! I'm sure I used it against other kids—including White kids. Even though I was African American, I didn't realize that the term was especially demeaning to other Black people like me. In fact, it wasn't until I was all grown up that I remembered this aspect of my childhood and realized how my socialization made it seem okay to put down Africans. I didn't even realize there was anything strange about it at the time.

When racist ideas, jokes, and images are treated as normal, they become deeply rooted in a society's culture. If we engage in racist insults or tolerate them—if we don't stand up and say *"This is not okay!"*—then we teach others that there is nothing wrong with racism. As you learned in the Introduction, white supremacy has been deeply woven into the fabric of our nation's culture for centuries. This means that racist violence, discrimination, and exploitation have been the norm throughout our history. One of the most important steps in unlearning racism is realizing that *it should not be normal* to oppress people because of their skin color or ethnic background.

o o o

Some people believe that the best way to unlearn racism is to just stop talking about race. But ending racial thinking isn't quite that easy. Let me give you an example.

One of my students, whom we'll call Lisa, was thinking of writing a paper about the problem of racial injustice in our criminal justice system, which involves everything from policing and the courts to laws and policies. Lisa felt that one of the biggest causes of racial inequality was the very fact that people like police officers and judges use racial labels. A police officer might refer to someone as White or Black, and then discriminate against them on the basis of their racial biases. In order to address this problem and create greater racial equality, Lisa thought it would be a good idea to ban the use of racial categories in the criminal justice system. In fact, she thought the best way to undo racism was for all of us to stop describing people and neighborhoods and schools in terms of race.

Leaning back in my chair, I asked Lisa to explain step-by-step how she thought a ban on racial categories might reduce racism.

"Well," she said, "if officers and judges aren't allowed to use racial labels to categorize people, then hopefully they would treat them equally."

"Okay." I nodded. "Let's go with your idea. Suppose a ban went into effect tomorrow and suddenly racial categories were no longer allowed in the criminal justice system. Police officers, judges, and everyone else can no longer call anyone White, Asian, Black, or Latinx. But let's also suppose that the officers and judges still have all of the racial ideas and prejudices that they had before the ban went into effect."

Lisa took a deep breath. She could see where I was going with this.

"Do you think that telling officers and judges that they can't use racial words would immediately prevent them from thinking about people through a racial lens?" I asked.

"No . . ."

"You see, it's very likely that the racial ideas they carried with them throughout their lives would persist even if they could not use the words. But what if you're right? It *is* possible that not being able to describe people in terms of race could lead some of the officers and judges to treat people more equally. But how could we actually *know* if things are getting better or worse unless we can track racism using racial categories?"

Think about it this way: Can you put out a fire by avoiding the word "fire"? I certainly wouldn't recommend it. Similarly, we have to be able to name racism and refer to racial categories in order to address racism. Very often, we have to name a problem in order to be able to do anything about it—for example, if we didn't invent the term "inequality," then how would we be able to describe the existence of that issue, let alone do anything about it?

In that same way, if we're going to address racism, we first need to learn how racist ideas and practices produce inequalities in our society. But trying to completely avoid acknowledging race would leave us without any tools to actually determine whether groups are being treated more or less equally. Sometimes, we also need to acknowledge the importance of racial identities—especially for Blacks and people of color who have been discriminated against and disadvantaged as a result of white supremacy.

Like Lisa, many people believe the way to end racism is to just stop talking about race. But that's not how the social world works. In truth, we absorb ideas about race throughout our lives, and those racial biases mold the way we see ourselves and others even when we avoid describing people in terms of race.

But in order to challenge racism, we also need to see beyond the made-up idea of race. We have to acknowledge that racial belonging is just one aspect of a person's identity and experience. If I see you only in terms of my preconceived notions about your "race," then I can't actually know you as a full person. Instead, we have to acknowledge our racial biases and prejudice. In order to do this, we have to learn how to notice when we are stereotyping people. We have to catch ourselves in the act!

As a social experiment, you might try to notice when and if you think about other people (or yourself) in terms of race or ethnicity. For an entire day, pay attention to the kinds of thoughts and feelings that come up when you think of racial labels. In order to guide you, here are a few questions to reflect on during your experiment:

1. When do you find yourself thinking about someone else's race?
2. When do you find yourself thinking about your own race?
3. What assumptions have you made about other people as a result of their race?

Be kind to yourself if you notice any racial assumptions or even negative beliefs about racial groups. Don't blame or judge yourself for your answers to these questions. The truth is, every person on the planet has biases and prejudiced beliefs. Although it can feel uncomfortable to acknowledge our racial beliefs, doing so can provide valuable insight into our socialization. The important thing is to realize that we've all absorbed our ideas about race from the society in which we live. As we grow up, we can challenge those ideas and commit ourselves to seeing everyone as equally valuable and worthy of respect.

o o o

Unlearning racism is not something that happens overnight. It's not something that happens after reading a book or taking a class. As a young antiracist, you need to know that the path ahead of you—the path ahead of us—will not be quick or easy.

One of my favorite activists and educators, Jane Elliott, is a White teacher who decided to commit herself to teaching White children and adults about racism after Martin Luther King Jr. was assassinated in 1968. Although she's been doing this for many decades and is now in her eighties, Jane Elliott acknowledges the work of overcoming her own racial prejudice is never done. Because she was socialized in a racist society, she knows that the racist ideas and images she absorbed from our nation's culture are still floating around in her mind. There's a lot we can all learn from her example.

Unlearning racism is an ongoing process. Even as an educator and researcher who works on these issues, I still notice my own racial ideas, stereotypes, and assumptions. But when I notice those assumptions, I try to consciously let them go. And I also acknowledge that there are ways in which race and racism influence my thinking even when I'm not consciously aware of it.

The good news is that you are beginning this work as a young person. The sooner we become aware of our own biases and prejudices, the sooner we can begin seeing beyond stereotypes and trying to treat people as individuals. Unlearning racism doesn't mean that we need to stop talking about race. Rather, we have to acknowledge how race and racism shape our society in order to change our society. We also have to learn to name the specific type of racism that exists in the United States—white supremacy. In the next chapter, we're going to take a deep dive into the history of white supremacy and examine how it continues to operate in our world today.

TWO

WHAT THE HECK IS WHITE SUPREMACY?

Are you still hangin' in there? I know we've covered a lot of ground, but the truth is, we're just getting started. So far, we've explored the origins of racial thinking and looked at the negative impact of racism on how we see ourselves and one another. But now, we have to tackle a vexing question: *What the heck is white supremacy?*

You may think you already have this one figured out. When many people hear those words "white supremacy," they automatically imagine members of the Ku Klux Klan wearing white hoods and burning crosses. Or, perhaps you associate white supremacy with skinheads and Nazis. If so, you're not alone—and you're not entirely wrong. In fact, most people think of white supremacy as hate groups and extreme forms of racial violence—like slavery or the Holocaust.

In 2015, while Barack Obama was still president, a twenty-one-year-old White man named Dylann Roof walked into an African

American church in South Carolina, quietly sat down during the service, and then shot nine Black people to death as they were praying. Roof's motive was clear: He proudly embraced Nazi symbols and expressed his belief that racial and ethnic minorities like African Americans and Jews should be killed. For many people, this is what white supremacy looks like—a terrible act of violence and a lone-wolf assassin.

But while white supremacy includes extremist groups and others who are willing to violently impose their racist views, there's a lot more to it than hateful ideas or targeting minorities in very obvious and shocking ways. What's important to understand is that the racism we all still live with is maintained through everyday interactions that teach people to discriminate on the basis of skin color and other physical features. Every single act of discrimination adds up on a daily basis and accumulates from one year to the next, creating unfair advantages for Whites and injustice for everyone else.

While extreme acts of violence are definitely *a part* of white supremacy, they aren't the *whole* story. In fact, white supremacy seeps into our politics and laws, our education system, the economic sector, the images we see in the media, and the way we stereotype and treat one another. If you want to rise up against racism, you'll also need to learn about white supremacy as a *social system*.

WHITE POWER

In this chapter, we're going to unpack the meaning of white supremacy and examine how it shapes our society, economy, and politics.

But before we go too far, here's a simple definition that I want you to keep in mind:

White supremacy is the social, political, and economic dominance of people socially defined as White.

Now, lemme explain what I mean by "socially defined as White." As we saw in Chapter 1, race is not fundamentally real—it's a social construction, a web of myths. The racial labels and definitions we use today are just made-up ideas that were created to justify colonialism and—you guessed it—w*hite supremacy*. But what exactly is "dominance"? Basically, dominance is about exercising power over others. And power is about your ability to get what you want.

If you've ever seen a bully on the playground, then you know exactly what abusing power looks like. In a white supremacist society, people who are considered White have more power than others. This means that members of the White population have an easier time gaining access to precious resources like nice neighborhoods, property, desirable schools, good jobs, healthcare, and political office than members of other ethnic or racial groups. It also means that White people are treated with more respect and deference than people considered "non-White."

This does not mean, though, that *all* White people are rich or that *all* White people feel powerful. Some Whites live in poverty, experience difficulties, or even belong to a minority group themselves.

For example, it may surprise you to learn that most of the children who live in poverty in this country are White. This is because White people are still the largest racial group in the United States.

Poor and working-class kids have a very hard time making it in our society because they often lack access to quality schools, healthy food, and economic opportunities. As a result, White children who live in poverty have a greater chance of being exposed to drugs, malnutrition, and family instability. This is all important to keep in mind because many news programs and textbooks give very little attention to White poverty.

We can also think of other kinds of experiences and disadvantages—like disability or gender discrimination—that can make life very difficult for some Whites. Some groups that are considered White today, like Jews of European origin, are religious minorities and experience bigotry and violence because of their ethnicity. In fact, the everyday struggles of certain White people like these lead others to believe that white supremacy is just a myth. Maybe you're even wondering how to make sense of all this. If our society is white supremacist, why aren't *all* White people wealthy, healthy, and living fabulous lives?[1]

RACIAL GAPS

The first thing to remember is that white supremacy doesn't *guarantee* every White person or White family a golden path to success and happiness. Instead, white supremacy makes it *easier* for Whites to get ahead and to bounce back during difficult economic times. But, because most White people live in majority White neighborhoods—far away from people of color—and don't have close friendships with people of a different race, they are often blind to the *huge* gap between their circumstances and the challenges faced by racial minorities.

What do these racial gaps look like? And how do we know that they exist? Let's start with economics. Most White families have far more material resources than Black and Brown households. Did you know that nationwide, the average White family holds *thirteen times* the wealth of the average Black family?[2] This is because for nearly **four hundred years**, discriminatory laws and racist beliefs allowed White politicians, bankers, and employers to favor other Whites while excluding people of color.

Of course, enslaved Africans and their descendants were not paid for their labor, and racist policies prevented most of them from having their fair share of economic opportunities. Only a few enslaved people were able to gain their freedom and buy land. But even after the abolition of slavery, many African Americans were robbed of economic opportunities. Racist laws and practices allowed White communities to legally mistreat minorities. At the same time, Whites were able to purchase land, create businesses, and pass on resources from one generation to the next.

In 1862, Congress passed the Homestead Act, which gave away *millions* of acres of Native American land to White individuals and families. This important law allowed White Americans to create settlements and farms for crops that would contribute to the national economy. The farmlands that Whites received at this time helped them make money and improve their families' lives and, yes, pursue life, liberty, and happiness. But racial minorities were almost completely excluded from this whopping government handout.

Sociologists have shown that tens of millions of White Americans were able to access great economic opportunity as a result of discriminatory policies like the Homestead Act.[3] Because Whites benefited from discriminatory housing policies, many Whites were able to become homeowners, and many families built wealth by purchasing and maintaining a home. Meanwhile, at the time of the Homestead Act, people of color were not allowed to buy homes, receive bank loans, or live without fear of white supremacist violence. In fact, some non-White minorities weren't allowed to enter this country at all.

For many years, Asians were not allowed to move to the United States due to racist immigration laws passed in the 1800s.[4] And, until the 1960s, racial quotas kept immigrants from Asia and Africa from entering the United States in great numbers.

An 1886 advertisement for laundry detergent with a racist caricature of a Chinese man. The image of Uncle Sam kicking the Chinese man is a visual representation of the racist idea that Asians do not belong in the United States. [Library of Congress]

White politicians' efforts to prevent people from outside Europe from entering the country aligned with efforts to suppress Black Americans and assert white supremacy. African Americans were routinely denied the right to vote, and civil rights activists were regularly met with violence and even the threat of death from racists. With the playing field intentionally made to be so unequal, many Whites were able to amass political power and economic resources while forcing other racial groups to work bad jobs for low wages—or keep them out of this country altogether.

Young civil rights protestors [Getty Images/Wally McNamee]

Of course, wealthy Whites benefited the most from this system. Working-class and poor Whites have been severely disadvantaged and have limited opportunities.

But white supremacy also encouraged poor and working-class Whites to feel better about their circumstances by looking down on people with darker skin. This is what sociologist W.E.B. Du Bois called the "wages of whiteness"—the psychological boost that people are taught to feel about being White—and not being a person of color. He used the word "wages" because in our society, it literally pays to be considered White.[5]

W.E.B. Du Bois (1919) [Library of Congress]

It has also been easier, historically, for Whites born into poverty to eventually work themselves up the class ladder. Why is it easier for poor Whites to move out of poverty than many other groups? Well, for one, poor White people are more likely to live in neighborhoods with greater opportunities and better schools than the neighborhoods where poor Native American, African American, and Latinx people live. Because of widespread housing discrimination and segregation imposed by Whites, many Black and Brown Americans have been forced to live in what social scientists call "concentrated poverty"—places with very few resources, subpar schools, and unsafe neighborhoods.

Meanwhile, many poor and working-class people of color have a hard time getting ahead because of widespread discrimination and limited opportunities. As a result, many researchers suggest that poverty operates differently across racial and ethnic groups—it is "stickier" (and harder to overcome) for African Americans, Native Americans, and Latinx people.[6]

Today, the economic consequences of racist ideas and policies are clear. Centuries of white supremacy have created what social scientists call the "racial wealth gap." To understand the wealth gap, let's take a step back and consider what the word "wealth" means. Wealth is a measure of your assets—the amount of valuable property that you own. Someone with a great deal of wealth might own a home (or multiple homes) as well as land, real estate, and expensive cars. A business tycoon might own factories and equipment.

On the opposite end of the spectrum are people with little to no wealth. People who are poor or who live in debt have very few economic resources. The important thing to keep in mind is that the wealth we have (or don't have) depends on many different factors, some of which are beyond our control. The most important factor shaping our access to wealth is the family into which we were born. Some families have resources (like houses and money) passed down from one generation, which is why children with wealthy parents have a head start over other kids. Think about it—who do you think has an easier time getting a good education, finding a well-paying job, or even creating a business—a kid from a poor family or a kid from a rich family?

If you guessed that wealthier kids are more likely to attend nice schools and get good jobs, you would be right! But what many people don't realize is that wealth (and poverty) is also shaped by racist policies and discrimination that have made it easier for White families to build economic resources over time.

In the middle of the twentieth century, many White families were able to attain economic security and become middle class as a result of social programs like the GI Bill, which helped veterans returning from World War II have a pathway to education, home ownership, and wealth. Unfortunately, most of the economic resources that were made available through these kinds of federal programs were given to Whites. African American soldiers were not spared the injustice of racial discrimination. Although it may be hard to believe, even Black soldiers who bravely fought for their country abroad were denied their fair share of opportunities when they came back home after the war.[7]

Shutting people of color (and especially African Americans) out of economic opportunities is not ancient history. Until the 1960s, when laws such as the Civil Rights Act of 1964 were enacted to help foster greater equality, White racism prevented most African Americans from having a fair shot at home ownership. If the '60s seems like a super long time ago, just remember that many people alive today (like my parents) were born in that era. As a result of centuries of unequal treatment, White households have an enormous wealth advantage that has not disappeared since the civil rights movement. According to the U.S. Census Bureau, about 10 percent of White kids are born into poor families, but these numbers are much worse for many kids of color. A whopping 33.8 percent of Native American children, 30.8 percent of African American children, and 26.6 percent of Latinx children are born into poverty.[8]

Now, you might be tempted to believe that White families have more wealth because they save up all their money in piggy banks, or because they are better at handling money. But research has shown that African American families actually save at a higher rate than their White counterparts.[9] What we know for sure is that the racial wealth gap—the disparity in resources owned by Whites and other groups—is mostly the result of the accumulated advantages that White families are able to pass on to the next generation. And the gap is shockingly gigantic. For example, when former President Barack Obama lived in the White House, White Americans in Washington, D.C., held *81 times* the wealth of African American families. To give you a sense of just how massive that gap is, consider this:

The Earth is 81 times bigger than the moon!

And, believe it or not, the situation is even *worse* in some other cities. In Los Angeles, for example, White families have 89 times more wealth than their African American neighbors. Latino families are similarly disadvantaged by the racial wealth gap. Scholars have estimated that it would take African American families over 200 years to reach the same level of wealth that Whites have today—and Latino families would need over 80 years to do the same.[10] Even education is not enough to make the racial wealth gap disappear.

Beyond land, home ownership, and wealth, research has also

shown that Black and Brown laborers are paid less than White workers and are more likely to earn a poverty-level wage.[11] This racial "wage gap"—the difference between the income paid to Whites and people of color for their work—is also a big source of inequality. For example, sociologists have found that even though African Americans have greater access to high-paying jobs today than in the past, they also end up being paid less than their White co-workers.[12] And although some Asian American ethnic groups now attain more education than White Americans, they still earn less than Whites with the same degrees and credentials.[13] So, while there are certainly White people who experience poverty and economic disadvantage, across the board, people of color often experience even *more* difficulties as a result of past and present discrimination.

POLITICS

Aside from economics, white supremacy also shapes our politics. For most of our nation's history, white power was the law of the land. The American Dream that the founding fathers imagined—a land of freedom and opportunity—looks great on paper. There's only one little problem: *They didn't plan to share this dream with everyone.* When the authors of the Declaration of Independence gathered in 1776 to celebrate "life, liberty, and the pursuit of happiness," they planned to limit these freedoms to people like them—other White men. Just about everyone else was left out—including Native Americans, enslaved Africans and their descendants, Asian Americans and Pacific Islanders, and women of all backgrounds.

Almost all of our presidents believed the myth that Whites are inherently superior to other groups, and that White men in particular should lead the country. Some of them, including George Washington, owned slaves. In 1785, Thomas Jefferson, a slave owner, published a book entitled *Notes on the State of Virginia*, in which he describes Blacks as "inferior to the Whites in the endowments both of body and mind."[14] Andrew Jackson, the guy on the twenty dollar bill, referred to Native Americans as "savages" and advanced racist policies like the Indian Removal Act, which resulted in the violent displacement and killing of thousands of Indigenous people.[15]

It took activists and freedom fighters many generations of resistance and struggle *against* the U.S. government in order to expand liberties and protections for a wider share of the population. Over the course of hundreds of years, abolitionists and civil rights activists like Harriet Tubman, Ella Baker, and Martin Luther King Jr. organized and pushed for more humane policies. But even today, although we live in a very diverse society and White men make up only one third of the population, they dominate *every* level of politics, from your local mayor's office to Congress, the Supreme Court, and the Presidency.[16]

When Barack Obama became the first Black president of the United States in 2008, many people were tempted to believe that White favoritism and extreme racism were things of the past. Unfortunately, this was not to be. Hate crimes, which target victims on the basis of their race, gender, or sexuality, rose sharply after Donald Trump won the presidency in 2016. Yet even before Trump took office, activism in Ferguson, Missouri, as well as the larger Black Lives Matter movement focused the nation's attention on police violence and brutality against African Americans, including the murdering of kids and teenagers.[17] Today, members of the neo-Nazi party are running for political office in the United States. White supremacist groups are more outspoken and visible than they have been in at least a generation, and some elected officials, like the former congressman Steve King, have openly described Whites as a superior race.[18]

EUROPEAN ETHNICS

It's probably obvious by now that white supremacist racism is harmful to people who are not considered white. But a major misconception about white supremacy is the idea that it only endangers people of color or people from outside Europe. In fact, there are many groups that are considered White today who were previously viewed as non-White—and subjected to horrific violence. As you'll recall from Chapter 1, social constructions of race are unstable. They shift and change over time. Throughout the early colonial period, the term "White" was mainly restricted to so-called WASPs. No, not the black-and-yellow insects that sting. The term "WASP" refers to "White Anglo-Saxon Protestants."

Anglo-Saxons were people descended from the Germanic people— typically those living in Great Britain. This means other Europeans— especially Italians, the Irish, and Jews—were often treated like second-class citizens and viewed as inferior. In some cases, members of these European ethnic groups were treated as though they were not "really" White.[19] Jews experienced antisemitism and bigotry, while some Italian immigrants to the United States were viciously lynched. History teaches us that white supremacy can target a wide variety of people, and the definition of who is and who is not White can change from one era to the next.

WHITEWASHING RACISM

One of the major problems we face in our society is the whitewashing of white supremacy. The myth of white superiority was deeply woven into our laws for centuries, and the injustice and harm inflicted on people of color has often been erased, minimized, and even justified throughout our history. Even today, our country continues to celebrate many White people, especially White men, who viewed Whites as superior to others—and ruthlessly mistreated Black and Brown people.

Every year, tens of millions of American families gather together in the chilly month of November for a Thanksgiving feast. A bountiful spread of turkey, stuffing, collard greens, and delicious pies is supposed to commemorate the first encounter between European colonists and Native people. You've probably heard the famous jingle: *In 1492, Columbus sailed the ocean blue.* You may have read about his ships—the *Niña*, the *Pinta*, and the *Santa Maria*. In schools throughout the country, teachers tell their young students that the original inhabitants of this land and the European explorers who came here greeted each other like old friends and happily shared a meal. Columbus and the other colonists are often celebrated like heroes for "discovering" the New World.

But many elements of this familiar Thanksgiving story are

completely made up. Christopher Columbus—an Italian immigrant to Spain—didn't discover the land that would come to be called America. There were already people living here! And, he never even made it to the territory that would become the United States. In fact, Columbus was quite lost when he ended up on the island of Hispaniola. He had actually set sail for the Far East and thought he was in India when he reached the Caribbean.[20] This is why he insisted on calling the inhabitants *Indians*. To this day, Native people are incorrectly called "Indians" because of Columbus's mistake.

The biggest lie of all, though, is in the way that our nation falsely portrays the encounter between Natives and Europeans. There was no joyful Thanksgiving meal shared in a spirit of peace and brotherhood. In truth, Columbus and his men had violent intentions as soon as they arrived in the Americas. Their plan from the start was to capture the "Indians," steal their land, and hunt for gold on behalf of the Spanish crown. The explorers used their Catholic religion to justify their sense of superiority over the Natives. They believed that their Christian faith gave them the right to colonize and exercise power over "inferior" people. Within just a few years, Columbus and other Europeans succeeded in conquering and murdering most of the Indigenous population. Many Native children were brutally killed by the colonizers, and Native women were violated. Europeans also enslaved hundreds of Native people and sent many of them to Spain in bondage.[21]

Despite these atrocities, Christopher Columbus is still celebrated today by many people as a hero. His violent racism and hatred of Indigenous people are often brushed aside. But for many years, Native Americans who survived colonization have been speaking out and raising awareness about their side of the story. For example, in 2016, a group of Native American girls created a video for *Teen Vogue* magazine to share their views on the *real* meaning of Thanksgiving. From their perspective, there is nothing family-friendly or enjoyable about this annual tradition. For them, Thanksgiving has always been a holiday for Europeans—those who would eventually call themselves White—to celebrate killing Native Americans and taking their land.[22] But this perspective—one shared by many Indigenous people—is all too often erased or ignored.

THE GREATEST SHOWMAN

As you can see, white supremacy involves a lot of misrepresentation. The past and the present are frequently distorted in ways that favor the White majority and silence the views of people of color—not just in how we talk about the history of the United States, but also in the various forms of entertainment we consume, like TV shows, movies, and books.

Recently, one of my friends suggested that we watch a supposedly heartwarming film—*The Greatest Showman*, starring Hugh Jackman. Released in 2017, the movie chronicled the life and times of P.T. Barnum (1810–1891), the founder of the world-famous Barnum & Bailey Circus. Every kid I knew growing up just loved the circus—and the Ringling Brothers and Barnum & Bailey circus was the biggest and greatest show on earth. I remember watching the circus shows on television and marveling at the gargantuan elephants, perfectly trained tigers, and acrobats dressed in colorful costumes.

Back then, I didn't know about the long history of circus shows mistreating people and animals alike. And, although I eventually learned about the terrors of circuses as an adult, I didn't know much about Barnum and thought it would be fun to check out the movie.

The Greatest Showman portrays P.T. Barnum, a White man from Connecticut who lived during the 1800s, as an advocate of diversity and inclusion who was ahead of his times. The so-called "freaks" in his show include a very short man, a bearded lady, several Black acrobats, and a man covered in tattoos. While these uniquely talented people were shunned and hated by the wider society because of their appearance, the movie depicts P.T. Barnum as someone who showed them love and acceptance. Without knowing the real history of Barnum's life, my friend and I loved every minute of the film. At one point, we were even moved to tears by its message of empowerment and diversity.

But after we finished the film and dried our tears, I decided to do what I do best—research. After doing a little digging into P.T. Barnum's life, I was shocked by what I found. The rosy fairy tale presented in the film—the image of a progressive White man who valued inclusion—couldn't have been further from the truth. In fact, P.T. Barnum violently mistreated and exploited vulnerable people—including children and people with disabilities—forcing them to work in horrible conditions. His circus routinely depicted Black people as savage beasts, drawing on popular tropes of white supremacy.

At one point, Barnum bought a blind, elderly enslaved African American woman named Joice Heth, held her against her will, and made her pretend to be George Washington's nurse in his circus show. In addition to subjecting her to torture—among other indignities, Barnum pulled out her teeth to make her look older for his audiences—Barnum continued violating her even after her death. When she died, Barnum actually sold tickets so that he could profit from "entertaining" crowds as her body was publicly dissected and torn apart.[23] Reading about this made me sick to my stomach.

Of course, none of these terrible things made it into *The Greatest Showman*. Instead of telling the truth about P.T. Barnum's racism and cruelty, the film sanitized his image for a new generation of young people. The lives of the children, disabled people, and racial minorities who were kidnapped and exploited by this powerful, wealthy White man were relegated to the dustbin of history.

What do you think happens when racial injustice is ignored, brushed aside, and misrepresented for hundreds of years?

THREE

STEALING AMERICA

Many kids across this country grow up learning the words to a popular song called "This Land Is Your Land." You've probably heard or sung this song at school or maybe even on the Fourth of July. It goes like this:

This land is your land, this land is my land . . .
This land was made for you and me.[1]

As a young girl, I never thought twice about singing these words. But have you ever stopped to ask whose land this really is? Roxanne Dunbar-Ortiz, a Native American scholar, suggests that we should all question the meaning of songs like "This Land Is Your Land".[2] Who actually has the right to this land? And whose rights were trampled on by the colonizers who eventually created the United States?

In order to really address these questions, we have to take a look at the history of our country from the perspective of the Indigenous people who were here before Columbus. This requires confronting some difficult truths and challenging many of the stories we've been told about the "discovery" of America. Many of us grew up being told that this land belongs to the United States government and its citizens. In some ways, it might even seem obvious that this land is "ours."

But in truth, this land was originally home to people from many different ethnic groups who were already living here when Europeans used extreme forms of violence and deceit to claim this continent as rightfully "theirs."

Long before European colonizers stumbled onto this continent, Native peoples lived, thrived, and created sophisticated societies in the land now referred to as the Americas. Scientists are still debating exactly when and how humans first arrived here, but the latest research suggests that this land was first settled at least 15,000 years ago, during the Ice Age.[3] It is believed that people of Asian and European descent traveled from Siberia to modern-day Alaska by walking over a patch of land that is now covered by the Pacific Ocean.

Back then, North America (where the United States and Canada are now located) was an extremely cold and difficult place to live— but the people who survived the journey found a way to establish sustainable cultures that would last for thousands of years. Over time, the descendants of these original inhabitants would eventually come to be known as "Native" or "Indigenous" Americans. They created complex forms of government, established strong values and belief systems, learned how to cultivate the land and grow agriculture (once the temperatures warmed up), and developed their own languages and civilizations.[4]

By some estimates, there were nearly twenty million Native people living in Turtle Island—the term some Natives used for North America—before colonizers arrived.[5] As a result of genocide and displacement, as of 2019, there are only about five million Native people in the United States.[6] But despite the ongoing oppression they face, Indigenous people continue to resist, and they sustain a diverse and rich community of over five hundred distinct Nations and societies.[7] They include groups like the Cherokee, Choctaw, Muskogee, and Seminoles across North America. Other Indigenous people have ancestral ties to the Aztec civilizations in what is now called Mexico.

Throughout this chapter, we will revisit some very dark and disturbing pages of our history. In particular, we will consider how white supremacy has been established through the unjust displacement, killing, and oppression of Indigenous Americans. As you will see, this land was not "made" for U.S. citizens but instead was violently stolen by heavily armed colonizers and their descendants. Along the way, colonizers created patriotic myths and racist ideas about the inferiority of Native people to justify their theft of Native land and their violence toward Native people.

At least one of our presidents—Andrew Jackson—built his political career on a platform of displacing and killing Native Americans. The legs of white supremacy—capitalism, colonization, genocide, and slavery—can all be seen in the experiences of Native people. This shameful legacy is not just a thing of the past. Even today, Native Americans are still being subjugated by the military and political forces of the United States, even as they actively resist those forces.

In order to rise up against racism, we need to stand up for the dignity and human rights of Native people. This means recognizing their right to their homeland as well as their right to *sovereignty*—the power to govern and exercise authority over their own societies and Nations.

THE FOUR LEGS OF WHITE SUPREMACY AND THE OPPRESSION OF INDIGENOUS PEOPLE

One of the reasons racism is so dangerous is that it teaches us to value some lives more than others. Indigenous lives have been repeatedly devalued over the last five centuries as European colonizers destroyed their homes and pushed them off their land. Racist ideas and religious bigotry played an important role in Europeans' attempts to force Indigenous people off their homelands. When Columbus and other Spanish colonizers arrived in the Caribbean islands in 1492, they described the Native people living there—the Carib and Taino people—as inferior savages. Immediately thereafter, they began scheming to take the Native people's land and resources.

The United States and many of the countries throughout the Americas were built on a special type of colonization called *settler colonialism*. This type of colonialism occurs when a group decides to move to another part of the world, remove the native population, and establish its society on that land.

But why did the European colonizers want Native land in the first place? The Spanish monarchy that employed Christopher Columbus was motivated by greed and sent "explorers" across the globe in search of gold and other precious materials that could enrich their kingdom back home.[8] Indigenous people were well aware that the colonizers were obsessed with stealing wealth. In fact, the Muskogee Nation, an Indigenous group, referred to the colonizing hordes as "people greedily grasping after the lands of the red people."[9]

Around this time, *capitalism*—one of the four legs of white supremacy discussed earlier—slowly began to spread new economic arrangements across the globe. In the 1400s and 1500s, Europeans in places like Spain and Portugal were on the hunt for new sources of wealth, such as land, because their own economies were in trouble. This is why colonization was an alluring enterprise for European leaders—creating a new colonial empire overseas could help create economic opportunities for their home societies.

After Columbus's initial voyage in 1492, Spaniards began growing a very profitable product called *sugar cane* on the Caribbean island of Hispaniola. During this time, colonizers increasingly began creating profit for themselves through the labor of enslaved Africans who were forced to grow and cultivate agricultural products like sugar on Indigenous lands.

At the same time, Indigenous people were also being displaced and killed—either intentionally through massacres or unintentionally through the spread of deadly, contagious diseases brought by Europeans. Unlike Indigenous people who relate to the land as stewards and caretakers, colonizers viewed land as available for the taking, to become their "private property." Moreover, Europeans turned to racist ideas about their superiority as well as the myth of Native inferiority to justify their mistreatment of Native people.[10]

Indigenous educators and historians like Dunbar-Ortiz and Dina

Gilio-Whitaker teach us that the displacement and killing of Native Americans is a form of *genocide*. The United Nations defines genocide as acts that involve:

> *Killing members of the group;*
> *Causing serious bodily or mental harm to members of the group;*
> *Deliberately inflicting on the group conditions of life calculated to bring about its physical destruction in whole or in part;*
> *Imposing measures intended to prevent births within the group;*
> *Forcibly transferring children of the group to another group.* [11]

All of these aspects of genocide have been enacted upon Native people as colonizers seized their land and assaulted their bodies. And, throughout our history, many political leaders of this nation openly promoted policies and actions designed to destroy Native lives.

For example, before George Washington became the first president of the United States, he served as a general in the rogue military that was seeking to overthrow the British government. As some Indigenous Nations aligned with the British forces, Washington made his intentions to destroy the Native communities crystal clear, instructing his officers to "overrun" and "destroy" the settlements of the Haudenosaunee Nation, a group living in what is now called New York.

Even more chilling, Washington urged his military to use "terror" as a form of psychological warfare in order to overpower the

Haudenosaunee.[12] Nearly a century later, U.S. General William T. Sherman would echo Washington's sentiments, coldly stating, "We must act with vindictive earnestness against the Sioux, even to their extermination, men, women and children . . ."[13]

How did European settlers and politicians convince themselves that it was acceptable to force Native people off their own land and oppress their communities? And how could they justify horrific acts like ethnic cleansing? Unfortunately, religion has been used throughout history as a justification for injustice and exploitation. Many settlers viewed themselves as superior not only because of their Europeanness but also because of their Christian faith. Colonizers like Columbus felt justified imposing their religious beliefs onto Indigenous people, whom they viewed as savages, and claimed that it was God's will for Native people to be ruled over (or removed) by Christians.[14]

Another key idea that was used to justify violence toward Native Americans was the notion of "Manifest Destiny"—the belief that the people of the United States were destined to expand across the continent and displace the Indigenous groups living here. You may recall from your history classes that when the United States was first formed in 1776, it was just a collection of thirteen colonies along the East Coast. The rest of what many of us now think of as "our land" still belonged to Indigenous Nations. But White settlers and politicians soon began to claim that it was inevitable for the United States to spread its territory "from sea to shining sea." Racist and false ideas about the superiority of Whites and the inferiority of non-Whites were used to claim that it was morally right for colonizers to take Indigenous territory.

This is a visual representation of the idea of "Manifest Destiny." The White
woman represents White American civilization—bringing "the light"
of technology, structural advancement, and knowledge. She is depicted
chasing Indigenous people off of their land. [Library of Congress]

BROKEN PROMISES AND TREATIES

Time and time again, the United States government has broken prom-
ises and treaty agreements with Indigenous Nations in order to steal
their land and expand the territory of the country.[15] In addition to
using violence and military force to dominate Indigenous people,
White politicians rigged the legal system and violated prior agreements with Native people. In the early 1800s, it became extremely
difficult for Native Americans to defend their interests within the
U.S. courts. Both local and national officials of the United States government were determined to take as much Native land as possible.
To accomplish this goal, they began deliberately "destroying tribal

governments, banning tribal assemblies, making it illegal to pass tribal laws, denying Native Americans the right to vote or sue or testify in court or even dig gold on their own land."[16]

Deprived of the right to participate in elections and speak in the court of law, Native Americans found themselves with very few legal options for protecting their homes and families. Despite these significant challenges, Indigenous Nations continued to resist U.S. efforts to violently push them off their land.

Sitting Bull, Chief of the Lakota people, led a strong resistance against European colonizers (1883) [David F. Barry]

Unfortunately, most U.S. government officials were determined to expand westward no matter the cost to Native Americans. The Indian

Removal Act of 1830, championed by President Andrew Jackson, was a brutal policy that forced approximately seventy thousand Indigenous people out of their homes.[17]

Thousands of Indigenous people died as a result of these forced removals, including at least four thousand Cherokees who lost their lives on the "Trail of Tears." In that same year, the state of Georgia broke legal agreements with the Cherokee Nation and created a lottery system to dole out jackpots of stolen Cherokee land to thousands of White men.[18]

This trend of enriching Whites with stolen Native land continued over the next decades with the support of many White Americans and politicians. In addition to Andrew Jackson, eight other U.S. presidents were involved in removing Native Americans from their land and authorizing hideous techniques like burning entire villages and destroying Indigenous people's food supplies.[19]

In 1862, the United States Congress signed the Homestead Act, which violated treaty agreements with Indigenous people and gave hundreds of millions of acres of Native territory—and wealth—almost entirely to White people.[20] Meanwhile, Indigenous Nations were increasingly restricted to living on small pieces of land called "reservations"—sometimes hundreds or even thousands of miles away from the places they traditionally called home.

Against considerable odds, Native people have launched resistance movements with some degree of success against their forced displacement. Have you ever heard the name "Geronimo"? This name became etched in history because Geronimo, a strong Apache warrior, helped his people resist the U.S. military. The Apache defended their nation from the violence of the U.S. government for nearly forty years—from 1850 until 1886—led, in part, by Geronimo. Around the same time, Cheyenne leaders Little Wolf and Dull Knife mobilized over three hundred individuals to stand up against the powerful U.S. military and partially return to their ancestral land in 1878.[21]

RESISTING SETTLER COLONIALISM

The true history of Indigenous people has been distorted and misrepresented in our schools and popular culture. My history classes in elementary school, middle school, and even high school did not address the genocide and injustice that Native American people have been experiencing and resisting for hundreds of years. Many of us were taught to believe the myth that Native people passively gave away their land or happily made agreements with European settlers. These misrepresentations are reinforced by cultural traditions that continue to teach us that "this land" was destined to belong to the U.S. government rather than sovereign Native people. Each November, hundreds of millions of Americans gather on Thanksgiving to "celebrate" a supposedly peaceful meeting between pilgrim settlers and Native people.

But, as we have seen in this chapter, the actual encounters between settlers and Natives were violent and unjust. Jaskiran Dhillon, a Native scholar, writes that the myth of Thanksgiving represents "the story White Americans like to tell themselves about who they are and what they stand for."[22] The true story of our nation's founding is a story of colonial oppression and white supremacy. But the story most Americans want to believe is one of freedom, liberty, and justice for all. Native Americans, however, have not been free to protect their families, communities, and land from ongoing theft and exploitation imposed by government officials and companies looking to find new sources of wealth.

Today, as in the past, many Indigenous people continue to resist and oppose the forces of racism and colonialism. In 2016, a company called Energy Transfer Partners sought permits to build the Dakota Access Pipeline to carry millions of barrels of oil across the United States.[23] However, the pipeline would run through land belonging to the Standing Rock Sioux Tribe. The Standing Rock Sioux argued that the pipeline construction would violate an 1851 treaty between the Sioux and the U.S. government. Both Indigenous advocates and environmental activists protested the pipeline and raised awareness about the risks of contamination and pollution that would result from oil leaks. Indigenous people marched, organized resistance campaigns, and spoke out against the pipeline proposal.

Many Native activists and supporters held signs that said "WATER IS LIFE"—signaling key Indigenous values such as our interconnectedness with life, as well as the need to protect our water supply from chemicals and contamination. Yet, despite our country's legal and moral obligation to respect this treaty, the U.S. government decided to grant the permit allowing for the creation of the pipeline, committing yet another violation of Indigenous treaty rights.[24] Since the pipeline was created, it has already leaked oil and dangerous contaminants into the local environment.[25]

The building of the pipeline did not bring an end to resistance efforts on the part of Native Americans. As I write these words, young people continue to play a very important role in leading the Standing

Rock movement. The International Indigenous Youth Council acts to protect local rivers from the environmental hazards of the Dakota Access Pipeline, and has built an organization stretching from California to Colorado, New Mexico, South Dakota, Texas, and Minnesota. Their movement, led by young people, is rising up for social justice, environmental protection, and Indigenous sovereignty. And their values are rooted in "prayer, honor, wisdom, and love."[26]

Creating a world with more peace and justice will require that we recognize the humanity, knowledge, and dignity of Native people—as well as their right to live happily and safely in their communities. Indigenous nations experience many forms of violence and health problems as a result of historical oppression. Some research suggests that Native Americans are killed by police at a higher rate than any other racial or ethnic group.[27]

Native people also have to deal with being largely invisible, demeaned, and misrepresented in the media as well as our history books.[28] Many sports teams have names and mascots that disrespect Native people with racial slurs and dehumanizing stereotypes—such as the R-word, which has been used throughout history as a racist insult toward Native people. Using a racial slur for the name of a sports team is deeply harmful, and no one deserves to have their heritage ridiculed or made fun of for entertainment.

Here, too, Native people demonstrate their collective strength and resilience by standing up to injustice. Adrienne Keene, a Cherokee scholar and activist, is leading efforts alongside thousands of other Indigenous people to protest racist mascots and improve the representation of Native Americans.[29]

On Long Island, where I teach, the Shinnecock Nation is resisting the efforts of developers and politicians who attempt to encroach on their land.[30] When I visited their 800-acre reservation in Southampton, New York, on a cold, windy November afternoon, I had the pleasure of discovering the work of Jeremy Dennis, a young Shinnecock artist who uses photography and digital representations to unearth the history and cultural heritage of Native American people.

One of Dennis's most exciting projects is called *On This Site* and consists of an interactive online map where you can click on different sacred Indigenous sites across Long Island to learn about local history from the perspective of Native American people. Dennis describes his vision this way: "My hope is that this project will create awareness of these sites and inform viewers, using the perspective of a Native American cultural vision and voice. This is where we once were, and are still here."[31]

White supremacy in the United States has always been deeply connected to settler colonialism and stealing land from Indigenous people. But, as we have seen in this chapter, Indigenous people have also been resisting and rising up against white supremacy for centuries. Now that we have established how racism is tied to colonialism, next we will take a closer look at slavery—another pillar of modern racism. In Chapter 4, we will consider how and why the enslavement and oppression of African Americans is still deeply relevant for understanding our society today.

FOUR

WHY SLAVERY STILL MATTERS

I magine walking into an eighth-grade classroom for a history lesson and having your teacher suggest that slavery might actually be a good thing. And, as if that's not shocking enough, now imagine being instructed to make a list of the "positive aspects" of enslaving and torturing human beings. This is exactly what happened to students at a school in San Antonio, Texas—not in 1718 or 1818, but in 2018!

The ordeal came to light when a student in the class named Manú Livar posted a copy of his required homework assignment—"The Life of Slaves: A Balanced View"—on Twitter.[1] In the "Positives" column, Manú wrote "N/A"—for not applicable—because he didn't believe there was anything good or positive about slavery. In the "Negative Aspects," he wrote, among other things:

- Forced strenuous labor
- Rape

- Forced religion
- Stolen culture
- No payment
- Occasional torture
- Hardly were fed

Manú's long list of "negatives" also referred to many of the terrible facts of life under slavery—that enslaved people were frequently separated from their families and loved ones, made to live in terrible conditions, subject to cruel violence, including sexual abuse by their "masters," and deprived of access to medicine and healthcare. When Manú came home from school, he showed his assignment to his parents and spoke up about feeling uncomfortable when his teacher instructed students in the class to justify slavery. After his concerned father shared a picture of the worksheet on social media, many people, including students, parents, community members, and even elected officials across the country were angered and upset by the incident.

What happened to Manú was not an isolated incident. As you know, transatlantic slavery is one of the legs of white supremacy and racial oppression. But what you might not know is that the racist idea that slavery was a "good thing" for Africans is still very much with us. There are, in fact, schoolteachers and even college professors who continue to promote the dangerous myth that enslavement and human rights abuses can have "positive aspects".[2] And, as we've already witnessed in this book, in classrooms across the country, generations of students have learned an upside-down version of history that downplays the violent atrocities and injustices experienced by enslaved people.[3]

For much of our nation's history, textbooks portrayed slave masters as "kind" and suggested that enslaved persons were actually happy and cheerful living under the whips and chains of bondage.[4] To a large degree, this misrepresentation of slavery is the result of continued racist ideology and anti-Black racism in particular. Unfortunately, the warped ideas that justified forcing Africans into slavery, including the twisted notion that it was partially for their benefit, have not gone away despite the fact that slavery was officially abolished by the Thirteenth Amendment in 1865.[5] And, the continued celebration of slavery in memorials to the Confederacy throughout the U.S. South reflects the ongoing racial oppression that haunts millions of African Americans.

It may seem odd or paradoxical that a country that prides itself on valuing "liberty and justice for all" could promote slavery. How could a nation claim to foster freedom and equality while keeping millions of people in chains?

According to historian George Fredrickson, the co-existence of racism and the belief in human equality may not be as contradictory as you might think. By portraying Blacks and other non-White groups as subhuman, inferior beings who didn't deserve freedom, White Americans found a loophole of sorts that allowed them to perceive the United States as the "land of the free" while keeping Blacks enslaved.[6] In other words, it was the "land of the free" only for those who supposedly merited freedom under this racist system: White people.

In this chapter, we will learn how and why slavery still matters for our society today. Like settler colonialism, slavery is a profoundly disturbing and traumatic topic due to the many forms of violence and

abuse to which enslaved people were subjected. But, just as Indigenous people resisted (and continue to resist) colonial oppression, so
did enslaved African Americans overcome outrageous odds to challenge the institution of slavery.

As we begin this part of our journey, it's important to recognize
that slavery is not merely Black history or the history of the southern
states. In fact, as we will see later on, slavery is connected to the
history of the entire world and is central to the social, political, and
economic structures of the United States.

In fact, our entire country was quite literally built on the backs
of enslaved people. The United States as we know it would simply
not exist without the physical labor and cultural contributions of
Africans and their descendants. The African presence on this continent brought new cultural practices, forms of knowledge, and artistic
expression as well as intellectual achievements. Over the course of
246 years, African slaves and their descendants created wealth and
economic opportunities for White Americans.[7]

Although most White Americans never owned slaves, White
Americans collectively benefited from generations of unpaid slave
labor. Toiling away on land stolen from Native Americans, slaves
became vital to the social, political, and economic relations of the
British colonies and, later, the newly formed United States. But
unpaid labor was not only the foundation of our economy—it was
also enshrined within our constitution and legal institutions. Many
U.S. presidents, Supreme Court judges, senators, and other powerful
individuals owned slaves and fiercely defended the institution. The
question of slavery was so central to our politics that it ripped the
nation apart during the bloody Civil War.

Manú, the student mentioned above, is not African American. Although he and his family are Mexican American and identify as Chicano, they felt moved to speak up about the moral and historical wrong of portraying any aspect of slavery as a good or positive thing. All of us, regardless of our racial or ethnic background, need to come to terms with the horrors of slavery and the ways in which this dreadful chapter of history continues to shape society in the present.

SLAVERY AND THE MODERN WORLD

Slavery is the practice of owning other human beings and forcing them to perform unpaid labor. It is an economic form of oppression. Sadly, enslaving humans is an ancient phenomenon that can be found in societies all over the globe.[8] Many people associate slavery with Africans in particular, but the word "slave" actually comes from the term 'Slav' which refers to an ethnic group in Eastern Europe. Before the modern era, it was common for Europeans to enslave other European ethnics—especially foreigners and captives of war.[9] As Europeans began to colonize the Americas and oppress Indigenous people in the fifteenth century, they also increasingly turned to slave labor in order to create profitable plantation economies.

At first, French, Spanish, and English colonizers all tried to enslave Indigenous people. Columbus himself captured hundreds of Native Americans and sent them to Spain in chains.[10] The enslavement of Native Americans was interwoven into the fabric of colonial life in the British colonies that would eventually become the United States.[11] During this time, colonizers also exploited the labor of poor

Whites and White criminals through a practice called *indentured servitude.* Unlike slaves, however, indentured servants were not legally bound to a lifetime of unpaid labor.

As the work of maintaining and expanding the colonies increased, Europeans turned to the continent of Africa for slave labor. It is important to bear in mind that Africans have a very long and rich history prior to transatlantic slavery. And, some people of African descent came to this continent as free individuals. As early as the 1500s, Africans (both enslaved and free) accompanied Europeans during colonial explorations of the American continent.[12] The very first non-Native person to settle in Manhattan (New York) was actually a free sailor and linguist of African descent named Juan Rodrigues.[13] But while some Africans did come to the Americas as explorers, most were brought here unwillingly in chains.

Human trafficking and enslavement quickly became a major economic engine for many Western nations while creating an immense amount of suffering for millions of Africans and their descendants. Between 1525 and 1866, European nations established the *transatlantic slave trade*, also referred to as the *triangular trade*. This trade route is sometimes called a "triangle" because of the three steps in the journey taken as European slave traders crossed the Atlantic Ocean.[14]

In the first stage of the "triangle," slave ships left coastal cities in Western Europe filled with merchandise such as weapons, alcohol, and jewelry and traveled across the Atlantic to coastal cities in West Africa. There, Europeans exchanged their goods for human beings captured and held in bondage by African traders.[15] During the second stage, called the *Middle Passage*, Europeans forced enslaved Africans onto their ships in brutal conditions and set sail for the Americas. In the final stage of the "triangle," valuable products created through unpaid slave labor like tobacco, sugar, and cotton were shipped back across the Atlantic to boost European economies—thus completing the "triangle" by returning to the point of origin.

THE UNIQUENESS OF TRANSATLANTIC SLAVERY

As mentioned earlier, slavery is a very old practice that can be found in societies across the globe. There is historical evidence that Native Americans, Europeans, Africans, and Asians all have a history of enslaving people. However, transatlantic slavery represented a very different kind of slavery than the systems that previously existed in cultures throughout the world.

In terms of scale, it was an unprecedented enterprise. Uprooting between 12.5 and 30 million people, the trade represented the most massive forced displacement of people in the history of the planet.[16] The vast majority of Africans who were kidnapped during the transatlantic trade were sent to European colonies in South America (including modern-day Brazil) and the Caribbean islands. Only about 388,000 enslaved Africans were sent to the colonies that would become the United States.[17] These individuals would eventually give rise to a population of over four million enslaved adults and children by the end of the Civil War in 1865.[18]

Approximately two million enslaved people died in the horrendous Middle Passage, which could last up to several months as the ships made their slow voyage across the Atlantic. Conditions aboard the ships were unbelievably gruesome and inhumane. African women, men, and children were ripped from their families and forced to lie naked in chains next to strangers for weeks and months at a time. They were provided very little food or water and did not have access to toilets and proper sanitation. This means that enslaved persons had to lie in pools of vomit, urine, and excrement, without the ability to clean themselves.

Enslaved people—including young people who were the same age as you are right now—were often abused and tortured. Many succumbed to disease, and others were brutally killed by European enslavers. At least a million slaves were tossed overboard to their death during the Middle Passage, either as a consequence of enslavers' cruel whims, or the illness and starvation that inevitably resulted from overcrowded and inhumane conditions.[19]

Beyond its horrific scope and scale, transatlantic slavery was also very different from prior forms of slavery due to racial ideology that was used to justify the "chattel" system. Chattel slavery is a type of exploitation in which a human being is owned as a piece of property and reduced to the status of an object—like a piece of furniture.[20] A chattel slave would be trapped in this oppressed condition for the entirety of their lives. In most other societies, including African societies, slavery was not a lifelong sentence. It was common for people to temporarily become slaves as a result of conquest or war—but it was usually possible to escape slavery and attain freedom.

However, during the transatlantic slave trade, Europeans gradually introduced the idea of race to justify enslaving Africans and their children indefinitely. Eric Williams, an influential Caribbean historian, put it this way: "Slavery was not born of racism: rather, racism was the consequence of slavery."[21] The myths of White racial superiority and Black racial inferiority were used to falsely portray enslaved people as barbaric, unintelligent, and deserving of nothing more than a life of servitude. As Europeans began to describe themselves as members of a biologically superior White race, they also started to think that enslaving other Whites was a bad thing.

By contrast, enslaving Africans was increasingly framed as the natural order of things.[22] Despite the fact that enslaved Africans came from many different ethnic groups with their own distinct languages and cultures, Europeans labeled them all as members of a single Black race and promoted the racist idea that Black people were naturally suited for slavery and unsuited for freedom.

Throughout plantation societies in the Americas, Whites established racist laws, which cemented Black people as the bottom of the racial hierarchy.[23] In many jurisdictions, it was illegal for African American slaves to learn how to read or write, assemble together, and carry weapons. Slaves were also prevented from testifying in court. And, in 1857, the Supreme Court issued a fateful ruling known as the *Dred Scott Decision*, which argued that the Constitution of the United States barred all Black people, regardless of whether they were enslaved or free, from ever being citizens.

Robert Taney, the chief justice of the court, went so far as to write:

> *[Blacks] had for more than a century before been regarded as beings of an inferior order, and altogether unfit to associate with the white race either in social or political relations, and so far inferior that they had no rights which the white man was bound to respect, and that the negro might justly and lawfully be reduced to slavery for his benefit.*[24]

Here we have an example of the highest court in the land openly expressing the white supremacist idea that Blacks are "beings of an inferior order" without any rights whatsoever.

But slavery wasn't just a life sentence for Africans and their descendants—it became an *intergenerational* prison of forced labor, daily humiliations, and brutal oppression. One of the ghastliest realities of this slave system is the fact that the children of enslaved African women automatically became "chattel" in the womb. They would be reduced to the status of slavery from the moment they were born. Can you imagine how heartbreaking it was for enslaved mothers and fathers to know that their kids would become slaves at birth?

Harriet Jacobs, an African American abolitionist who escaped slavery, gives us some insight into how devastating enslavement was for Black families. In her famous book, *Incidents in the Life of a Slave Girl* (1861), Harriet describes the horrible predicament of enslaved children and their parents. Enslaved people had to live with many different kinds of trauma, including the trauma of knowing their loved ones could be taken away from them at any moment, as White slave masters regularly sold their property to the highest bidder. Jacobs recounts one such incident:

> On one of these sale days, I saw a mother lead seven children to the auction-block. She knew that some of them would be taken from her; but they took all. The children were sold to a slave-trader, and their mother was bought by a man in her own town. Before night her children were all far away. She begged the trader to tell her where he intended to take them; this he refused to do. How could he, when he knew he

would sell them, one by one, wherever he could command the
highest price? I met that mother in the street, and her wild,
haggard face lives to-day in my mind. She wrung her hands
in anguish, and exclaimed, "Gone! All gone! Why don't God
kill me?" I had no words wherewith to comfort her. Instances
of this kind are of daily, yea, of hourly occurrence.[25]

As we can see from this tragic account, the slave system involved Whites' utter disregard for the humanity and dignity of those held in bondage. Such callous indifference caused profound despair, pain, and agony for those who were bought and sold like objects for the enrichment of White Americans. In Harriet's words, slaves were "no more, in the sight of their masters, than the cotton they plant, or the horses they tend."[26]

RESISTANCE AND REVOLUTION

"What, to the American slave, is your Fourth of July?" This question was posed by Frederick Douglass in 1852 to an audience of nearly 600 White abolitionists in New York.[27] They had asked him to speak to their group on Independence Day—but he'd refused. Instead, Douglass arrived on July 5. So, what was the meaning of the Fourth of July for Douglass—a man who had been born into slavery and risked his life to gain freedom? He continued his fiery speech:

I answer; a day that reveals to him, more than all other
days in the year, the gross injustice and cruelty to which he is

the constant victim. To him, your celebration is a sham; your boasted liberty, an unholy license; your national greatness, swelling vanity; your sounds of rejoicing are empty and heartless; your denunciation of tyrants, brass fronted impudence; your shouts of liberty and equality, hollow mockery; your prayers and hymns, your sermons and thanksgivings, with all your religious parade and solemnity, are, to Him, mere bombast, fraud, deception, impiety, and hypocrisy—a thin veil to cover up crimes which would disgrace a nation of savages. There is not a nation on the earth guilty of practices more shocking and bloody than are the people of the United States, at this very hour.

Frederick Douglass (1879) [David F. Barry]

For Douglass, Independence Day was not a genuine celebration of freedom. Instead, it was a hypocritical farce. By speaking up and denouncing the evils of slavery throughout his abolitionist writing and speeches, Douglass used his pen and the podium as powerful tools of resistance.

Like Douglass, many African Americans found numerous ways to resist slavery—usually nonviolently but occasionally through the use of force. Harriet Jacobs, mentioned earlier, dedicated much of her life to the abolitionist movement. Another heroic Harriet, Harriet Tubman, risked her life again and again to bring enslaved people to freedom through a network of safe houses known as the *Underground Railroad*. In 1831, Nat Turner led a bloody insurrection against enslavers in Virginia in which White women and children were brutally killed.[28]

Harriet Tubman (c. 1868–69) [Collection of the National
Museum of African American History and Culture]

Some White Americans joined forces with enslaved people to rise up against the injustice of slavery. In 1859, a White man named John Brown worked with a small group of collaborators to launch an attack on a federal arsenal in Virginia. Brown's objective was to smuggle the weapons in the arsenal to enslaved Blacks so that they could undertake an armed rebellion. Although the plan did not succeed—and Brown was executed as a result of his actions—the bloody episode demonstrated that there were Whites who were willing to die for the worthy cause of ending slavery.[29]

John Brown (1856) [Boston Athenaeum]

Undoubtedly, the most massive uprising against slavery occurred outside the United States. In 1804, the Black residents of Saint Domingue (now known as Haiti) achieved the first successful slave revolt in history as they defeated their French enslavers and created the first Black republic. They had been led by General Toussaint

L'Ouverture until his death in 1803. As a result, "every white-slave owner, in Jamaica, Cuba, or Texas, lived in dread" of new uprisings and rebellions.[30]

But Haitians would pay dearly for their freedom. With the backing of Western powers—including the United States—the French king "demanded that Haiti pay an 'independence debt' to compensate former colonists for the slaves who had won their freedom in the Haitian Revolution" and threatened to unleash its powerful military if the new Black nation refused to comply.[31] The amount of "debt" unjustly imposed by France added up to between seventeen and twenty-four billion dollars—a crushing amount that plunged the Haitian economy into chaos and instability.

It may surprise you to learn that the French were not alone in demanding to be paid for losing the value of their enslaved property. In fact, slave owners—*not slaves!*—received *reparations* in the United States and in the European plantation economies. Reparations are monetary payments or other kinds of resources that are given to someone as a form of compensation to "repair" a past wrong. In 1862, President Lincoln "signed a bill . . . that paid up to $300 for every enslaved person freed" while England paid millions of dollars in reparations to over 46,000 enslavers in their Caribbean colonies following the abolition of slavery.[32] Enslaved people themselves, however, never received just compensation for their labor.

THE AFTERLIFE OF SLAVERY

Saidiya Hartman, a cultural historian, argues that we are all still living with the "afterlife of slavery." For descendants of enslaved Africans in the United States, this "afterlife" takes the form of "skewed life chances, limited access to health and education, premature death, incarceration, and impoverishment."[33]

According to Joy DeGruy, a social worker and scholar, Black people today are still experiencing "post-traumatic slave syndrome" as a result of intergenerational trauma.[34] You may have heard of the term "PTSD," which refers to "post-traumatic stress disorder." The basic idea behind PTSD is that experiencing violence or abuse causes psychological harm that can last many years and even an entire lifetime. Scholars like DeGruy argue that trauma can be collectively passed on from one generation to the next. From this perspective, nearly two hundred and fifty years of violent oppression under slavery produced psychologically harmful beliefs and behaviors that continue to negatively affect descendants of enslaved people today. For example, African Americans who internalize negative beliefs about being Black may be experiencing post-traumatic slave syndrome.[35]

James Loewen, a sociologist, also points out that in addition to the social and economic oppression of African Americans, the ongoing effects of slavery also include "the cultural racism it instilled in Whites."[36] This means that one of the most important legacies of slavery is White Americans' wrongful belief in White superiority and Black inferiority.

The continued misrepresentation of slavery as well as the history of African people within our educational system and popular culture is also a consequence of the transatlantic trade. As seen at the onset of this chapter, there are still teachers across the United States who portray slavery as having "positive" aspects, and research has shown that many educators and textbooks fail to provide a comprehensive and honest assessment of this difficult past.[37] How can we truly move forward and right the wrongs of history if we don't honestly acknowledge what came before?

More generally, the racist ideas that Europeans created to justify enslaving Africans have resulted in the erasure of African histories and African contributions to human civilization, language, science, technology, and knowledge. To take just one example—Did you know that the world's oldest university and library are both located in an African nation? The Qarawiyyin University and Library in Morocco were both established in the year 859 by a wealthy African Muslim woman named Fatima al-Fihri.[38] If you're anything like me, you certainly didn't learn this history in school!

The important thing to remember is that the problems created during generations of transatlantic slavery did not magically disappear when the enslaved were freed. For centuries, the inhumane treatment of enslaved Black people was deeply embedded in American culture. And, the culture of anti-Black racism that Whites gradually created to legitimize slavery didn't disappear after abolition. Not only did racist ideas outlive slavery—so did white supremacy as a system of power. The passage of the Thirteenth Amendment to the Constitution abolishing slavery did not eradicate widespread discrimination, racial violence, and extreme disparities in economic, social, and political resources. Those who were freed during and after the Civil War did not find a nation ready or willing to provide any substantial degree of help. According to historian Jim Downs:

> Little if any thought was given to what would happen to Black people after emancipation. Questions about where they would go, what they would eat, how they would work and,

most important, how they would survive . . . were not consid-
ered, either by policy makers in Washington or the majority of
generals in the field.

In fact, "freedom" for African Americans often meant a lack of
resources and adequate help from the federal government. Many
emancipated people died of starvation and illness as a result of
neglect and disregard by White authorities.[39]

And, as it turned out, emancipation didn't result in true freedom.
In the wake of the Civil War, white supremacy continued to be institutionalized throughout the United States in the form of Jim Crow
segregation laws in the South and limited educational and employment opportunities, as well as the threat of White mob violence and
lynchings. The intertwined legacies of slavery and racial oppression
deprived African Americans of basic human and civil rights, all of
which hampered their ability to enjoy the full freedoms of citizenship.

Opposing racism in our society today requires that we see the connections between the past and the present. Antiracism also requires
making a conscious effort to reject the culture of white supremacy
that has taught generations of Americans to hate, fear, and ridicule
Black people. From the Middle Passage to everyday indignities of
being vulnerable to torture and deprived of freedom, enslaved people in the United States overcame unthinkable atrocities through
their resilience and determination to survive. Rising up against racial
injustice involves learning to empathize with the plight of African
Americans and others who have been harmed—and are still being
harmed—by racism.[40]

How can we honor the memory of those who helped build this

country through their blood, sweat, and tears? What do you think should be done? Some experts argue that the United States government still owes a debt to African Americans for slavery *and* centuries of discrimination that can and should be paid.[41] Where there's a political will, there's a way. Young people just like you can play an important role in shifting the political culture of this country by advocating for reparations.

But Saidiya Hartman also points to the need for something more than economic repair. "The demands of the slave on the present have everything to do with making good the promise of abolition . . ." she writes. "It requires the reconstruction of society, which is the only way to honor our debt to the dead."[42]

FIVE

SECOND-CLASS CITIZENS

Akiko Kurose was only sixteen years old when Pearl Harbor, a military base in Hawaii, was bombed by the Japanese in 1942. Born to Japanese American parents, Akiko grew up in Seattle, Washington. As a U.S. citizen, Akiko did not realize that she had any reason to worry about her own safety when the United States entered World War II after the Japanese attack. Many years later, Akiko reflected on the moment when she began to understand her predicament:

> Well, I'd just come home from church and then we kept hearing, you know, "Pearl Harbor was bombed" . . . I had no idea where Pearl Harbor was. My geography was not that sophisticated . . . And my father said, "Uh-oh. There's gonna be trouble." And I said, "Well, how come?" . . . He says, "Well, Japan just bombed Pearl Harbor . . . We're at war with Japan." But, I thought, "Why should it bother me?"

The next day, Akiko returned to her high school and came face-to-face with the "trouble" her father had warned her about:

> . . . when I went back to school that following morning . . . one of the teachers said, "You people bombed Pearl Harbor." And I'm thinking "My people"? All of a sudden, my Japanese-ness became very aware to me, you know. And then . . . I no longer felt I'm an equal American . . . I felt kind of threatened and nervous about it.[1]

Akiko was right to feel nervous. Just a few months later, on February 19, 1942, her life was turned upside down when President Franklin Delano Roosevelt signed Executive Order 9066 authorizing the "internment" of Japanese Americans. The infamous order facilitated the removal of nearly 120,000 Japanese Americans from their homes and their forced relocation to concentration camps in eight states.[2] Most were citizens of the United States and about one third were children.[3]

Akiko and her family suddenly found themselves displaced and sent to a concentration camp in Puyallup, Washington.[4] There, along with thousands of others, they were incarcerated in dehumanizing conditions and fenced in with barbed wire. Some were made to live in barns and stalls that previously had housed horses and pigs. "People would drive around in cars, calling us names," Akiko said. "You'd feel like an animal in the zoo."[5]

How could the United States justify the incarceration and psychological abuse of over one hundred thousand people—including its own citizens—without due process for years at a time? As we will see later, much of the justification for Japanese internment had to do with racist ideas about who does (and does not) truly belong in this country. Despite the fact that the United States was at war with Germany, Italy, and Japan in 1942, only Japanese Americans were targeted for internment. Neither German Americans nor Italian Americans were sent away to concentration camps. Officially, people of Japanese descent were labeled "an enemy race" by the U.S. government and treated like criminals as a result of racist beliefs about Asians and other people labeled non-White.[6]

Akiko's experience vividly demonstrates that citizenship is not enough to protect people defined as non-White from the violence and injustice of racism. In fact, the United States has a long history of treating its citizens unequally. Many of these inequalities are directly tied to racist ideology and misguided beliefs about the racial worthiness (or unworthiness) of human groups. As scholar Tanya Golash-Boza points out, politicians in the United States "consistently have used immigration policy to influence the racial and ethnic makeup of the nation."[7]

In this chapter, we will deepen our understanding of systemic racism by considering the relationship between white supremacy, citizenship, and immigration. We have already seen that the United States was established through unjust and oppressive racist practices, including the genocide of Native Americans as well as the enslavement of Africans and people labeled Black. But once it was formed as a nation, the United States continued to enforce racist laws and practices governing who could become a citizen—and how citizens would be treated.

Racism is related to citizenship in two major ways. First, racist beliefs and practices can limit the group of people who are allowed to become citizens. This means that racism can exclude people from accessing the nation's resources on the basis of their perceived race by preventing them from entering the country or becoming citizens. Very often, racist exclusion of this type is fueled by *xenophobia*—fear and hostility directed toward foreigners or "outsiders."[8] Secondly, racist beliefs and practices can also create inequalities and injustices *among* citizens of the same nation who are defined as members of different racial groups. In this way, racist ideology can create an unjust hierarchy of citizens with the White majority on top and other groups positioned on the bottom.

Although much of our discussion will touch on immigration, it's important to bear in mind that some members of our society are not immigrants at all. Native Americans are, of course, the original inhabitants of this land and most African Americans are the descendants of people who were involuntarily kidnapped and enslaved. Many Chicanos actually became U.S. citizens when the United States violently seized Mexican land. After the Mexican-American War, which took place between 1846 and 1848, more than half of Mexican territory was absorbed into U.S. states.[9]

For most of our country's history, immigration and citizenship policies were tools of racial exclusion—not inclusion. Because the United States was first conceived as a nation to be ruled by and for White men, our immigration and citizenship laws were restrictive from the start. The slow expansion of rights to a wider circle of humanity only occurred as a result of protest and political engagement on the part of courageous activists and visionaries. Promoting true equality in our society requires acknowledging the ways in which laws related to citizenship and immigration have historically benefited Europeans defined as White—especially those from Western and Northern Europe.

WHITE SUPREMACY AND CITIZENSHIP

In principle, a nation is supposed to provide equal rights, protection and dignity to all of its citizens. But the sad reality is that many nations, including our own, fail to realize this ideal. It may surprise you to learn that one of this country's very first laws governing citizenship was overtly white supremacist. The **Naturalization Act of 1790** provided access to citizenship to "free White persons"—a category that, at the time, only included White men. This meant that foreigners living within the United States could only become citizens if they were considered White and male.[10]

As we explore this history, it is important to recognize that social factors like racial classification, gender, and class position shape our access to (or exclusion from) the resources and benefits of U.S. citizenship.[11] The key idea is that, as a result of structural oppression, we do not all experience citizenship in the same way.

Historian Linda Kerber identifies a number of groups that have received unequal treatment with regard to our nation's citizenship laws. As indicated above, women were excluded from the Naturalization Act of 1790 and did not receive the right to vote until 1920. Native Americans, survivors of genocide, did not receive citizenship until 1924. And, even after attaining citizenship, many states continued to systematically deny Indigenous people the right to vote on the basis of racist ideology. Native Americans—including veterans who fought for the United States—would have to wait until the Voting Rights Act of 1965 to have legal access to elections in every U.S. state.

Today, Indigenous people still face significant barriers to full political participation. This is especially true for those who live on reservations and do not have the kind of mailing addresses or identity cards required by the United States government. As a result, nearly 1 million Native Americans are not registered to vote.[12]

Enslaved Africans were also excluded from citizenship until the Fourteenth Amendment to the Constitution was ratified in 1868. But even after the Civil War, African Americans were relegated to the status of second-class citizens, subject to White mob violence and systematically denied voting rights as well as opportunities for economic advancement.[13] In the words of race scholar George Fredrickson, "Emancipation could not be carried to completion because it exceeded the capacity of White Americans—in the North as well as in the South—to think of Blacks as genuine equals."[14]

Asian Americans who immigrated to the United States were barred from becoming citizens for much of our country's history and faced severe restrictions and quotas that limited their ability to reside in the United States until the 1960s. In the end, the only group of people who have always had access to citizenship in the United States are Caucasian males.[15]

According to sociologist Vilna Bashi Treitler, racist ideology has played a central role in shaping immigration policies and practices in the United States. She argues that various groups—including immigrants from Europe, the Americas, and Asia as well as Native Americans and African Americans—have all historically attempted to move up the hierarchy by improving the reputation of their ethnic group.[16] How does an ethnic group improve its reputation? Analyzing a diverse range of groups and migration histories, Treitler concludes that being socially labeled as White or *as close to White as possible* is the magic ticket for gaining acceptance into American society and greater access to valued resources like citizenship and property rights.

For example, Irish American and Italian American immigrants were both considered lower on the hierarchy of European "races" when they arrived in the United States. By assimilating into White American society, both groups were able to gain greater acceptance, access to good jobs, and political power.

But Treitler's analysis doesn't end there. Because the meaning of "blackness" has historically been defined in opposition to "whiteness," and as the bottom of the racial hierarchy in the United States, gaining acceptance by the White majority also requires that members of ethnic groups distance themselves from African American descendants of slaves. In short, the pathway to "ethnic success" has been accepting the racial hierarchy of white supremacy and stepping on the backs of African Americans.[17]

THE DIMINISHED CITIZENSHIP OF AFRICAN AMERICANS

Ida B. Wells, a crusader for women's rights and racial justice, learned through painful experience that citizenship did not provide protection for African Americans. As a Black woman living in Memphis, Tennessee in the late 1800s, she came face-to-face with the shocking violence and oppression that rocked the lives of African American communities after their "emancipation" and transformation into U.S. citizens. In the spring of 1892, one of Wells's friends—a Black business owner—was brutally lynched by a group of White domestic terrorists in Memphis. When local authorities refused to hold the perpetrators accountable, she decided to use her platform as the owner of a major newspaper to begin a lifelong campaign against lynching.

Three years later, Wells published one of her most influential pamphlets: *A Red Record: Tabulated Statistics and Alleged Causes of Lynching in the United States*. In stirring prose, Wells addressed the ways in which racist ideas and practices prevented African Americans from enjoying their rightful status as full citizens:

> *By an amendment to the Constitution the Negro was given the right of franchise, and, theoretically at least, his ballot became his invaluable emblem of citizenship. In a government "of the people, for the people, and by the people," the Negro's vote became an important factor in all matters of state and national politics. But this did not last long. The southern White man would not consider that the Negro had any right which a White man was bound to respect . . . It was maintained that "This is a White man's government," and regardless of numbers the White man should rule . . . The government which had made the Negro a citizen found itself unable to protect him. It gave him the right to vote, but denied him the protection which should have maintained that right. Scourged from his home; hunted through the swamps; hung by midnight raiders, and openly murdered in the light of day,*

the Negro clung to his right of franchise with a heroism which would have wrung admiration from the hearts of savages.[18]

The startling and horrific truth about lynching revealed by Ida B. Wells was that African Americans were actually *more* vulnerable to racist violence as *citizens* than they were as enslaved property. Local and government officials alike openly allowed White Americans to murder their African American countrymen. This sobering historical precedent provides insight into how other groups faced harrowing discrimination and mistreatment as a result of being racially labeled and stigmatized.

ANTI-ASIAN RACISM AND IMMIGRATION POLICIES

The first major wave of immigrants from Asia were the Chinese and a growing community settled first on the West Coast of the United States. During the 1860s, twenty thousand Chinese American workers labored to build the first transcontinental railroad. Yet, despite their significant contributions to the nation, White politicians and influential leaders routinely portrayed Chinese people as "alien, dangerous, docile, and dirty."[19] In addition to being racially disrespected and viewed as invaders, Chinese workers were also underpaid and exploited. Gordon Chang, a history professor at Stanford University, notes that "Chinese workers were paid 30% to 50% less than their White counterparts and were given the most dangerous work."[20]

White hostility toward Asian Americans and Pacific Islanders resulted in the adoption of overtly discriminatory immigration laws as well as efforts to colonize and control territories in Asia and the Pacific Ocean. The Page Act of 1875 was the nation's very first law limiting immigration—and it targeted Chinese women. The Chinese Exclusion Act of 1882 had the effect of banning Chinese workers from entering the United States. It remained in effect for over sixty years. The Immigration Act of 1917 went even further and banned all people from the "Asiatic Zone."[21] During the late 1800s and early 1900s, the United States also began to expand its power overseas, resulting in the brutal colonization of Hawaii, the Philippines, and many other societies.[22]

These policies of exclusion and domination were justified by White officials with blatantly racist ideology. In 1923, Franklin Delano Roosevelt—the same man who would go on to authorize the internment of Japanese Americans two decades later—openly expressed his white supremacist views. In an article he wrote that year, he proclaimed: "[The] mingling of White with oriental blood on an extensive scale is harmful to our future citizenship."[23]

The importance of White identity to citizenship and property rights was no mystery to Asian immigrants. Accordingly, two different Asian American men petitioned the Supreme Court to be categorized as "White" in the early 1900s. In 1914, Takao Ozawa, a Japanese immigrant, applied for U.S. citizenship in Hawaii but was denied. At this time, naturalization—the act of becoming a citizen—was still limited to Whites and African Americans, while Asians remained excluded. Ozawa protested the denial and took his complaint all the way to the Supreme Court, contending that he should be considered "White" and granted citizenship because of the light color of his skin. But in 1922, the Supreme Court decided against Ozawa, arguing that Japanese people cannot become citizens because they are not Caucasian.

Just a few months later, in 1923, the Supreme Court switched gears and made up another excuse to exclude Asian people from citizenship. Bhagat Singh Thind, an Indian immigrant, argued that he should be considered White and granted citizenship because of his Caucasian heritage. In the *United States vs. Bhagat Singh Thind* decision, the Justices abandoned their prior argument that Whiteness really means "Caucasian" and instead made the nonsensical claim that although Indians were technically Caucasian, they were not entitled to citizenship because the "common man" did not consider them White.

Such a blatant flip-flop on the part of the Supreme Court clearly demonstrates that the meaning of racial categories like "White" are completely made up and based on subjective, shifting arguments that do not stand up to logic or scrutiny. But European-descended people who proclaimed themselves to be "White" had the power to make the word mean whatever they wanted it to mean—protecting their own economic and political positions in the process.[24]

RACIST EXCLUSION AND DEPORTATION OF LATINX PEOPLE

One of the strangest—and most persistent—features of white supremacist racism is the way in which European colonizers and immigrants from a continent thousands of miles across the Atlantic have consistently felt entitled to establish artificial borders and tell people who were living on this land before their arrival that they do not belong in the United States.

People of Hispanic or "Latinx" ethnic origin include some of the Indigenous inhabitants of the North and South American continents. Yet, Latinx Americans who were born in the United States sometimes experience xenophobia and have been told to *"Go back to your country!"* This is especially ironic since, as mentioned earlier in this chapter, some Mexicans became citizens of the United States not because of immigration, but because the U.S. invaded their homeland of Mexico. Many Americans forget that much of what is now the United States was, in fact, Mexican land until the middle of the 1800s. The states of California, Arizona, and New Mexico were largely Mexican territories until the U.S. invasion. The Treaty of Guadalupe Hidalgo, signed at the end of the Mexican-American War in 1848, "transferred the northern half of Mexico to [U.S.] control."[25]

A Mexican laborer harvesting tomatoes on a farm during the *Bracero Program*, which brought people from Mexico to the United States as temporary, exploited workers [Wikimedia Commons]

Throughout our history, Latinx people have been the targets of racist ideology, exploitative labor practices, mass deportations, and shocking violence.[26] Spanish-speaking people from South America, Central America, and the Caribbean are frequently negatively stereotyped in the media as criminals or low-status workers.[27] Between 1848 and 1928, thousands of Mexican people were murdered by lynch mobs throughout the United States.[28] Tragically, such violence has not disappeared. In 2019, a white supremacist terrorist drove ten hours to El Paso, Texas, in order to target and kill Latinx people. Twenty-two people died as a result of his actions.[29]

That same year, Francisco Galicia, an eighteen-year-old Mexican American, was detained at the U.S./Mexican border for twenty-three days despite having documents that showed him to be a U.S. citizen. During this time, he was forced to live in inhumane conditions in an overcrowded space with sixty other people and "[not] allowed to call his family or a lawyer, brush his teeth, or get access to a toilet, shower or bed." His young brother, who was undocumented, was deported to Mexico and separated from his family. Francisco and his mother have since filed a lawsuit against government officials for possible racial profiling.[30]

We continue to see evidence of bias against many different immigrant groups—including Latinx Americans—at the highest levels of government. Former President Donald Trump often used hateful language describing Hispanic individuals as violent criminals and dangerous invaders to justify exclusionary immigration policies. As some observers have pointed out, in portraying Latinx immigration as an "invasion," Trump and other politicians are drawing upon some of the same dehumanizing tropes that were used against Asian Americans and Pacific Islanders in the 1800s and early 1900s.[31] And, importantly, such hostile and hurtful language is almost never applied to European immigrants that are considered "White."

CHALLENGING RACISM IN CITIZENSHIP AND IMMIGRATION POLICIES

Throughout this chapter, we have considered how ideas about race shape the ways in which groups of people are viewed as legitimately belonging—or not belonging—in the United States. Over the last several centuries, White identity has been most closely associated with citizenship while members of groups defined as non-White continue to struggle for civil rights, social acceptance, and equal protection from harm. Yet despite this unfair treatment, it is important to acknowledge that at each stage of our history, activists and leaders— including citizens and noncitizens—have not stood idly by in the face of inequality. There's a long line of heroic figures who have resisted unjust policies and organized to create significant changes to our laws and policies.

Akiko Kurose, the Japanese American teenager incarcerated by her own country during World War II, grew up to be an award-winning teacher and a powerful human rights advocate, working with groups like the Congress of Racial Equality and joining in solidarity with African Americans and other people of color.[32]

Fred Korematsu, another Japanese American citizen, actively refused to comply with the internment policy. At the age of twenty-three, he was branded a criminal by the U.S. government for resisting the internment order. Undeterred, Korematsu bravely took his grievance to the Supreme Court. Although the Justices ruled against him in 1944, he continued to stand up for justice. Forty years later, with the support of legal experts and organizations, Korematsu successfully managed to have his conviction overturned when the U.S.

government finally admitted that the internment policy was racist and conceded that innocent Japanese Americans had been victimized by unfair suspicion and propaganda.[33] In 1998, his heroism was honored by President Bill Clinton with the Presidential Medal of Freedom.[34] Ten years prior, President Ronald Reagan signed The Civil Liberties Act of 1988, which provided a formal apology and monetary reparations to the survivors of Japanese internment.[35]

Fred Korematsu, who bravely resisted the racist internment of Japanese Americans during World War II (1983) [San Francisco Chronicle/Hearst Newspapers/Getty Images]

Today, young leaders and activists across this nation are following in the footsteps of human rights advocates like Kurose, Korematsu, and Ida B. Wells—the African American anti-lynching campaigner mentioned earlier.

United We Dream, the "largest immigrant-youth-led community in the country," supports the mobilization of young people called *Dreamers*—youth who were brought to the United States as children but do not have citizenship.[36] Connecting four hundred thousand individuals through one hundred local groups in twenty-eight states, United We Dream reaches over four million people and aims to amplify the voices and interests of both documented and undocumented immigrants.

Young people mobilize in support of Dreamers at a 2017
rally held New York City [Rhododendrites]

Power California is another group bringing together youth of color—including immigrants and undocumented people—to exercise political influence. Their inspiring vision imagines a future in which "[all] who call California home—regardless of citizenship—participate fully in decision-making for a just, safe, and culturally-vibrant state."[37]

In the next chapter, we will continue to explore the theme of politics and citizenship by taking a closer look at racial inequalities in the criminal justice system and learning how young people are working to transform our legal institutions.

SIX

CRIME AND PUNISHMENT

They killed my baby brother! They killed my baby brother!"

These are the words that fourteen-year-old Tajai Rice screamed again and again as her twelve-year-old brother Tamir lay dying on the ground with two gunshot wounds to the abdomen. It was a cloudy Saturday afternoon in November of 2014—just a few days before Thanksgiving. Tamir had been playing in the park with a toy gun near their family's home in Cleveland, Ohio. Around 3:30 p.m., a man sitting in the park became frightened and called 911: "There's a guy with a pistol, and it's probably fake," the caller said. "But he's like, pointing it at everybody." At one critical point, he added that "the guy's probably a juvenile." Soon thereafter, the 911 dispatcher summoned officers to the scene—but left out crucial information. Not only did the dispatcher neglect to tell the police that the "guy" might be a child, but they also didn't inform the officers that the gun could be fake.[1]

The fact that Tamir Rice's boyhood was not acknowledged—that he was described as an adult—cannot be separated from antiblack racism. When police officer Timothy Loehmann arrived at the park, along with two other officers, he immediately shot Tamir without hesitation. Video footage of the incident revealed that only two brief seconds elapsed between the moment Loehmann first saw Rice and the moment he discharged his weapon. In the minutes after the shooting, the Cleveland officers showed no concern whatsoever for Tamir's injuries. Rather than administer any kind of emergency medical attention to attempt to save his life, the responding officers proceeded to physically assault Tajai, Tamir's older sister, shoving her to the ground and roughly restraining her in handcuffs even though she had done nothing wrong. Four minutes after Loehmann shot Rice, an FBI agent arrived on the scene and became the first adult in the vicinity to try to save Tamir's life. Almost ten minutes after the shooting, paramedics finally reached the park and provided medical care. Tamir was eventually taken to the hospital but died from his injuries the following day.[2]

Tamir's mother Samaria and sister Tajai joined others in protesting the officers' violent actions and filed official complaints as well as a wrongful death lawsuit. One year after his death, the city of Cleveland refused to admit any wrongdoing but agreed to pay six million dollars to Tamir's family and estate. Officer Loehmann, a White male who had been previously cited for poor performance and incompetence with his firearm when he'd worked for another town's police department, was later fired—not for killing Tamir Rice, but for lying on his job application. He was eventually hired by another police department in Ohio but withdrew his application after protests led by community members as well as the family of Tamir Rice.[3]

Unfortunately, what happened to Tamir was not an isolated incident. Black men and boys alike experience the highest risk of dying at the hands of the police. One out of every thousand African American men and boys will die during encounters with police officers and law enforcement—about 2.5 times the rate at which White men and boys are killed by police.[4] African American and Native American women, men, and children as well as Latino men and boys are killed by police at higher rates than White Americans.

o o o

All too often, Black and Brown children and adults alike are viewed as criminal threats, increasing the likelihood of violent and tragic outcomes when law enforcement is involved. Take the clear and upsetting differences between the cases of Tamir Rice and Dylann Roof, who we first discussed in Chapter 2. Tamir, a Black child, was immediately shot to death by police simply for holding a toy gun. Yet a White adult, Dylann Roof, the domestic terrorist who killed nine African Americans while they were praying in church, was safely apprehended by police.

Despite the fact that White people and especially White men are historically responsible for the genocide of Indigenous people as well as acts of violence against African Americans, Latinx people, and other non-Whites, White men and boys are rarely depicted as violent threats in our media and popular culture.

Our laws and policies should be fairly applied regardless of our skin color. But this nation's ongoing history of white supremacy has produced a criminal justice system distorted by racism and other forms of bias. Samuel Walker, an expert on policing, observes that at "every point in the history of criminal justice, the people arrested, prosecuted, and punished have been mainly the poor and the powerless."[5] This means that the rich, privileged, and powerful have greater influence in the criminal justice system and, as a result, are not held accountable or policed as harshly as poor people, working-class people, and people of color.[6]

White men—including those who commit acts of violence—have traditionally held positions of power within our police forces. The same is true for our military and political offices. As a result, Whites have been able to use their power to label other racial groups as threats while creating and breaking laws in order to maintain dominance. Adam Malka, a professor of history, suggests that "[because] violent White men have historically been the policing authorities, not the criminals, they helped to create a racialized legal system sympathetic to them and hostile to minorities."[7]

Throughout this chapter, we will explore the difficult topic of systemic racism within our legal system. Laws and legal practices developed by White Americans have historically disadvantaged Indigenous Americans, African Americans, and people of color.[8] As we delve into this history, we will come face-to-face with the reality that our laws are not neutral. We will also look at the relationship between *the law*, on the one hand, and *moral beliefs about right and wrong* on the other. While we usually think of our laws as moral, just, and good, the history of racism teaches us that laws can be used to oppress groups deemed to be racially inferior.

Because racial bias and discrimination were embedded within our nation's legal structures and practices, many of our laws have, in fact, been immoral. One of the most prominent examples of immoral laws includes the legal system that allowed Whites to lawfully enslave and torture African Americans at the very same time that our founders declared that *"All men are created equal."* During this time, it was even illegal for Black people to read! Enslaved people who sought literacy—as well as those who helped them obtain education—were breaking the law.

We might also consider the many treaties and agreements that the United States disregarded as the nation stole land from Native Americans and enacted genocide. We can also see the immorality of the *Dred Scott* Supreme Court decision of the nineteenth century—which asserted that Whites had no duty to respect the human and civil rights of African Americans—as well as the racist internment of Japanese Americans in the twentieth century. For most of our nation's history, racist practices were not only legal—they were described by powerful Whites in positions of authority as morally correct.

All of these examples demonstrate that the "justice system" can actually be a source of injustice. Accordingly, antiracists often find themselves challenging their own society's legal institutions and law enforcement in the pursuit of justice and equal protection. Sadly, civil rights activists and peace advocates have often been labeled "violent" and treated like criminals and terrorists for challenging white supremacy and injustice. Martin Luther King Jr. famously wrote his "Letter from a Birmingham Jail" after being arrested by police in Alabama while leading direct action against racial injustice. In his letter, Dr. King noted that even White civil rights activists "languished in filthy, roach infested jails, suffering the abuse and brutality of policemen."[9]

Martin Luther King Jr. being arrested in Montgomery,
Alabama (1958) [Associated Press]

The nightmarish truth is that some of our country's most highly ranked law enforcement officials, including those working within the FBI and other authorities, have expressed sympathies with white supremacists while subjecting Native American, African American, and Muslim American civil rights organizers to persecution, violence, and surveillance.[10]

It is important for students of antiracism to understand how our laws and legal institutions can be instruments of oppression as well as instruments for social change. Unjust laws and practices can be challenged and abolished. Constitutions can be amended and rewritten. Protest and organized action can urge our political leaders to fulfill the promise of equal protection before the law. Political participation and voting can transform our legal policies and structures.

And new systems and ways of addressing harm can be imagined and implemented by young people just like you.

CRIMINAL JUSTICE AND SYSTEMIC RACISM

The *criminal justice system* refers to the laws, institutions, policies, and practices involved in arresting, judging, defending, incarcerating, and monitoring people suspected of or found responsible for committing crimes.[11] The trouble with the justice system, however, is the fact that laws and policing practices reflect the biases and worldviews of those in positions of power.

You will notice that the word "system" has already come up quite a lot in this book. That's because we can't make sense of the impact of racism by just focusing on the actions or prejudice of *individuals* such as police officers, judges, or lawmakers. Yes, it is certainly true that some incidents of racism result from individuals' prejudice. However, we also have to examine the way *collective* structures and practices produce unequal treatment and outcomes.

Recall that earlier in this book, we talked about how racism has become *institutionalized* in the United States. This means that racism has infiltrated our social institutions—our electoral system, police departments, courtrooms, classrooms, places of worship, and even our families.

So if we want to understand why African American boys like Tamir Rice have a higher chance of being killed by police than White boys of the same age, we have to consider the historical, social, and cultural forces that make people racially labeled as non-White more vulnerable to disadvantage, mistreatment, and harm. We also have to acknowledge that racism has become deeply embedded in our culture, which means that people of *all* racial and ethnic backgrounds working within our criminal justice system can be influenced by biases that have historically benefited White Americans.

One major source of inequality in our criminal justice system is the historical exclusion of people of color and women of all racial and ethnic backgrounds from positions of power in our legal institutions. Every single president of the United States to date, with the exception of one, has been a White man—and, as we have seen, many of them openly embraced white supremacist views and supported racist policies. Expressing racism and engaging in racist behavior have not been treated as disqualifying for public office and positions of authority in our criminal justice system. To the contrary, racist views and beliefs have often been validated and normalized by authority figures.

Although non-Hispanic Whites make up only about 60 percent of the population, they represent 90 percent of all elected officials, 77 percent of Congress, and over 70 percent of police officers.[12] White men represent 31 percent of the U.S. population but comprise 65 percent of elected officials and nearly 60 percent of all state court judges.[13] The role of a prosecutor is very important in our legal system—they are lawyers who represent the government and pursue cases against individuals accused of crimes. A whopping 95 percent of all elected prosecutors are White. Even more shocking? Three out of five U.S. states have *zero* Black prosecutors.[14] By 2060, most women in the United States will be women of color. But as of this writing, there has only been *one* woman of color on the Supreme Court—Justice Sonia Sotomayor, a Latina.[15]

Supreme Court Justice Sonia Sotomayor (2009) [Collection of the
Supreme Court of the United States/Steve Petteway]

As a result of systemic racism, the perspectives and prejudices
of White citizens are more likely to be represented in our laws and
criminal justice policies than the perspectives and prejudices of other
groups. Diversifying our legal system and elected officials is one of
the requirements for a just and fair democracy. As journalist German
Lopez points out, "this kind of diversity matters because people's
backgrounds and life experiences can influence what issues they
think are most important."[16] Although diversity alone is not enough
to end racism in the criminal justice system, it is an important tool for
creating antiracist change.[17]

RACIAL GAPS IN THE CRIMINAL JUSTICE SYSTEM

In Chapter 2, we learned about *racial gaps*—disparities in the resources and treatment given to people on the basis of their perceived race. These gaps carry over into the criminal justice system. According to historian Samuel Walker, modern police departments were first established in the 1830s and demonstrated "no commitment to public service or to the rule of law." Their aim was not to preserve the peace or serve the greater good. Instead, police officers "served the will of the dominant White majority" and helped uphold the racial hierarchy.[18] The myth of White superiority historically portrayed people of color as criminals and threats while fostering the belief that Whites are less suspect, violent, and dangerous.

Today, Whites are significantly less likely than people of color to experience confinement in jails and prisons. Within state prisons, African Americans are confined at 5.1 times the rate of their White counterparts. Latinx people are confined at 1.4 times the rate of non-Hispanic Whites.[19]

Because these gaps and disparities begin very early in life, scholars of inequality refer to the *cradle-to-prison pipeline* to describe the accumulated disadvantages that make children of color more likely to be policed and incarcerated.[20] As we've seen with Tamir Rice, kids of color are just as likely as adults of color to be treated more harshly than their White counterparts.

Black girls are also subject to being treated like criminals, brutalized, or even executed by police.[21] At the age of only seven years old, Aiyana Stanley-Jones was killed by a police officer in Detroit,

Michigan, while she was sleeping.[22] The officer who killed her was never held accountable. In 2020, a Florida police officer arrested a six-year-old Black girl at school as she sobbed and pleaded: "Please, give me a second chance!"[23]

A protest poster honoring Aiyana Stanley-Jones. (2010) [Ted Eytan]

Monique Morris, a filmmaker and scholar, describes the harsh discipline many African American children experience from a very early age:

> *Black children are 19 percent of preschool enrollment, but 47 percent of preschool-age children who have had one out-of-school suspension. Black girls are 20 percent of female preschool enrollment, but 54 percent of girls receiving one or more out-of-school suspensions . . . Black girls with one or more disability experienced the highest suspension rate of all girls.*[24]

As a result of centuries of discrimination and negative stereo-types, children of color are often treated as adults by the educational and criminal justice systems alike, leading to harsh and sometimes violent forms of punishment.[25] Researchers at Georgetown University found that African American girls are "viewed as more adult than their White peers *at almost all stages of childhood*, beginning most significantly at the age of five." Similarly, Terry Cross, an advocate for Indigenous people, observes that Native children "are much more likely to be subjected to the harshest treatment in the most restrictive environments and less likely to have received the help they need from other systems."[26]

THE WAR ON DRUGS

How did we get to this point in our society? A lot of what we have already discussed in this book about the history of racism explains the roots of inequality in our criminal justice system. But there are also recent events, like the "War on Drugs," that have created additional harms and vulnerabilities for people of color.

When I was in elementary school in the '80s and early '90s, my classmates and I were introduced to the D.A.R.E. program—*Drug Abuse Resistance Education*—by a local police officer. We learned about the dangers of substance abuse and were told to *"Just say no to drugs."*[27] Back then, I had no idea that the D.A.R.E. program was part of a broader set of policies that would criminalize communities of color and fill our prisons with millions of Black and Brown people on the basis of nonviolent drug offenses.

During the 1970s, President Richard Nixon called for a War on

Drugs that would address the use of illegal substances with harsh penalties and punishment rather than treatment and rehabilitation.[28] In 1982—the year after I was born—President Ronald Reagan actively promoted this "drug war" and signed three pieces of legislation that profoundly transformed our criminal justice system: (1) the 1984 Crime Control Act, (2) the Anti-Drug Abuse Act of 1986, and (3) the Anti-Drug Abuse Act of 1988.[29]

Sociologist Tanya Golash-Boza points out that all three of these laws established *mandatory minimum sentences* for offenses like selling, possessing, or using illegal drugs that had a disproportionate effect on people of color. Although research suggests that Whites use and sell illegal drugs more often than people of color, Whites are *less* likely to be targeted by police for drug use or subject to long prison sentences.[30]

During the War on Drugs, substances often used by African American people were criminalized and policed more harshly than drugs used by Whites. For example, the Anti-Drug Abuse Act of 1986 treated "powder cocaine" (typically used by Whites) differently from "crack cocaine" (typically used by Blacks). It established an automatic prison sentence of five or more years for five hundred grams of powder cocaine or just five grams of crack cocaine. That means someone in possession of five grams of crack cocaine would be given the same sentence as someone in possession of one hundred times the amount of powder cocaine!

These kinds of discriminatory policy changes during the War on Drugs encouraged police officers, prosecutors, and judges to target communities of color, creating even larger racial disparities in the criminal justice system.[31]

The War on Drugs also ushered in what is known as the era of mass incarceration—a period in which the United States exponentially increased the number of people held behind bars in jails and prisons. Up until the 1970s, about one out of every one thousand persons was incarcerated in the United States. By 2013, that number jumped to seven out of every one thousand persons—an increase of over 700 percent.[32] But, these increases have not affected all racial and ethnic groups equally, and communities of color have been the primary targets of mass incarceration.

RACIST IDEOLOGY AND CRIME

As we have been learning throughout this book, the idea that Black and Brown people are inherently criminal is a key component of racism. Historically, the ideology of white supremacy taught people to fear racial minorities despite the fact that our country was established through acts of violence committed by Europeans targeting Native Americans, people of African descent, and other marginalized groups. These racist beliefs, in turn, are used to justify the kinds of biased policies discussed in this chapter.

Today, racist websites publish false statistics about race and crime in order to portray Black and Brown people as inherently violent. These false statistics can inspire hate crimes and murder as in the case of Dylann Roof—the White nationalist who killed nine African Americans in Charleston, South Carolina. Before carrying out his act, Roof wrote a manifesto that expressed his hateful beliefs and pointed to made-up statistics about "Black on White crime" that he found on the internet using Google. In making these kinds of arguments, hate groups and extremists typically ignore, downplay, or defend acts of violence committed by White people.[33]

Unfortunately, the problem is not confined to racist websites or extremist groups. Some of our most influential politicians continue to use white supremacist ideology to portray non-Whites as criminal threats. For example, Donald Trump launched his presidential campaign by suggesting that Mexicans are "rapists" and has expressed negative stereotypes about people of color to generate support for anti-immigration policies.

The tendency to collectively blame Latinx Americans, Asian Americans, African Americans, and Indigenous Americans for social problems is a hallmark of white supremacy. And, as we will see in Chapter 7, media images and representations also continue to perpetuate the belief that Whites are racially innocent whereas non-Whites are dangerous threats to society.

In fact, research has shown that White people *with* a criminal record are actually viewed more favorably than African Americans *without* a criminal record. In a classic study on racial discrimination, sociologist Devah Pager found that Whites who served prison time for felony drug convictions were actually called back for job opportunities more often than African Americans who had never been convicted of a crime.[34]

Because racism is deeply ingrained in our culture and institutions, all of us living in this society have been exposed to harmful ideas about people of color—including people of color! Black and Brown people working in the criminal justice system are also at risk of absorbing and perpetuating racist ideas about non-Whites. This is why diversity alone is not enough to challenge systemic racism.

Redditt Hudson, an African American former police officer,

experienced the culture of racism within the criminal justice system throughout his career. According to Hudson, "It is not only White officers who abuse their authority. The effect of institutional racism is such that no matter what color the officer abusing the citizen is, in the vast majority of those cases of abuse that citizen will be Black or Brown. That is what is allowed."[35]

CONCLUSION: RISING UP FOR JUSTICE

What do antiracists need to know about race and crime to debunk the myths and misconceptions that we've explored in this chapter? First, it's important to understand that the majority of violence occurs *within* racial and ethnic groups—not *between* them.[36] This means that Whites are far more likely to experience violence at the hands of another White person—largely as a result of racial segregation.

Secondly, social scientists have found that living in poverty is a major factor that promotes crime. Indigenous Americans, African Americans, and Latinx Americans all experience greater poverty rates than White Americans.[37] In Cleveland, the city where Tamir Rice lived and died, nearly half of all children live in poverty.[38] Scholars and antiracist advocates argue that reducing poverty and improving economic opportunities are effective strategies for providing greater safety and well-being for communities of color.[39]

Another important lesson for students of racism and antiracism is that *our laws and policies can be changed*—and you can play a role in changing them! As we have already seen throughout this book, civil rights activists and ordinary people have transformed our legal institutions by engaging in protest, political organizing, voting, and even running for office. Abolitionists like Mariame Kaba, mentioned at the beginning of this book, believe that racial justice requires imagining and building a world without prisons and policing. From this perspective, antiracism activism should include ongoing efforts to abolish harmful institutions and shift resources to marginalized communities.[40]

Finally, dismantling racism requires bringing greater attention to those who have been harmed by racial discrimination in the criminal justice system. In 2016, two years after the tragic killing of her son Tamir Rice, Samaria Rice established a foundation to honor his legacy. The Tamir Rice Foundation seeks to provide a safe space for youth to engage in constructive and enriching activities rooted in the experiences and history of African-descended people.[41] Through her work, Samaria hopes to "change laws and implement new policies . . . with community oversight for police accountability and community reform dialogue."[42]

SEVEN

THE IMAGES WE SEE

Anyone can wear the mask. You can wear the mask. If you didn't know that before, I hope you do now. Cuz I'm Spider-Man. And I'm not the only one."

When Miles Morales spoke these words in the hit 2018 film *Spider-Man: Into the Spider-Verse*, he ushered in a brand-new era for Marvel comics. For the very first time, audiences saw a more inclusive vision of Spider-Man on the big screen—an Afro-Latino kid from Brooklyn who transforms into a powerful superhero. The image of a Black and Puerto Rican Spider-Man represents a huge shift. Before Miles Morales swung into action, the masked crusader had always been portrayed as Peter Parker—a White man.[1] With Miles Morales now starring in comic books, animated series, and even the signature game of the new PS 5 video game console, young people of color and multiethnic kids can see themselves depicted as one of the most iconic characters in the Marvel universe.

Miles Morales, the newest Spider-Man (2018)
[Sony/Columbia/Marvel/Kobal/Shutterstock]

You've probably heard the saying: *"A picture is worth a thousand words."* Images in media and popular culture matter because they reflect and circulate ideas, stories, myths, and beliefs that influence how we see the world, ourselves, and one another. Visual portrayals also influence what we think and how we feel about so-called "racial groups." As a result of white supremacy, the vast majority of champions and "good guys" in movies, books, and TV shows have traditionally been shown as White. Until quite recently, most Asian, Indigenous, Latinx, and Black Americans grew up without seeing people who look like them represented in positive and inspiring roles. Instead, racially marginalized groups have typically been reduced to negative stereotypes, villains, and sidekicks. Against these forces of exclusion, people of color have had to fight for greater access to positions of power and influence in order to change cultural representations in society.

In the last chapter, we explored how racism corrupts the justice system. Images are also an important part of that story. A recent study found that news networks in New York City overwhelmingly show African Americans as criminals. On one program, 82 percent of *all* stories about crime focused on Black offenders.[2] Latinx people are also frequently portrayed as criminals on television and in films.[3] When we see groups of people regularly depicted as lawbreakers or delinquents, we are more likely to think of them as violent or dangerous. These harmful images fuel discrimination and injustice.[4]

For far too long, people of color have not had a wide range of images to represent members of their community in diverse and dignified ways. Peggy McIntosh, a White antiracist educator, argues that racial biases in the media reinforce racism. As a White person, McIntosh notes that she can "turn on the television or open to the front page of the paper and see people of my race widely represented."[5] When White men are shown as violent criminals in films and on TV, White people as a whole are not stereotyped as dangerous gangsters. But Black and Brown individuals do not have that privilege. Instead, "[the] bad behavior of a person of color, when it occurs or is thought to occur, is unfairly projected onto his or her entire group."[6]

Despite the fact that our society is becoming increasingly diverse, contemporary cultural images continue to elevate Whites above other groups. Racism even warps our perception of who is—and is not—beautiful. Leah Donnella, a writer and cultural critic, points out that the same European intellectuals who created the idea of race also believed that Europeans—their own group—were more physically attractive than others:

> [A] lot of current Western beauty standards celebrate Whiteness—not some objective, biological, evolutionary thing, but literally just being a White person. In fact, if you go back

and look at the work of some early racial theorists—people like Christoph Meiners and Johann Blumenbach—they defined the category of "White," or "Caucasian," as being the most beautiful of the races.[7]

Indeed, the *Encyclopedia Britannica* associated "Caucasians" with beauty well into the 1900s.[8] Meanwhile, groups labeled racially inferior are more often described as unattractive and ugly.

Indigenous people, Black people, and people of color have been historically *underrepresented* and *poorly represented*. As a result of centuries of racial discrimination, White Americans are represented more often and more positively than people of color. Marvel's decision to reimagine Spider-Man as a Black Puerto Rican teenager is an exception to the rule, as cartoons, video games, magazine covers, and major Hollywood films still overwhelmingly feature Whites in starring roles.[9]

But a lack of diverse images is not the only thing that needs to change. Racial groups are also *misrepresented* in the images we see at the movies, on television, in art, video games, comics, and even on our computer screens.[10] One of the major consequences of racism is the fact that wealthy White men make up the vast majority of top positions at media companies, and thus overwhelmingly determine the kinds of images produced and spread throughout society. Rising up to build an antiracist world means involving a broader range of people in the production of cultural images and challenging harmful stereotypes in visual culture. In other words, it's not enough to just include Black and Brown faces in storylines, art, and entertainment. We also need to change our power structure so that people of color can take a leading role in telling their own stories and shaping our visual culture.

In the pages that follow, we're going to take a deep dive into the relationship between racism and cultural images. From illustrations and cartoons, to movies, commercials, and video games, white supremacy distorts *what* we see and *how* we interpret the world around us on a daily basis. As we will discover later in this chapter, systemic racism is even programmed into the internet. New technologies reflect the stereotypes and biases of their human creators. For example, search engines like Google have a history of associating Black people with racist slurs, demeaning photographs of animals, and other kinds of disrespectful imagery.[11] This is largely due to systemic racism behind the scenes, which results in the exclusion of Black and Brown people from decision-making positions and jobs such as engineers, content creators, artists, editors, and media executives.

By uncovering hidden racial biases in the media and popular culture, we'll discover how systemic racism subtly operates through the art and entertainment we consume. But just as images can spread racist beliefs, so, too, can they be challenged and changed to debunk stereotypes, dismantle racism, and transform society. From the past through the present day, activists and everyday people alike have organized to protest racist images and create new representations featuring a wide range of colors, ethnic identities, and cultural heritages.

POWER AND REPRESENTATIONS

As we explore the topic of racial images, we'll want to consider how media amplifies *racial stereotypes*—generalizations and simplified representations of racial groups.[12] Visual representations in educa-tion, art, entertainment, news, and media operate like lenses that color how and what we think about racial labels. Not only are Whites often represented as superior and more powerful than others in cul-tural images—they are also portrayed in more complex and nuanced ways. Black people and people of color, on the other hand, are often reduced to *racist caricatures*—insulting depictions that reinforce neg-ative stereotypes.[13] As antiracist advocates, we have to recognize how the history of racism still reverberates in the stereotyped images we see in society today.

Although racial stereotypes generalize entire groups, there are also specific meanings that are uniquely applied to images of people based on other aspects of their identity, including their gender and sexuality—this idea is called *intersectionality*.

"Intersectionality" is a term introduced by social theorist Kimberlé Crenshaw to explain the links between racism, gender inequality, and other forms of disadvantage in the lives of Black women. As an illustration, Crenshaw asks us to imagine vehicles traveling along two streets that meet at an intersection. "Discrimination," she writes, "like traffic through an intersection, may flow in one direction, and it may flow in another. If an accident happens in an intersection, it can be caused by cars traveling from any number of directions and, sometimes, from all of them." In this example, the cars and traffic passing along the streets represent forms of bias, mistreatment, and disadvantage. Crenshaw argues that "if a Black woman is harmed because she is in the intersection, her injury could result from sex discrimination or race discrimination."[14]

While the idea was first developed to explain the unique

challenges faced by Black women and women of color, intersectionality is now used to show how racism operates differently depending on our social location—where we are standing and how we are positioned in society. Intersectionality helps us understand how racist beliefs and generalizations are applied differently to images of people of color depending on multiple factors, including race, sexuality, gender, and class.[15]

Earlier in the book, we encountered the stereotyped image of the Mammy that has historically portrayed African American women as dark-skinned servants with exaggerated red lips. Asian American actresses, on the other hand, have been burdened with stereotypical roles "like the vindictive dragon lady, the submissive China doll, [or] the nerdy overachiever."[16] Indigenous women and girls have often been limited to flat representations as "princesses" or disrespectful imagery of "squaws"—a racist caricature that dehumanizes Native women as sexual objects.[17]

For men and boys of color, racism and gender inequality produce a different set of stereotypes and representations. Because White men are positioned at the top of the status hierarchy, Black men, Indigenous men, and men of color are generally shown as less worthy, less moral, and less powerful than their White counterparts. To take just a few examples: African American men are visually imagined as thugs, athletes, or dangerous sexual predators, while Latinos get boxed into caricatures like the "Latin lover" or criminals. Arab men are often reduced to "terrorists" while stereotypes of Asian American men include being shown as frightening foreigners or martial artists. Notably, the limited roles that exist for Asian men in television and film tend to deprive them of love interests—rarely are Asian and

Asian American men given starring roles in romances and romantic comedies. Taken together, these racialized and gendered images function to dehumanize the representation of Black and Brown people.[18]

Finally, because racism is a system of power, it's important to acknowledge that discrimination traditionally prevented Black people, Indigenous people, and people of color from being able to create and control visual representations. Because the "table" of white supremacy was designed to serve the interests and tastes of wealthy White men, they are also the group that has had the most power to impose their views and perspectives onto the visual landscape of our everyday lives.

Now that we've laid the groundwork with these key ideas, we are better equipped to detect and challenge racism in the images that circulate in our society. In the next section, we'll travel back in time to consider how racial images have historically represented the biases of Europeans and their descendants.

RACIAL IMAGES THROUGHOUT HISTORY

What physical features come to mind when you think of Jesus Christ? Today, many people throughout the world imagine Jesus as a blue-eyed White man with long, golden blond hair. Although the historical Christ was ethnically Jewish and living in Palestine, modern paintings and films created by Europeans and Westerners typically portray him as Caucasian.

The story of how Jesus came to be viewed as "White" is actually intertwined with the history of Western racism and xenophobia. In the United States during the early 1900s, in an era of rising immigration from Europe and bigotry against newly arrived Jews and Catholics, many White intellectuals and elected officials warned against the dangers of allowing immigrants deemed racially inferior, including Italians and Jews, to enter the country.[19] It was in this context of rising xenophobia, anti-immigrant attitudes, and white supremacist violence against people of color that the image of Jesus Christ was whitewashed and visually detached from his Jewish roots.

o o o

When I was growing up in Chattanooga, Tennessee, I vividly remember seeing a small painting of Jesus hanging in my grandmother's home. As a young person, I never questioned whether the light-skinned, blue-eyed man in the portrait was, in fact, a historically accurate representation. Decades later, I would eventually learn that the painting was created in 1940 by an artist named Warner Sallman. His painting—"The Head of Christ"—became one of the most recognizable images in the world, with hundreds of millions of copies circulated across the globe.[20]

Despite the popular and widespread image of a Caucasian Jesus, modern science affirms that the historical Christ was, in fact, a "dark and swarthy Middle Eastern man."[21] In 2002, a team of forensic anthropologists and archaeologists from Israel and Britain produced a 3-D, digital model of what the head of Christ might have *really* looked like. The image depicts a man of bronze complexion with dark brown eyes and nearly black, bushy hair—someone who probably looked a lot like some of the very same immigrants who were labeled "racially inferior" by white supremacists a century ago! If white supremacy can be used to distort the image of Jesus Christ, how do you think it shapes the way we see ourselves and other human beings?

RACIST CARICATURES AS ENTERTAINMENT

Creating unflattering portraits of people of color became a very profitable form of entertainment in the 1700s and 1800s. Before the invention of film and television, actors of European descent drew audiences to theaters with parodies and performances that vividly illustrated the racial hierarchy. Instead of allowing people of African, Asian, and Indigenous origin to represent themselves and tell their own stories, White performers began covering their faces and bodies with colored makeup and wearing exaggerated, stereotyped costumes to embody "non-White" characters on stage. The practice of White actors donning *blackface, yellowface,* and *brownface* solidified racist beliefs and reduced people of color to dehumanizing caricatures.

Ironically, Europeans from ethnic groups that were deemed inferior by white supremacists helped popularize yellowface and blackface performances.[22] In 1768, an Irish playwright named Arthur Murphy premiered *The Orphan of China* in New York, a theatrical performance in which White actors wearing yellowface played Asian characters.[23] During the nineteenth century, "minstrel shows," which featured "comedic performances of 'blackness' by Whites in exaggerated costumes and makeup," became one of the most popular forms of entertainment in the United States.[24]

An 1899 cartoon entitled "The Yellow Terror in All His Glory"
depicting a caricature of a Chinese man violating Western nations,
represented here as a White woman [Ohio State University]

Thomas Dartmouth Rice, a White performer from Manhattan, became a global sensation when he introduced his "Jumpin' Jim Crow" minstrel act in the 1830s. Rice claimed to have encountered an enslaved Black man in the South who inspired his routine, which included covering his face in burnt cork to give his skin a jet-black appearance, applying red coloring to his lips, and wearing disheveled clothing. Rice's blackface "Jim Crow" character became a hit for White audiences who enjoyed demeaning portrayals of blackness.

Many other performers, including Jewish and Irish actors, followed in Rice's footsteps and created minstrel shows that made a mockery of enslaved people and their descendants. By belittling African Americans with parodies of their ways of dressing, speaking, and dancing, blackface minstrel shows transformed the brutal system of slavery into a form of entertainment and allowed newly arrived European immigrants to differentiate themselves from Black people and assimilate into the mainstream.[25]

Over time, "Jim Crow" became a term used to describe African Americans and, after the Civil War, it was the name given to discriminatory laws and policies designed to maintain white supremacy, impose segregation, and separate Black people from the rest of society.[26] Unfortunately, blackface is not merely a relic of the past. Every year—especially during Halloween—young people and adults alike continue to paint their faces black and impersonate African Americans, often without acknowledging the racist history that gave birth to minstrelsy.[27]

1830s image depicting White actor Thomas D. Rice, the originator
of "Jim Crow" blackface minstrelsy [Institute for Advanced
Technology in the Humanities at the University of Virginia]

THE BIRTH OF RACIST CINEMA

Technological innovations of the twentieth century allowed for racist imagery to circulate in new ways, reaching larger audiences than ever before. The advent of motion pictures was a major milestone in the history of racial images. Why is film such an influential form of media? Historian Vincent Brown explains that "[cinema] is so important to American popular culture . . . this is where people go to see their fears and fantasies realized. It's also where they go to learn history. It's probably the single most important medium in American popular culture."[28]

Racial fantasies and fears became big business for White filmmakers in the early days of cinema. In fact, the *very first* Hollywood blockbuster was a film that celebrated white supremacy.[29] In February of 1915, the world of cinema was forever changed when *The Clansman* premiered in Los Angeles to praise from its fans as well as protests from African American activists and White allies. Written and directed by a White man named D. W. Griffith, *The Clansman* took its name from a novel and a play authored by a white supremacist named Thomas Dixon. In describing his own philosophy, Dixon declared that "the White man must and shall be supreme."[30] D. W. Griffith agreed and turned Dixon's texts into a cinematic saga that quickly became the most successful silent film of all time.

The title of the film was eventually changed to *The Birth of a Nation*, which was meant to celebrate "the birth of the new white supremacy."[31] Despite opposition from Black activists and antiracist organizations, *The Birth of a Nation* was wildly popular and "considered mainstream entertainment."[32] Its plot was designed to tell the history of the United States in a way that would glorify the Klan and demonize Black and multiracial people.

Poster for the 1915 film *The Birth of a Nation* [Wikimedia Commons]

Following the lives of two White families from the days of slavery through the Civil War and the period of Reconstruction, the movie presented African Americans as a backward race and depicted Black and multiracial men in particular as violent threats to White women. Black politicians in the post-Civil War era were shown as uncivilized, dirty, and unfit for elected office. The film also portrayed interracial marriage and relationships as abominations. And, above all, members of the Klan were upheld as cultural heroes while Black and mixed-race people—particularly men—were the villains.

These ideas were embraced and amplified by White community leaders and politicians, including Woodrow Wilson, then president of the United States. With his approval, *The Birth of a Nation* became the first film to ever be projected at the White House.

Blackface was prominently featured in the production, with White actors covering their faces in dark makeup to play the role of African Americans. In an infamous scene, a Blackface character named Gus chases a White woman through the woods. Terrified and disgusted by his romantic pursuit, the woman jumps off a cliff to her death. Later, Gus himself is killed by members of the Ku Klux Klan, prompting many White audiences to cheer.[33] In this way, *The Birth of a Nation* fueled violent racial hatred and openly encouraged White Americans to fear and even kill Black people. One of the major consequences of *The Birth of a Nation* was the rebirth of the KKK, which became more active and emboldened after the film's release.[34]

But activists and community members who believed in the value of Black lives stood together to oppose D. W. Griffith's hateful message and harmful imagery. In Boston, William Monroe Trotter, an African American Harvard graduate and newspaper owner, led a radical protest movement against *The Birth of a Nation*. His massive campaign of civil disobedience and protest drew together thousands of Black and White Bostonians in an attempt to prevent the film from being shown.[35] By organizing collective action and raising consciousness about the dangerous impact of the film, Trotter promoted "radical black self-determination—the militant push by colored people to defy white supremacist 'truths' propagated in the culture at large."[36]

Some White activists, including those working with the National Association for the Advancement of Colored People (NAACP), also joined forces with African Americans to stand up against the film. Mary Childs Nerney, then secretary of the NAACP, wrote this letter of protest to local officials in Chicago:

> I am utterly disgusted with the situation in regard to "The Birth of a Nation" . . . we have fought it at every possible

point. In spite of the promise of the Mayor to cut out the two objectionable scenes in the second part, which show a White girl committing suicide to escape from a Negro pursuer, and a mulatto politician trying to force marriage upon the daughter of his White benefactor, these two scenes still form the motif . . . The harm it is doing the colored people cannot be estimated.[37]

Jane Addams, a social reformer and one of the most famous White Americans in the country during her lifetime, also denounced *The Birth of a Nation* as a "caricature of the Negro race."[38] Even though the protest movement was unable to convince officials to delete the most offensive scenes or prevent the film from being shown, these acts of resistance allowed community members to join in solidarity across racial lines to demand humane and just images of African Americans. Their efforts also debunk a common claim about historical racism—that such attitudes simply reflected the views of the day. The protests against *The Birth of a Nation* in 1915 show us that racist views were strongly opposed at the time by Black people and some White allies as well.

RACIAL STEREOTYPES AND REPRESENTATION TODAY

With major Hollywood films like *Black Panther* and television shows like *Stranger Things* featuring a diverse cast of characters, it might seem like racial misrepresentation and underrepresentation are no longer major problems. Unfortunately, this is not the case. Although our society has made progress, the images that we see still reflect our ongoing history of white supremacy. People of color remain severely underrepresented on the big and small screens. While Whites make up only about 60 percent of the population, they represent 83.3 percent of leading roles in film and 93.5 percent on broadcast television.[39] Latinx people are especially excluded in the industry. Nearly one out of every five individuals in the United States is Hispanic—but they only make up 5 percent of film roles and 2 percent of television roles.[40]

Racism also shapes the kinds of roles and representations that are made available to Black people, Indigenous people, and people of color. Sociologist Nancy Yuen explains that "racial bias in Hollywood . . . allows White actors to play different characters but limits actors of color to stereotypes."[41] Brian Young, a Navajo actor, has written about being asked to portray stereotypical roles that disrespect the history and culture of Native Americans. Once, he agreed to play an "Indian shaman," which required wearing feathers and "war paint." With so few opportunities in Hollywood for Native Americans, Brian felt pressured to take the part even though the film did not honor his community:

> . . . as I climbed into the feathered costume and began to apply "war paint" to my face, I began to feel very uncomfortable. Even though I'm not of a Plains tribe . . . I knew that this kind of regalia was not meant for casual, every-day wear. For many tribes, including mine, feathers are sacred. Looking at myself in the mirror in full costume, I felt shameful for mocking my spirituality. I promised myself I'd never play "Indian" again—and since then have turned down several auditions for big budget films.[42]

One of the dangers of reducing Black and Brown people to caricatures and stereotypes in films is that those images often take the place of real human interactions. Due to centuries of segregation and racist housing practices, many White Americans do not live with or have meaningful relationships with people of color. When stereotypes are accepted as the "truth" about other people, racial biases remain intact and everyone suffers. Brian has encountered the negative impact of being reduced to a stereotype firsthand:

> I have personally experienced the level of ignorance that results from one's only exposure to a culture being what one sees in movies. During my orientation week freshman year in 2006, many of my classmates, when they discovered my Navajo heritage, seemed to think I lived in a teepee and hunted buffalo in the plains on horseback.

Brian's painful experience teaches us about the importance of questioning racial stereotypes and creating more inclusive cultural representations.

NEW TECHNOLOGIES, OLD BIASES

As with the advent of motion pictures, modern technologies have not eliminated racial biases. For example, online search engines like Google provide biased results, linking images of Black people to insults, slurs, and even arrest records.[43] Data scientists have also shown that artificial intelligence and facial recognition technologies discriminate against darker-skinned people. A study conducted by Joy Buolamwini and Timnit Gebru—both of whom are leading data scientists—reveals that facial recognition software encodes racial and gender biases as a result of designers' decisions to predominately train the programs on White male faces. Using the concept of intersectionality introduced at the onset of this chapter, the authors show that dark-skinned women are far more likely than others to be misrecognized—and misrepresented by biased software.[44]

In the digital realm of video games, between 70 percent and 80 percent of lead characters are White men.[45] Like other areas of our culture, video games center the stories and aspirations of White men while Black and Brown people mostly appear in the role of sports stars (as in the *Madden NFL* and *NBA2K* series), or as minor supporting characters that reinforce negative tropes.[46] Scholars Kishonna Gray and David Leonard describe gaming as "a world of good and evil, of domination and annihilation, where Whiteness and American manhood characterize protectors and heroes."[47]

For André Brock, an expert on racism and technology, the 2009 game *Resident Evil 5* presents a prime example of raced and gendered stereotypes. The virtual environment unfolds in a fictional African society. A woman of color named Sheva is depicted as subordinate to a White male hero. She is rendered as a romantic object rather than an individual empowered with her own storyline and sense of self. In effect, she exists only to serve a White character. Brock suggests that *Resident Evil 5* paints Africa as "a setting to be cleansed and civilized . . . At no point are the Africans allowed to be anything other than savage; they are never seen within familiar Western contexts such as high-rise buildings, shopping centers, or at leisure." In this way, the game spreads false destructive beliefs about Africa and Africans.

Given the patterns of underrepresentation we've already seen, you probably won't be surprised to learn that people of African descent are almost totally excluded among video game developers. Only 2 percent of gaming programmers, coders, and designers identify as Black. And, despite the fact that almost 20% of the U.S. population is Hispanic, a mere 7% of workers in the game industry are Latinx.[48] These numbers reflect broader diversity problems in the field of technology. Black and Latinx people are particularly underrepresented in jobs as engineers and computer programmers. There are, however, some regions and cities where African Americans thrive in the tech industry. For example, back in my hometown of Chattanooga, Tennessee, Black people make up about 12 percent of all employees working in computing and mathematics—a number that matches their share of the overall population.[49]

CONCLUSION: REIMAGINING REPRESENTATIONS

As we have seen throughout this chapter, racist caricatures are still with us—but they can also be challenged and changed. Activists and cultural creators are increasingly rising up and calling for change. At the ripe old age of eleven, Marley Dias decided that she was fed up with stories that revolved around "White boys and their dogs." So, she decided to create the #1000BlackGirlBooks project, an initiative to collect a thousand books featuring Black girls. In the process, Marley exceeded her goal and brought widespread attention to the need for diversity in our cultural images and narratives. Now, Marley is a teen author herself as well as the star of her own television show called *Bookmarks* on Netflix where she interviews famous people on topics such as identity and representation.[50]

Marley Dias, author, television host, and creator of the #1000BlackGirlBooks project [Andrea Cipriani Mecchi]

As we have seen time and time again, collective action remains one of the most important tools for making a positive difference. When Abercrombie & Fitch released a line of "humorous" T-shirts in 2002 depicting Asians as racist caricatures with exaggerated figures and slanted eyes, more than one hundred Asian Americans demonstrated in San Francisco to raise awareness about the harm of racial stereotypes. The company was forced to remove the T-shirts from all 311 of its stores.[51] In 2018, the European clothing company H&M

made headlines around the world for creating a brazenly racist ad. A photograph featured on their website showed a young Black boy wearing a green hoodie emblazoned with the words "Coolest Monkey in the Jungle." It took protests and social media campaigns for the ad to be removed.[52]

In recent years, *The Simpsons*, one of the world's longest-running and most popular television series, came under fire for reducing people of color to narrow stereotypes. In a documentary called *The Problem with Apu*, South Asian comedian Hari Kondabolu expressed his frustrations with the representation of Apu Nahasapeemapetilon—an Indian American character who owns a store called Kwik-E-Mart. For thirty years, Apu was voiced by Hank Azaria, a White actor who used an exaggerated accent for the role, and his dialogue on the show was also mostly written by White writers.

For Kondabolu, who grew up in Queens, New York—one of the world's most racially and ethnically diverse regions—Apu's signature accent sounded like "a White guy doing an impression of a White guy making fun of my father."[53] By portraying Apu as a foolish and uncultured immigrant, *The Simpsons* reinforced negative stereotypes about Indian immigrants and reinforced the idea that it's okay to mock and make fun of foreigners. The big problem, as Kondabolu explains, is that in the 1980s and 1990s, when *The Simpsons* first became a global phenomenon, there were very few representations of South Asians on television. As a result of this severe underrepresentation, Apu's stereotyped character became extremely influential for millions of *Simpsons* fans and shaped beliefs about South Asian people. For decades, Indian American kids didn't have other examples of people from their community who looked like them on television. It became common for South Asians to be mocked by others with Apu's well-known line *"Thank you, come again!"*

The misrepresentation of Indian Americans in *The Simpsons* is linked to the exclusion of South Asians as writers, editors, and cultural creators. Hari Kondabolu, himself a lifelong fan of the show, admits that Apu "is funny." However, from his perspective, the character is "based on this faulty foundation of . . . a caricature. So, you know, fundamentally everything that he's going to do is based on a caricature. And that's weird. Like, this whole character is what White writers thought of us 30 years ago, thought of our community. This isn't how we represent ourselves. This is how they view us."[54]

In 2020, Hank Azaria announced that he would no longer voice the character of Apu. At first, he didn't want to listen to criticism about the role. But, eventually, Azaria had a change of heart. After years of protest from Hari Kondabolu and other South Asians, *The Problem with Apu* forced him to rethink his responsibilities as a White actor. Azaria, who is Jewish, realized that if members of his community were reduced to a single stereotyped character on television, he would also probably feel offended: "I started thinking, if that character were the only representation of Jewish people in American culture for 20 years, which was the case with Apu, I might not love that . . ."[55] Although the fight against racism on television is far from over, the fact that Kondabolu and other South Asians spoke up made a difference.

And, while the pace of progress is excruciatingly slow, the film industry is beginning to shift. In 2015, after it was announced that all twenty of the nominees for the Academy Awards for Best Actor and Best Actress were White, activist April Reign created the

#OscarsSoWhite hashtag, which brought attention to systemic racism in Hollywood. Performers have also engaged in activism to demand better images for people of color. In 2015, Native American actors organized a protest and walked off the set of *The Ridiculous Six*, a western starring Adam Sandler, due to the film's blatant disrespect of Native women and Indigenous culture.[56] Native Americans, like other historically excluded groups, have also resisted their underrepresentation and misrepresentation in Hollywood by creating their own films and independent productions.[57]

Crazy Rich Asians, which hit theaters in 2018, was the first American film in a quarter of a century to feature an all-Asian cast. Starring actors of Asian heritage like Constance Wu, Henry Golding, Michelle Yeoh, and Awkwafina, the movie was a critical and commercial success.[58] Peter Ramsey, one of the filmmakers behind *Spider-Man: Into the Spider-Verse*, brought the story of Miles Morales to life and became the first Black director to win an Oscar for an animated movie.

Ramsey aims to create change by portraying people of color in vivid, richly nuanced ways: "We don't want to keep watching the problem of the week, or stories about 'Isn't it so tragic that you happen to be this skin color?'" he insists. "We want to see stories about real people that have the depth and the power and the subtlety of any other story you'd see in the mainstream."[59]

EIGHT

RACISM AND ANTIRACISM IN SPORTS

On the evening of July 9, 2016, the women of the reigning WNBA champions Minnesota Lynx prepared to hit the court in a home game against the Dallas Wings. Inside the basketball arena's media room, journalists working the sports beat gathered to hear from the players. At an ordinary pre-game press conference, athletes face the cameras, answer questions about an upcoming matchup, and discuss how they plan to take on their opponents. But this would be no ordinary pre-game press conference.

Instead of talking about the game, the Lynx decided to make a different kind of statement. Wearing warm-up shirts emblazoned with the words "BLACK LIVES MATTER" and "CHANGE STARTS WITH US," the four team captains—Maya Moore, Rebekkah Brunson, Seimone Augustus, and Lindsay Whalen—stood shoulder to shoulder in front of reporters. Their shirts honored the names of Philando Castile and Alton Sterling—two African American men killed by police the week before. But the shirts also displayed the shield of the Dallas police department, which had just lost five officers in a mass shooting perpetrated by an African American veteran.

The killing of Philando Castile occurred just miles away from the Target Center in Minnesota, Minneapolis, where tip-off was scheduled for later that night. With racial unrest and mourning sweeping the nation, the Lynx wanted to use their platform to take a stand for solidarity and justice. They condemned racist policing as well as violence directed against police.

Speaking on behalf of the team, Lynx star Maya Moore explained that the players wanted to bring attention to "a longtime problem of racial profiling and unjust violence against Blacks in our country . . . But we do not in any way condone violence against the men and women who service in our police force. Senseless violence and retaliation will not bring us peace."[1] The women—Black and White—called for unity and accountability. "This is a human issue," Moore said, "and we need to speak up for change together."[2] After ending their press conference, the Lynx players handled their business on the court and won their game in a blowout.

The players' protest went viral on social media, stirred controversy, and inspired other athletes to take a stand. Off-duty police officers who had been providing security at the stadium that evening were so upset about the Lynx support for Black Lives Matter that they walked off the job. Other WNBA teams—including the Washington Mystics, New York Liberty, Indiana Fever, and Phoenix Mercury—joined the collective protest, wearing black warm-up shirts to practice in order to raise awareness about police shootings of African Americans. WNBA officials threatened players and teams with fines and penalties for altering their uniforms, but the women refused to be silenced.

Members of the Washington Mystics take a knee to protest the shooting of Jacob Blake, an African American who was shot seven times in the back in 2020 [Julio Aguilar/Getty Images]

The activism and leadership of the WNBA athletes echoed across the world of professional sports. Just one month later, Colin Kaepernick of the San Francisco 49ers sent shockwaves through the NFL and the country when he famously took a knee during the pre-game national anthem. For Kaepernick, the anthem and the flag were both painful reminders of racial injustice. Reflecting on the motivation behind his protest, Kaepernick explained:

I am not going to stand up to show pride in a flag for a country that oppresses Black people and people of color . . . To

*me, this is bigger than football and it would be selfish on my
part to look the other way. There are bodies in the street and
people getting paid leave and getting away with murder . . .
There's a lot of racism in this country disguised as patriotism
and people want to take everything back to the flag but that's
not what we're talking about . . . We're talking about racial
discrimination, inequalities and injustices that happen across
the nation.*[3]

Other athletes—including fellow NFL players as well as Megan
Rapinoe, a White American soccer star—joined in solidarity by
kneeling or putting their fist up during the anthem. But Kaepernick
became the public face of the movement, and as a result he faced
death threats and harsh criticism from powerful politicians, including
former President Donald Trump. Eventually, he lost his job with the
49ers and was pushed out of the league entirely.

The athletes who protested during the summer and fall of 2016
were not the first to use their platform to speak up about racism. In
fact, fifty years earlier, Jackie Robinson—the famous African American baseball player—wrote: "I cannot stand and sing the anthem.
I cannot salute the flag; I know that I am a Black man in a White
world."[4] From the twentieth century through the present day, African
American athletes in particular have taken a leading role in breaking
racial barriers and rising up against white supremacy. At times, such
athletic activism has been demonized by critics as "unpatriotic" or
"divisive."

Some think of sports as unbiased competitions, where people are
judged solely on the basis of their hard work and athletic performance. But sports are far from neutral. Racist beliefs and practices

create unfair playing fields for all of us—including athletes. But this can be difficult for some of us to see given the global impact of superstars like Serena Williams and LeBron James. After all, doesn't the success of Black and Brown athletes prove that anyone can rise to the highest ranks in sports?

Well, not quite. When we listen to the voices of Black people, Indigenous people, and people of color in athletics, we learn that systemic racism creates inequalities and unfair burdens that negatively impact their lives.

The unfortunate truth is that racism has been interwoven into the fabric of sports for generations. Although it's become common for people of different racial identities and ethnic backgrounds to play together in athletic competitions, this was far from the case for most of our country's history. For hundreds of years through the middle of the twentieth century, racial segregation in athletics was the norm as most White Americans declined to engage in sports and leisure activities alongside groups that they labeled racially inferior. And, even in those instances when sports included people of diverse backgrounds, Black people, Indigenous people, and people of color have historically been on the receiving end of discriminatory treatment.

Despite the presence of many Black and Brown sports stars today, racially discriminatory practices continue to create unique disadvantages for people racialized as "non-White." The vast majority of major sports franchises are owned by White men, and relatively few people of color hold leadership positions as coaches and managers. Throughout the country, hundreds of high school teams still bear racist names and feature harmful caricatures of Native Americans as their mascots. And, as we will see later, vicious acts of racial hatred still occur within athletic events. For these and many other reasons, athletes of color have historically played a major role in shifting the national and even international conversation about race.

In this chapter, we're going to tackle the topic of racism and antiracism in sports. Given the cultural significance of sports in the United States and around the globe, it's important to understand how and why athletes have been at the center of debates over race and justice. Whether you consider yourself a jock, a nerd, or something in between, all students of antiracism have a lot to learn from athletics activists who refused to be satisfied with just winning games, titles, and championships. In the pages to come, we'll consider the long-lasting effects of racist beliefs and discriminatory practices in athletics and discover how the courageous actions of contemporary athletes like Colin Kaepernick and the WNBA players are part of a long history of antiracist protest in the world of sports.

THE (RACIAL) POLITICS OF SPORTS

It might not be obvious to you that sports are deeply political. Harry Edwards, a world-renowned sociologist, put it this way: "Sports unavoidably reflect society . . . [it] is this fact that makes sports and politics inseparable."[5]

For many of us, it *is* surprising to learn that sports have historically been intertwined with systemic racism. There are at least two reasons why this is the case. First of all, as we've already established, many people did not grow up learning the true history of racism— including the history of racist practices and harmful ideas that have become deeply embedded in our culture, politics, and economy. This means, among other things, that the ongoing struggles of Black and Brown athletes have typically been brushed under the rug.

Another reason why many are surprised by (or in denial about) the existence of racism has to do with the myth of political neutrality in sports.[6] The idea that sports are not—or should not be—political has been historically used by White politicians, team owners, and journalists to suppress free speech, squash athletic protest, and keep the system of white supremacy intact. Athletics activists have had to struggle against and overcome an enormous amount of political opposition in order to speak up about injustice.

In 2018, after NBA star LeBron James spoke passionately about political issues in a postgame interview, a FOX News host proclaimed that LeBron should "Keep the political comments to [himself] . . . Shut up and dribble." But LeBron refused to stay silent and continues to use his platform to bring awareness to important issues, including voting rights. This is just one recent example of the way Black athletes have long used their influence to courageously shed light on social problems despite opposition from racist critics.[7]

Despite recent progress, for most of our country's history, the racial hierarchy was harshly enforced in all spheres of society, including athletics and recreation. This meant that, with few exceptions, Whites chose to play sports and games among themselves.

But in the twentieth century—and especially during the Civil Rights era—many White Americans began to point to the presence of African Americans in professional sports as proof that the United States was becoming a land of opportunity. When Black athletes like baseball star Jackie Robinson broke the color line in professional leagues, White journalists enthusiastically described sports as more inclusive and welcoming than the rest of society.[8]

However, as we will see later in this chapter, these trailblazers faced daily discrimination and disrespect from White athletes, fans, officials, managers, and commentators. And instead of finding support among teammates and coaches, these marginalized athletes were discouraged from speaking up about their experiences of mistreatment or openly criticizing the country that actively oppressed them. Instead, they were expected to just "shut up and play."[9]

o o o

Have you ever stopped to wonder why the national anthem is played at sporting events? The tradition has become such a routine part of sporting culture that most of us take it for granted. Listening to Whitney Houston's awe-inspiring rendition of the anthem during the 1991 Super Bowl halftime show is an indelible memory from my own childhood. (And if you haven't already heard it, you really should look it up!) The ritual of singing the national anthem and displaying the flag at sporting events provides important clues about the deeply political nature of sports. For many Americans, sports have become closely tied to the ideas of patriotism and even nationalism. But how and when did this happen?

The story of the song that would eventually become our national anthem revolves around *three* different wars. Francis Scott Key, a lawyer from Washington, D.C., wrote *The Star-Spangled Banner* in 1814 when the United States was at war with Britain.[10] His poem— later set to music—was an openly political song and a celebration of national identity—especially *White* national identity. Nearly half a century later, the tune was played at the dedication of a baseball field in Brooklyn, New York, on May 15, 1862, during another violent conflict—the Civil War. It was the very first time that the song was performed at an athletic event.[11]

The politics of the Civil War would come to play an important role in the controversies that surrounded the song throughout the latter half of the 1800s.[12] That's because "The Star-Spangled Banner" isn't just a song about war and patriotism. It's also a song about race and slavery. Few people realize that the man who wrote our anthem was a white supremacist and a slave master. In fact, Francis Scott Key so despised Black people that he described them as a "distinct and inferior race."[13] And, in the full version of "The Star-Spangled Banner," Key included lyrics wishing death and destruction upon enslaved Black people who fought for (and obtained) their freedom by joining forces with the British against the United States in the War of 1812. As journalist Jon Schwarz points out, the anthem *"literally celebrates the murder of African-Americans."*[14]

Some Northerners believed the song's lyrics should be changed to honor the fight against slavery. But Southern supporters of the Confederacy, the pro-slavery states that committed treason by declaring war on the rest of the nation, became strong advocates for keeping the song as is—including its hateful words about African Americans.[15]

It was in 1918—at the height of World War I—that "The Star-Spangled Banner" achieved widespread popularity in sports. That year, when the all-White Boston Red Sox and Chicago Cubs battled in the World Series, the stadium band played the song to liven up the crowd. Eventually, the patriotic ode spread like wildfire through sporting events across the country. When it was finally selected as the nation's anthem in 1931, some White Americans marched in the streets while "hoisting the Confederate flag."[16] It was in this way that a deeply political song with racist roots came to be integrated into the fabric of our country's sports culture.

RACIAL SEGREGATION IN SPORTS

Most of us have become accustomed to seeing players of diverse ethnic and racial backgrounds playing sports with and against each other. But the color line was heavily enforced in athletics and leisure activities for centuries. During slavery, African Americans were held in bondage and not allowed to freely participate in games and sports alongside others as equals. Although some slave owners occasionally allowed enslaved people to engage in play and physical exercise among themselves, such activities were designed to maintain a sense of "harmony in bondage" under a brutal system of oppression.[17] Just as prisons often provide daily periods of recreation for people in confinement, so, too, did plantations provide some limited opportunities for sports.

The abolition of slavery led to the emergence of interracial games and athletics in the late 1800s, but the rise of Jim Crow segregation reinforced the system of white supremacy and imposed a rigid racial hierarchy separating African Americans from Whites. While many Whites refused to play sports with former slaves, the rise of African American educational institutions empowered Black people to create their own athletic organizations and engage in structured sports.[18]

During a period of time after the Civil War, some Black athletes competed alongside White counterparts. Although Jackie Robinson is often credited with integrating professional baseball, that distinction actually belongs to Moses Fleetwood Walker.[19] Walker, a biracial man from Ohio, started playing in the minor leagues with the previously all-White Toledo Bluestockings in 1883—only eighteen years after the Civil War. The next year, the Bluestockings became a major league team, making Walker the first Black player in the majors.

One journalist described Walker as the most valuable catcher in the sport. Before breaking the color barrier in pro baseball, this trailblazer became the first African American baseball player at Oberlin College as well as the University of Michigan, where he attended law school.[20] Just as incredible is the fact that Moses's brother—Weldy Wilberforce Walker—became the *second* Black man to play in the major league when he joined the Bluestockings in 1884.[21]

But the presence of the Walker brothers in major league baseball did not mean that Whites actually accepted them as equal human beings. Moses was spat on and insulted. The racist abuse he experienced from "fans" and even other players on his own team was shocking and violent:

> He was derided by spectators angered by his presence on the field with White players. An inviting target for opposing pitchers, he was plunked by pitches six times in 152 at-bats. His own pitcher . . . admitted years later that he ignored signals relayed by his African-American catcher and threw whatever he wanted. As a result of not knowing what to expect, Walker suffered numerous injuries, including a broken rib.[22]

Eventually, racist players refused to take the field with the Walker brothers. As Jim Crow laws and a resurgence of white supremacy swept across the United States in the early 1890s, Black players were forced out of the major leagues and professional baseball once again became an "all-White" sport.

The Walkers' experience painfully illustrates a pattern that would repeat itself again and again as Black, Brown, and mixed-race players joined Whites-only teams and leagues: They were still viewed by many Whites as inferior and were frequent targets of hateful behavior. But the Walkers defied White racism and excelled professionally, athletically, and intellectually against monumental odds. Moses went on to become a businessman, writer, and inventor. After the end of their baseball careers, Moses and Weldy teamed up yet again—this time to publish a newspaper that encouraged Black Americans to reconnect with their African roots.[23]

Another history-making athlete who defied the Jim Crow color line was Marshall "Major" Taylor—an African American who became the top cyclist on the planet in the late 1890s and "the world's first black sports superstar."[24] Born in Indianapolis, Indiana about a decade after the Civil War, Taylor discovered a special talent for riding bikes as a kid and won his first cycling championship at the age of thirteen.[25]

His relationships with members of the White community illustrate the complexities of the time. Despite widespread racism, Taylor had many strong and meaningful friendships that bridged the color line.[26] One of his very best friends was a White boy named Dan—the son of his father's wealthy employer. The two were incredibly close, played games and sports together, and even wore matching clothes![27]

Dan's family also bought Marshall Taylor his very first bike—a gift that changed the course of his life forever.

Groundbreaking cyclist Marshall "Major" Taylor shown with his family in the early 1900s [Major Taylor Association, Inc.]

There were a number of other Whites who provided Taylor with social, educational, and economic support, including a famous cyclist named Birdie Munger who took him under his wing and opened many doors for his athletic career. But, like the Walker Brothers, Taylor also experienced exclusion, disrespect, and violence from many White racists. Pursuing his dream of becoming the best cyclist in the world meant having to overcome social barriers, racist insults, vicious attacks from White opponents during racing competitions, discrimination from officials, and even death threats.[28]

The question of whether Taylor would even be allowed to

participate in races was always a thorny problem—even with the support of wealthy benefactors like Birdie Munger. Some competitions allowed "Negroes" while others did not. At times, Taylor had to sneak to the starting line in order to even have a chance. Once there, he couldn't simply focus on winning—he also had to deal with racist slurs as well as the constant threat of White cyclists trying to knock him down and injure him.

But Taylor remained supremely confident in his abilities and refused to back down. His courage extended beyond competing— he also boldly protested unequal treatment. In 1894, the League of American Wheelmen—an organization that controlled many cycling competitions—introduced a proposal to exclude Black members. Although he was only fifteen years old, Marshall stood up against the racial prejudice of the League and wrote a public letter of protest to the editor of *The Bearings*, a cycling magazine.[29]

When the local YMCA would not allow Taylor to train alongside Whites, Birdie Munger offered to take him to Worcester, Massachusetts, where the White community was more welcoming. There, the teen cycling phenom received ample help and support to develop his skills and physique. Just a few years later, Taylor's hard work paid off when he won the world's cycling championship at the age of twenty-one.[30] Described by one reporter as "the peer, if not the master, of every White rider in the world," he competed throughout Europe and won the respect and admiration of professional cyclists across the globe.

In his autobiography, Taylor wrote proudly of his achievements— but he also acknowledged the hateful treatment he'd been forced to endure: "It was not always the mere excitement of . . . out-racing my opponents around the track and across the tape first that gave me the greatest thrill," he wrote, "but the real climax was the glory of vindication and the joy of retribution following each success, which was always indeed a personal triumph, because of their prejudice and unsportsmanlike methods."[31] As it turns out, overcoming racism made his many victories all the more sweet.

ATHLETICS AND COLONIAL OPPRESSION

Like people of color, Native Americans have often been subjected to racism in the realm of sports. In the late nineteenth century, White government officials began forcibly removing Indigenous children from their families and sending them to boarding schools where the required curricula included physical education and athletics. These institutions were frequent sites of violence, harm, and abuse directed against Indigenous children. The Bureau of Indian Affairs, which controlled the schools, viewed Indigenous people as "fundamentally equal but culturally inferior human beings."[32]

Although White settlers who created the boarding schools described their aims as benevolent, in truth they used Western education, recreational activities, and sports to "strip Native people of their cultures and languages by indoctrinating them with U.S. patriotism."[33] White educators and school administrators believed that they needed to help "civilize" Native people by teaching them discipline and hard work.

Indigenous nations have their own rich traditions of athletics, including lacrosse, which was invented by the Iroquois, as well as stickball, a game practiced by the Chickasaw, Seminole, Cherokee, and other Native nations.[34] But the physical education programs at the boarding schools were not designed to celebrate Native culture—they were designed to promote assimilation.

In terms of sports, this meant introducing Native children to "mainstream" games like football "as part of a larger effort to erase Native American culture and history from memory."[35] Unlike African Americans, who were largely prevented from competing against Whites in the nineteenth century, Native students at boarding schools were often pitted against all-White teams from the country's top schools in order to demonstrate their "successful" assimilation.[36]

Before the period of colonization, it was common for Native women and girls to participate in sports.[37] Boarding schools, however, imposed the rigid gender roles and expectations of White society. Because Whites in the United States and Europe thought of rigorous sports as "masculine" activities, they encouraged boys to play team sports but provided very few opportunities for athletic development to Native girls. Instead of cultivating female athletes or even investing in their intellectual development, boarding schools mostly aimed to transform Indigenous girls into "good farmers' wives."[38]

But despite the abuse they were subjected to, some Native athletes managed to excel in athletics. One of the most famous graduates of the boarding school system was Jim Thorpe, a member of the Sac and Fox nation who has been celebrated as the greatest athlete in history. Thorpe's athletic prowess was mindboggling. As a student, he excelled at just about every sport you can think of, including "football, baseball, track and lacrosse" as well as "hockey, handball, tennis, boxing and ballroom dancing." At one track and field competition, he managed to place first in "high hurdles, low hurdles, high jump, long jump, shot put *and* discus throw."[39] During the 1912 Olympic Games, Thorpe earned two gold medals in the decathlon and the pentathlon.[40] He went on to play in multiple professional sports leagues until the age of forty-one and was chosen to be the very first president of the National Football League.

(Per NFL.com) Jim Thorpe, one of the greatest athletes of all time, joined the Canton Bulldogs professional football team in 1915 and became the first president of the NFL in 1920
[Heritage Auctions]

BREAKING BARRIERS AND RECORDS

The dawn of the twentieth century brought new opportunities for athletes to play and compete against each other across the color line—and new opportunities for white supremacists to push back against racial progress. When Jack Johnson became the world's first Black heavyweight champion in 1908, White boxing fans demanded a "Great White Hope"—a White athlete who would reclaim racial dominance in the sport.⁴¹ Two years later—in 1910—a White boxer named Jim Jeffries faced off against Johnson in what was then called the "fight of the century." Jeffries wanted to prove the superiority of the White race and "demonstrate that a White man is king of them all."⁴²

White journalists and community leaders worried that a victory for Johnson would encourage African Americans to demand equal rights. Before the match, a writer in *The New York Times* warned: "If the black man wins, thousands and thousands of his ignorant brothers will misinterpret his victory as justifying claims to much more than mere physical equality with their White neighbors." This wasn't just a boxing match—it had morphed into a political event.

In the end, Johnson won decisively. His success in the ring was not his alone—it represented a symbolic triumph for Black people against the forces of white supremacy. Reflecting on the match, Johnson wrote: "I realized that my victory in this event meant more than on any previous occasion. It wasn't just the championship that was at stake: it was my own honor, and in a degree the honor of my own race. The 'White Hope' had failed."⁴³

In response to that failure, angry, violent White mobs rioted across the United States, killing African Americans and leaving behind a wake of destruction.⁴⁴ Such extremist violence on the part of White vigilantes vividly illustrates the fact that sports are not just about fun and games—they can also be profoundly political—and bloody—battlefields.

White supremacist politics were also on display during the infamous 1936 Olympics in Munich, Germany, where Hitler had recently seized power. In the year before the competition, a multiracial group of activists and athletes joined forces to protest the Nazis' discriminatory treatment of German Jewish athletes. Some members of the U.S. delegation threatened a boycott. Leading the charge was Jeremiah Titus Mahoney, a White American of Irish descent who was then president of the Amateur Athletic Union and in charge of selecting the U.S. team.

Known for his opposition to racism and bigotry, Mahoney protested the Nazi regime's escalating mistreatment of Jewish athletes. "There is no room for discrimination on grounds of race, color, or creed in the Olympics," he insisted.[45] Mahoney was joined by a coalition of supporters including the National Association for the Advancement of Colored People (NAACP) as well as Jewish and Catholic organizations in advocating for a boycott of the Munich Olympics.

But others, including some Jewish American and African American athletes, believed that participating would provide an opportunity to disprove the myth of Aryan superiority. Still others argued for participating on the grounds that politics should be kept out of the Olympics—sound familiar?—which ultimately meant supporting Hitler. After much debate, the U.S. Amateur Athletic Union narrowly voted to compete in Germany.[46]

The achievements of African Americans at the 1936 Olympics were considerable. Gold medalists like Jesse Owens, the famous track star, broke historic barriers. But such advances were not enough to uproot white supremacy. Racist ideologues began to portray Black people as athletically gifted but intellectually inferior. And, when African American Olympians returned home, they were greeted with continued discrimination and Jim Crow segregation. Many struggled to find good jobs and provide for their families. Back in Germany, Hitler enjoyed a political boost from successfully presiding over the Olympics. Just five years later, Nazis would begin systematically murdering Jewish people in the mass genocide known as the Holocaust.[47]

○ ○ ○

You've probably seen the iconic photograph: Two Black men solemnly stand together on a podium with their heads bowed and their fists in the air, each wearing a single black glove. The political action that has been called "the most widely recognized protest in sports history" took place during the medal ceremony for the 200-meter race during the 1968 Olympics held in Mexico City, Mexico. As the United States' national anthem played in the stadium to honor Tommie Smith, the 24-year-old African American sprinter who won the gold, televisions across the world broadcast a stunning display of athletic activism.[48] Smith described the symbolism of the protest this way:

> *The right glove that I wore on my right hand signified the power in Black America. The left glove my teammate John Carlos wore on his left hand made an arc, my right hand to his left hand, also signifying Black unity. The scarf that was worn around my neck signified Blackness. [We] . . . wore socks, black socks, without shoes, to also signify our poverty.*[49]

Many people don't realize that this Black human rights protest was also a moment of interracial solidarity. Smith, along with John Carlos, an African American who won bronze, were joined by Peter Norman, a White Australian silver medalist who strongly supported the protest. In fact, it was Norman's idea for Smith and Carlos to each wear a glove since they only had one pair. His participation was all the more significant given Australia's status as an openly white supremacist society in the 1960s.[50]

Most people do not realize that Norman, Carlos, and Smith were all wearing a round white patch that was also a key component of the protest. Although it's impossible to see in the photo, the patches bear these words: "Olympic Project for Human Rights." The Olympic Project for Human Rights (OPHR) was founded in 1967 by athletics activists to mobilize around racism and social justice. Harry Edwards, a sociologist of sports mentioned earlier in this chapter, was one of the main organizers of the OPHR. As a scholar, athlete, and activist, Edwards rallied members of the U.S. team to protest racial injustice in the United States and proposed a boycott of the Mexico City games.

The year 1968 was one of shocking violence, revolt, and uprisings both in the United States and abroad. The Vietnam War raged on—as did antiwar protests. Marches and demonstrations swept across multiple countries. The Civil Rights and Black Power movements were directly challenging the White power structure. Martin Luther King Jr.—who supported the boycott—was brutally assassinated months before the 1968 Olympics. In this atmosphere of social upheaval and collective grief, the OPHR athletes refused to just "shut up and play."

They asked for the International Olympic Committee to exclude South Africa from participating in the games due to the country's racist system of apartheid and white supremacy.[51] South Africa had previously been barred from the Olympics in 1964—and athletes wanted to ensure that the ban would continue so long as the apartheid regime remained in power. They also wanted to reinstate the famous Black boxer Muhammad Ali's heavyweight championship, which had been taken away from him as a result of his protests against the Vietnam War. Finally, they called for the hiring of Black coaches as well as the removal of a White racist named Avery Brundage from leading the International Olympic Committee. Decades earlier, Brundage had pressured the U.S. team to participate in Hitler's Olympics and even defended the use of Nazi salutes during medal ceremonies. Now, he was defending white supremacy in South Africa.[52]

Ultimately, the U.S. athletes threatened to boycott the Olympics if South Africa was allowed to participate. Their powerful act of protest—along with international pressure from nearly forty countries—successfully forced the Olympic Committee to take a stand against apartheid in South Africa and exclude them from the games.[53] As a result of this significant win, many athletes decided to compete in Mexico City—and to use the event to publicly take a stand against racism. It was this collective organizing and political resistance that led to the unforgettable "Black Power" protest.

The Olympic ban against South Africa would continue until 1991, when the apartheid system was dismantled. Athletics activism and boycotts all played a powerful role in undermining white supremacy in South Africa.[54]

But their courage came with a heavy price. Tommie Smith, John Carlos, and Peter Norman all faced terrible backlash for using their platform to promote racial justice. After the playing of "The Star-Spangled Banner" at the medal ceremony in Mexico City, racist "fans" shouted the N-word, told the runners to "go back to Africa," and threw trash and debris from the stands.[55] The U.S. team kicked Tommie Smith and John Carlos out of the Olympic Village, the area that houses all Olympic athletes, forcing them to leave Mexico immediately.

Back home, the White-controlled press harshly attacked the athletes, accusing them of being "un-American"—a harmful label that would also be applied, almost fifty years later, to athletes like Maya Moore and Colin Kaepernick. One journalist compared Smith and Carlos to Nazis.[56] They received death threats—even members of their families were targeted.[57] But while many U.S. Olympians kept their distance, some showed support. The all-White Harvard crew team publicly expressed their solidarity after the protest:

> We—as individuals—have been concerned about the place of the Black man in American society in their struggle for equal rights . . . As members of the US Olympic team, each of us has come to feel a moral commitment to support our Black teammates in their efforts to dramatize the injustices and inequities which permeate our society.[58]

Peter Norman also faced significant hardships as a result of taking a public stand against racism. When he returned to Australia, he was treated like a "pariah" by other Whites and eventually pushed out of athletics despite being one of the nation's most distinguished sprinters.[59] Decades after the events of 1968, he continued to express support for racial justice. He also maintained an enduring friendship with the Black athletes who stood with him on the podium that night in Mexico City. When Norman died in 2006, John Carlos and Tommie Smith traveled all the way across the world to attend his funeral and help carry his casket.[60]

CONCLUSION: RACISM AND ANTIRACISM IN SPORTS TODAY

As we have seen throughout this chapter, the presence and participation of Black and Brown athletes has not been enough to eliminate racism. In fact, integrating sports has often been met with White backlash and violence. That pattern continued in 1947, when Wataru Misaka became the first person of color to play for the Basketball Association of America (which would later become the NBA), breaking an important racial barrier.

A Japanese American athlete from Utah, Misaka joined the New York Knicks only a few years after the internment of Japanese Americans during World War II. The first two Knicks games of the season were played at home, in New York, where Misaka was largely embraced by supporters. But when the Knicks went on the road to Providence, Rhode Island, racist fans didn't hold back their anti-Japanese bigotry. Unwilling to risk losing business as a result of White racist backlash, the Knicks kicked Misaka to the curb and cut him from the team.

Although Misaka did not publicly protest the racism he experienced, he paved the way for future basketballers to break racial barriers and stand up for justice.[61] Some six decades after the Knicks fired Misaka, they signed Jeremy Lin, the NBA's first Asian American player of Chinese or Taiwanese origin. Lin—who would go on to become the league's first Asian American to win an NBA championship—has been outspoken about the racism he has had to overcome throughout his athletic career.[62]

In the midst of the COVID-19 pandemic, as hate crimes against Asian Americans spiked, he made headlines by acknowledging that a fellow athlete referred to him as "the coronavirus" during a game. And, he's used his platform as an athlete to raise awareness about racism and antiracism. On his Facebook page, he wrote:

> *Something is changing in this generation of Asian Americans. We are tired of being told that we don't experience racism, we are tired of being told to keep our heads down and not make trouble. We are tired of Asian American kids growing up and being asked where they're REALLY from, of having our eyes mocked, of being objectified as exotic or being told we're inherently unattractive. We are tired of the stereotypes in Hollywood affecting our psyche and limiting who we think we can be. We are tired of being invisible . . . or told our struggles aren't as real.*[63]

Lin is joined by a diverse group of modern athletes across a wide range of sports who are rising up against racial oppression. From national anthem protests to boycotts, public statements, and political action, contemporary athletes continue to carry on a long and rich legacy of antiracist activism. Their efforts are still very much needed. Racist incidents occur at sporting events in the United States and globally every year and result in the targeting and humiliation of athletes of color.[64]

Even young athletes are not protected from such incidents. As recently as 2021, a White announcer at a high school basketball game in Oklahoma referred to young Black girls using the N-word after members of the team knelt during the national anthem.[65] In 2018, sportswriter Bob Cook described a wave of overt racism at youth athletic events that unfolded over a period of several weeks in 2018. Examples included:

- "Racial slurs directed by White fans at Black opposing players are suspected of fueling a post-game brawl at a high school basketball game in San Antonio."
- "White students at a posh Cincinnati prep school chanted racial slurs at two minority players on an opposing basketball team."
- "The captain of a high school soccer team in the Fresno, California, area was suspended for two games after directing a racial slur at two Black players on the opposing team."
- "The owner of an Idaho youth soccer club whose members are mostly minority or immigrant families said a racist, threatening letter was placed on his car."
- "The seventh-grade girls basketball team from Licking County, Ohio, kneeled before the playing of the national anthem in protest of the racial slurs that had been directed at it all year by its mostly all-White opponents."[66]

Native Americans are also regularly targeted by vicious attacks during athletic events—especially at high schools. Anti-Indigenous racism in these settings includes everything from property damage and vandalism to openly hateful comments such as "Hey Indians, get ready for a Trail of Tears Part 2," and the use of slurs such as "prairie [N-word]" and "dirty Indians."[67]

The destructive influences of racism and white supremacy on

sports go beyond attacks against athletes—they also affect who is and isn't granted access to power. Although African Americans represent the majority of NFL players, they hold less than 10 percent of all head coaching jobs.[68] Systemic racism also prevents many Black athletes from even being considered for the quarterback position due to the racist belief that they lack the intellect for the leadership role.[69] In terms of economic power, only two NFL teams are owned by people of color—both of whom are Asian American. There are no African Americans at all who own an NFL team.[70]

Beyond the power dynamics in sports, racism also impacts the gaps in health outcomes for different racial groups. Alicia Whittington, a Black woman scientist, has dedicated her professional career to addressing racial health disparities. As the assistant director of engagement and health equity research for the Football Players Health Study at Harvard University, Whittington has worked to investigate the health conditions that many NFL players face after retirement. In 2020, her team's research showed that White former players experience better physical and mental health than African Americans, Asian Americans and Pacific Islanders, and other players of color. The largest disparity was between White players and Black players. Black athletes were 89 percent more likely than Whites to report physical impairments and 50 percent more likely to experience depression and anxiety, among other health conditions.[71] For Whittington, who comes from a big football family, the results really "hit home":

> My siblings and I were all first-generation college students. Three of my brothers earned scholarships to play collegiate football. Two played in the NFL. Twenty-six years ago (in

1994), the oldest of the three earned a spot on an NFL roster. So, I've seen firsthand the amount of dedication, sacrifice, discipline, and motivation it takes to play football at the highest level. So, these results are . . . concerning.

The groundbreaking work being done by Whittington and her colleagues ultimately aims to reduce these health gaps and even the playing field for Black athletes and athletes of color.

While we've mostly discussed male athletes thus far, it is also important to acknowledge the intersection of sexism and racism in sports. Until the 1970s, women and girls were largely excluded from athletics in school.[72] We've talked about how Americans have historically defined sports as "unfeminine"; this myth—which persists even today—creates unique barriers for female athletes. Black girls and girls of color have had to overcome negative stereotypes and limited opportunities to pursue sports. Yet their refusal to back down in the face of discrimination has led to incredible achievements.

Dianne Durham, a trailblazing African American gymnast, became the first Black girl to win a national championship at the age of fourteen. But her history-making victories in a sport previously dominated by White athletes came with a painful price. "In my own life and gymnastics career," she wrote, "I encountered discrimination and prejudice . . . It didn't stop me from reaching all of my goals, but it did play a role in preventing me from reaching some of my biggest goals."[73]

Despite these obstacles, women and girls have made significant contributions to diversifying athletics and advancing social justice. As a sixteen-year-old, Wilma Rudolph overcame disability, poverty, and racism to compete on the track and field team at the 1956 Olympics, where she earned a bronze medal. In 1960, she went on to become the first woman from the United States to earn three gold medals at a single Olympics.

Wilma Rudolph posing with the three gold medals she earned
at the 1960 Olympics in Rome [Bettman/Getty Images]

But she wasn't satisfied with just winning competitions and worldwide acclaim. Following her victory, a tickertape parade was held in her hometown of Clarksville, Tennessee. In the past, such an event would have been attended by Whites only. But Rudolph insisted the parade should be open to anyone, which led to the first interracial celebration of its kind in the city's history. According to sports historian Maureen Smith, Rudolph went on to participate in a protest that led to a local restaurant becoming integrated, even before racial groups were allowed to share space in pools and schools.[74] She has been credited with blazing a trail for Black women athletes like tennis star Serena Williams.[75]

In recent years, an increasing number of Latinas are breaking barriers and finding a home in the sport of softball.[76] Aleshia Ocasio, a rising star who is Puerto Rican and Black, has been outspoken about racial discrimination and gender bias as well as homophobia.

"We experience racism in sports," she says, "because of the systemic racism that we experience in life." Her racial advocacy work focuses on voting and political action.[77] Ocasio's wife, WNBA star Natasha Cloud, also shares a deep commitment to creating positive change. In fact, she sat out the entire 2020 basketball season in order to dedicate her time to antiracist activism.[78]

Women and girls are powerful leaders in the fight for a more equitable world. Like Natasha Cloud, Maya Moore—the WNBA champion and two-time Olympic gold medalist who led Black Lives Matter protests in 2016—decided to walk away from basketball in 2019. Organizing with community leaders and activists, Moore worked for several years to successfully free an African American man named Jonathan Irons who had been wrongfully imprisoned for nearly a quarter of a century. Today, she continues to use her visibility as a sports star to shine a light on racial inequality in our judicial system.[79]

Writing in *Time* magazine, Sean Gregory observes that "[no] basketball player of Moore's stature has ever willingly taken a sabbatical from the game, in her prime, to advocate for social reform."[80] Moore's incredible sacrifice and dedication to the cause of justice is an inspiring example for us all and shines a bright light on the ways athletes, past and present, have refused to simply "shut up and play" in the face of racism.

NINE

HOW YOU CAN CHANGE
THE RACIAL FUTURE

When the World Health Organization announced in March of 2020 that the COVID-19 virus had become a world-wide pandemic, many of our lives were turned upside down. In a frantic collective effort to prevent the spread of the virus, global quarantines closed many schools and businesses, forcing one out of every two human beings on the planet to socially isolate at home.

But the risks of death and suffering were not evenly distributed—some of us were more vulnerable than others.[1] As infection rates and death tolls began to rise, the novel coronavirus ravaged poor and working-class people as well as Black communities, Indigenous communities, and communities of color. Throughout the pandemic, Native Americans have experienced higher death rates than any other group and African Americans have died at more than twice the rate of White Americans.[2] In New York City, where I live, the most diverse neighborhoods with Asian American, Latinx, and Black populations were also the most likely to host COVID-19 outbreaks.[3]

What explains the greater prevalence of disease and death among economically and racially marginalized people? One of the major ideas we have discussed throughout this book is the massive impact of racist ideology and discriminatory policies on the lives of Black and Brown people. Systemic racism and white supremacy create unequal living conditions, opportunities, and resources—and these disparities limit access to safe neighborhoods, quality education, good jobs, intergenerational wealth, and healthcare.

Well before the COVID-19 pandemic, scholars and activists were raising the alarm about the links between discrimination and health outcomes. Hundreds of Black people die every single day as a result of *racial health disparities*—the gaps in health outcomes for different racial groups. Over time, these numbers add up to a monumental loss. During the twentieth century alone, structural racism caused the premature deaths of over *four million* African Americans.[4]

Historically, prejudices and racist stereotypes have lowered the quality of medical care that Black people and other marginalized communities receive. And while there is a connection between wealth and health, research has shown, for example, that even financially successful African Americans are still more vulnerable to health problems like heart disease and strokes than White counterparts. African Americans, Native Americans, and Hispanic populations also experience an elevated risk of diabetes when compared to Whites.[5] Some groups, like Asian Americans, also experience mental health challenges such as depression due to the weight of racism and pressures to assimilate into mainstream culture.[6]

At the beginning of this book, I introduced the image of a table to explain how the system of white supremacy was built. We have seen how the structure of white supremacist racism has been supported by four "legs": capitalism, colonization, Indigenous genocide, and transatlantic slavery. This system of oppression puts the lives of Black and Brown people at risk on a daily basis.[7] Scholars like sociologist Whitney Pirtle teach us that racially marginalized people are more vulnerable to COVID-19 and other harmful conditions because of social, economic, and political reasons—not biology or genetics.[8] These systemic vulnerabilities are a result of the choices that have been made in our society—the destructive ideas, policies, and practices that perpetuate the myth that some lives are more valuable than others.

Given the devastating impact of COVID-19 in Native communities, Black communities, and communities of color, it's never been more important to understand the links between health and racial justice. As a student of antiracism, you can help dismantle white supremacy by supporting efforts to eliminate structural barriers to health and well-being.

Yet despite these inequities, many Black and Brown people are leading figures in the area of health equity. When members of the Standing Rock Sioux nation began to protest the building of the Dakota Access pipeline in 2016, many chanted *"Water Is Life!"* The phrase is more than a slogan—it's literally true. Community members knew that the pipeline of crude oil could leak and contaminate their water supply. The resistance at Standing Rock—which continues until this day—is one of the most important frontlines in the battle against environmental racism.

Kizzmekia Corbett, an African American immunologist, is also on the forefront of combating health inequality. As of 2021, she is the country's top scientist leading the coronavirus vaccination program at the National Institutes of Health and helped design the Moderna vaccine.[9] During college, she double majored in Sociology and Biological Sciences and developed an interest in racial health disparities before going on to complete her Ph.D. In addition to her lifesaving research, Dr. Corbett frequently volunteers her time to connect with members of the Black community to advance vaccine outreach.[10]

Kizzmekia Corbett, one of the leading immunologists who helped create the Moderna vaccine (2017) [Kizzmekia Corbett]

In many ways, the global pandemic intensified racial inequities documented throughout this book. In addition to the widening health disparities described above, there was also a rise in racist attacks against Asian people. As mentioned in the last chapter, violent crimes targeting Asian Americans skyrocketed following the spring of 2020. After former President Trump used language like "Kung Flu" and "The

Chinese Virus" to describe COVID-19, reports of anti-Asian attacks increased by 150 percent in big cities.[11] The president's comments implicitly encouraged anti-Asian racism and inspired others to blame Asians for the deadly pandemic. But it's not just White Americans targeting Asian American people. African Americans and people of color—communities that are also harmed by racism—have frequently engaged in vicious assaults against Asians during the pandemic.

All of these crises also converged with an unprecedented rise in antiracist activism. The tragic deaths of African Americans, including Breonna Taylor, George Floyd, and Ahmaud Arbery—all of whom were killed by police officers or White vigilantes—inspired hundreds of thousands of people in the United States and across the world to take to the streets in mass protest for justice.

Protestors in Minneapolis, Minnesota, honoring the memory of George Floyd
before the 2021 trial of police officer Derek Chauvin [Chad Davis]

The summer of 2020 was filled with unending marches against white supremacy and vigils in support of the #BlackLivesMatter movement. These uprisings ushered in a wave of symbolic and political change. Companies finally bowed to pressure to change the imagery of brands and logos that demeaned African Americans and Native Americans, including Aunt Jemima, Uncle Ben's, and Land O' Lakes.[12] Confederate monuments and statues honoring white supremacists were toppled. And, in 2021, another hashtag emerged—#StopAsianHate—as well as marches and protests to stand in solidarity with Asian Americans and Pacific Islanders.

If it wasn't already clear that white supremacy is a serious problem in this country, the shocking Capitol attack of January 6, 2021, made the issue impossible to ignore. As mobs of Trump supporters and insurrectionists attacked police officers and overran the Capitol building, many displayed white supremacist symbols and some even built a gallows with a noose.

Given the ongoing racial violence in our country and the world at large, it would be understandable to feel overwhelmed, sad, angry, or afraid. These are all emotions that I sometimes feel in my work as an antiracist scholar and educator.

But there's something else I feel, too—something that inspires me to carry on when the going gets tough. That feeling is *hope*. One of my favorite quotes comes from Mariame Kaba, an influential organizer and educator mentioned earlier in this book. "Hope," she says, "is a discipline." But what does that mean? Kaba describes hope as more than just an emotion—it's also a commitment to believe in the possibilities of positive change:

> *It's work to be hopeful. It's not like a fuzzy feeling. Like, you have to actually put in energy, time, and you have to be*

clear-eyed, and you have to hold fast to having a vision. It's a hard thing to maintain. But it matters to have it, to believe that it's possible, to change the world . . . [We] have an opportunity at every moment to push in a direction that we think is actually a direction towards more justice.[13]

Hope is not just about believing that it's possible to improve our society now and reshape the future. It's also about recognizing the change that's already occurred. As we have seen over the course of the previous chapters, Black people and people of color have courageously overcome obstacles and incredible odds to resist racism, rise above limiting beliefs, protest injustice, raise awareness, change laws, and even overthrow oppressive regimes. And there have also been White Americans who refused to remain silent about the wrongs of racism and committed themselves to supporting interracial solidarity—sometimes at great personal sacrifice.

A child holds a sign at a #StopAsianHate rally in Oakland,
California [Xinhua News Agency/Getty Images]

And yet, as the era of COVID-19 reminded us, the struggle against racism is far from over. How can we possibly maintain a sense of hope when there's still so far to go in the march toward justice? For me, practicing the discipline of hope means remembering and honoring the work of our ancestors and those who came before us—people who refused to accept the status quo even when others believed that change was impossible. If we rewind the clock several centuries, many people believed that the transatlantic slave trade would never come to an end. But some dared to imagine otherwise. It was enduring hope and the courageous work of enslaved people, freedom fighters, and White abolitionists that ultimately brought the system of chattel slavery to its knees. So, not only is positive change possible— it's already happened!

Together, we have the power to transform our society. And this is where *you* come in! Young people just like you have an important role to play in making sure that our future is better than our past. But it's going to take more than good intentions. We have to find ways to turn our growing knowledge into action that will dismantle injustice and create a more equitable society. **Equity** involves changing society and removing structural barriers in order to create fair outcomes for everybody regardless of their background or identity. In a racially equitable society, all young people would have the support they need to reach their full potential.[14]

Although we are all equal in terms of our worth as human beings, we do not all have equal access to the resources that allow us to thrive. This is why antiracist educators and organizers believe in the value of "giving everyone what they need to be successful."[15] In other words, it's not enough just to believe in the principle of equality. Antiracist advocates take active steps to support policies and practices that will undo the harm of white supremacy and level the playing field.

In these final pages, we will review some key ideas that are essential for creating a more inclusive and just world and consider concrete steps you can take on your own antiracist journey. But before we move on, I'd like you to take a moment to think about the following questions:

1. What would it be like to live in a society without racist beliefs, racial violence, and discrimination?
2. Can you think of any political, economic, and social transformations that might help bring an end to racism and other forms of oppression?
3. What does the word "freedom" mean to you? What would it feel like to be free?

THE MYTHS OF RACIST IDEOLOGY

One of the most important things we can do to resist white supremacy is reject the myths of racist ideology. Systemic racism is upheld by a web of harmful beliefs that distort reality and prevent us from being able to recognize our common humanity. For generations, the lies of racism have taught us that:

- Our worth is determined by the color of our skin or the texture of our hair
- Races are natural, biological groups, and we are more genetically similar to other people who share our race

- White Americans should be entitled to more land, power, and resources than others
- Learning about the history of racism is harmful or divisive
- Opposing white supremacy is unpatriotic
- People who take a stand against racial injustice are the problem

The truth is that there is nothing natural about the idea of race. Chapter 1 revealed that racial categories and labels were created by human beings during the period of European colonialism and transatlantic slavery. But the social construction of race—the fact that it was made up—doesn't mean that its consequences are any less real. The myth of race has been embedded in real policies, laws, and institutions. These social and political processes shape our behavior as well as how we view each other and ourselves. In a powerful documentary called *RACE: The Power of an Illusion*, anthropologist Alan Goodman explains that "you don't see race—you just think you see race." Sociologist Melvin Oliver agrees:

> *Race in itself means nothing—the markers of race, skin color, hair texture, the things that we identify as the racial markers, mean nothing unless they are given social meaning and unless there's public policy and private actions that act upon those kinds of characteristics. That creates race.*[16]

What this all means is that we are taught to see each other as members of racial groups. We also learn the myth, at a very early age, that some races are better than others. This ideology has warped our economy and our educational and judicial systems, as well as the media that we see on our televisions, computers, and smartphones every day.

Civil rights leaders and antiracist activists know that it is not enough to say that "races don't exist." In fact, we have to acknowledge how the idea of race—and the myth of White superiority—has created durable inequalities and unequal opportunities. Dr. Martin Luther King Jr. understood that white supremacy is much more than the Ku Klux Klan or neo-Nazis. In a 1967 sermon entitled "Love in Action," Dr. King described white supremacy as a system of power designed to justify slavery and oppression. Over time, he explained, the myth of white superiority was "imbedded in every textbook and preached in practically every pulpit. It became a structured part of the culture."[17]

Shifting our society toward justice requires honestly confronting the culture of racism that Dr. King struggled against. You may have noticed that the name of that sermon included the word "love." And that's important—because Dr. King understood antiracism as an act of love. The ideology of racism is based upon the lie that some people are unworthy or undeserving. In truth, every human being is special, unique, and worthy of dignity and respect. Dr. King believed that if we join together in solidarity and take action to dismantle injustice, we can create what he called a "beloved community"—a new way of relating to each other as equal members of the same human family.[18] Jane Elliott, a White antiracist educator, makes the same point when she says that "[there] is only one race—the human race."[19]

But despite the fact there is only one human race—one human species—the myth that racial groups are biological persists even today. In her research on college students, sociologist Ann Morning found that this is especially the case for beliefs about blackness. Her study revealed that students typically viewed Black people's participation in certain sports as the result of biology or natural differences rather than culture.[20] So, for example, students imagined that if many players in the NBA are Black, it must be because they have a genetic trait that makes them great basketball players. By contrast, students explained the presence or absence of White athletes from sports as being a result of cultural or historical differences.

Sports, the subject of Chapter 8, have historically perpetuated the belief that racial groups are biological.[21] Racist ideology portrays Black bodies—and Black athletes—as physically gifted but intellectually inferior. Remarkably, the idea that Black people are biologically distinct from other groups endures even though many African Americans have mixed ancestry.[22] The bottom line is that racial groups are social, cultural, and political constructions—not biological realities.

As antiracists, we reject the idea of race as genetics. The biological group we all belong to has a name: the human species. We also reject the harmful beliefs, misrepresentations, and racist stereotypes that have historically distorted society. Over the course of this book, we have seen countless inspiring examples of people who refused to accept these myths of racial inferiority and superiority—people who defied the limitations of racial prejudice and discrimination. You do not have to accept or conform to the narrow stereotypes that have propped up the system of racism.

THE IMPACT OF ADVOCACY

But simply challenging racist ideas is not enough. We also need to promote cultural and structural change. And this is why antiracist advocacy is so important. If we are to build the "beloved community" that Dr. King described, we'll have to find ways to show up and support one another. This begins with learning about the challenges faced by groups that have been historically disadvantaged by systemic racism—and by class inequality and other forms of oppression, too. Dr. King understood the fight against racism as deeply tied to the fight against poverty and war.[23]

All too often, the struggles, knowledge, and contributions of Indigenous people are left out of the conversation about racial and economic justice. This needs to change. Today, Native people continue to boldly resist the violence of settler colonialism. Indigenous advocates mobilize for the recognition of their diverse cultures and their national sovereignty as well as the return of their ancestral lands.

Websites and social media networks are also vibrant spaces of Indigenous mobilization and resistance. As a seventeen-year old, Theland Kicknosway used his platform on TikTok (@the_land) to educate others about his Cree and Potawatomi heritage and cultural traditions.[24] Indigenous advocates and organizations have also created hashtags including #NotYourMascot to bring greater visibility to Native causes. Such online activism has played a role in pressuring sports teams to end the racist practice of using Native American caricatures as mascots. But the movement had already been building for decades, led by the activism and scholarship of Indigenous community leaders.[25]

Young people—including non-Native youth—have also been involved in the effort to change Native American mascots. In 2013, a White high school student named Emily Greenberg participated in a summer program in New Hampshire. There, she met a number of Indigenous students, including Kenard Dillon, who is of Navajo, Apache, and Hopi heritage. As they began to develop a friendship,

Kenard asked Emily about her high school mascot. Embarrassed, she admitted that her school back in Cooperstown, New York, named their sports teams after the R-word—a slur against Native Americans. Hurt and offended, Kenard said that the mascot "goes to show how objectified, how marginalized, we've become to mainstream Americans."[26]

These words had a powerful influence on Emily. When the summer program came to an end, she went to the school board in Cooperstown to ask for the team names to be changed. From there, a youth movement began to build as Emily joined forces with her friend Hope Dohner, and later, another student named Catherine Borgstrom, to generate support in their community for a new sports mascot. Although they faced opposition, the students succeeded in raising consciousness and convincing the school district administrators to change the teams' name from the R-word to The Hawkeyes.

A 2014 protest against the Washington Football Team's former
use of a Native American slur [Fibonacci Blue]

The Oneida Nation, located in upstate New York, contributed $10,000 to support the shift and also took a leading role in mobilizing against the use of offensive Native mascots by other teams.[27] As a result of their advocacy—as well as the impact of protests for racial justice—the NFL's team in Washington, D.C., finally stopped using the R-word as their name and mascot in 2020. Later that year, the Cleveland Indians major league baseball team also agreed to change their name.[28]

While progress is being made, the struggle against racist mascots continues. As of 2014, over 2,000 high schools had Indigenous mascots as part of their team names. By 2020, that number dwindled by nearly half—but there are still 1,232 high schools with Native American slurs and caricatures being used as names and mascots.[29] Not only does this widespread practice contribute to a culture of racism—it also causes pain and suffering for Indigenous people.[30]

Adrienne Keene, a Cherokee scholar and activist, reminds us that Native mascots are not just problematic because they're hurtful, offensive and exploitative—they're also psychologically harmful. Stephanie Fryberg, an Indigenous psychologist and scholar of the Tulalip Tribes, has documented the negative impact of racist mascots on the mental health of Native people. And the damage begins early in life. Research suggests that Native mascots diminish the self-esteem of Indigenous youth.

But for Keene and many other Indigenous advocates, changing mascots is just one step in a much larger project of reclaiming their sovereignty, rights, and resources: "I don't want to just be talking about representations . . . I want to be talking about our land and water rights, about our treaty rights, about education in our communities, about nation building . . ."[31]

FIVE STEPS FOR CREATING ANTIRACIST CHANGE

All right. We've covered a *lot* of ground and explored many different kinds of advocacy. Now we've come to the most important part. How can *you* get involved and transform your knowledge into action? What specific steps can you take to join the fight against white supremacy? Here are five things anyone can do to help build a more just and equitable world.

1. MAKE A LIFELONG COMMITMENT TO ANTIRACISM

A system of oppression that was created over the course of centuries can't be magically fixed overnight—or even in one lifetime. Working toward justice is kind of like a relay race.[32] We pick up the baton from our ancestors, freedom fighters, and activists who came before us. And then we have to do our part to run toward the finish line and make the world a little better—not just for ourselves, but for those who will pick up the baton when we're gone. So, one of the most important things you can do right now is to decide that you're in it for the long haul.

We have a collective responsibility to stand up for what's right—and there's no expiration date for the cause of justice. Antiracism is a set of values and a way of life—an enduring commitment to upholding human rights. Hopefully, this book is just one of many that will guide you on your antiracist journey. Read about the history and present-day realities of racism in your local neighborhood or region.

Seek out diverse perspectives online and offline to learn about the experiences of a wide range of racial and ethnic groups. Watch films or listen to podcasts on the subject and then discuss them with your friends and family. Educate yourself about the work of antiracist community leaders, organizers, artists, and activists. The more you know, the better equipped you will be to help bring about positive change.

2. BUILD RELATIONSHIPS ACROSS RACIAL AND ETHNIC LINES

Earlier in this chapter, we saw how a friendship between a Native American student and a White American student eventually transformed an entire school. Unfortunately, due to centuries of segregation, interracial friendships are still not the norm in our society. In fact, polls have shown that 75 percent of White Americans report having no Black or Brown friends at all.[33] Moreover, the interracial friendships that some people experience at school sometimes fall apart as they grow up and neglect these relationships. You can help buck these trends by creating—and maintaining—a diverse social network. Building connections with a diverse range of people can help debunk stereotypes, introduce us to new perspectives, broaden our cultural horizons, and fuel our commitment to promoting racial justice.

But interracial friendship can also involve the hard work of navigating painful subjects. One Haitian American writer put it this way: "I think the real reason these friendships are hard to maintain is that in order to be truly authentic, I need to feel like I can share all the parts of myself with my friends . . . If I can't do that, our 'friendship' isn't as close as the ones I have with my Black friends and other [people of color]."[34] If we truly want to break down racial barriers, our friendships and close relationships should be spaces where we can build enough trust to talk honestly about difficult topics like white supremacy.

3. SPEAK UP AGAINST RACIST IDEAS, IMAGES, AND BEHAVIOR

Have you ever heard the phrase "If you see something, say something"? We might add: "If you hear something, say something." You can advance the cause of antiracism by getting into the habit of speaking up when you notice racist images in the media or harmful verbal comments.[35]

It's especially important to recognize the link between the history of racist ideas and present-day stereotypes. Speaking up against racist jokes is also an important aspect of antiracism. Research demonstrates that such jokes are, in fact, no laughing matter. In their study of White college students, sociologists Leslie Picca and Joe Feagin found that racist jokes were common and widespread. Such behaviors contribute to a culture of racism and encourage discriminatory behavior.

You probably won't be surprised to learn that most racial joking targets Black people and people of color, as well as Jewish people. This pattern reflects our society's history of white supremacy, anti-Black racism, and antisemitism. Disrupting this culture of racism involves speaking up when we hear offensive statements.

Consider this scenario as reported by a White student in Picca and Feagin's study:

I headed over to a dorm next to mine to see some guy friends of mine (five White males and one Middle Eastern male) . . . We were all hanging around in the dorm rooms, being social. I started talking to one of the visiting friends, Chad, about his college and fraternity. The Middle Eastern [student], Brad, was walking around like everyone else, when all of a sudden Chad said, "Hey. Hijacker!! How are you?" As soon as Chad said this, the whole room went silent. Brad calmly went up to Chad and said that was very offensive and to never call him that again.[36]

In this case, none of the White students spoke up to condemn Chad's racist remark. Instead, Brad had to speak up for himself. Now, imagine if things had turned out a bit differently. What if the other White students had spoken up and told Chad that what he said was wrong? What if someone had actively supported him? What would you have done if you were in the room? And what might you have felt if you were in Brad's shoes—or if you've been in Brad's shoes—alone and unsupported?

Shifting from a culture of racism to a culture of antiracism means that we all need to get more comfortable speaking up for one another and for ourselves. But sometimes we might not know how to respond when confronted with hateful speech or actions. If you're wondering what to do if you witness hate speech or even violence, I recommend seeking out resources on bystander training that can help empower you with a variety of tools for addressing harmful or bullying behavior. One great place to start is ihollaback.org.[37]

4. SUPPORT INTERSECTIONAL JUSTICE

In Chapter 7, I introduced the term intersectionality—a concept coined by Black feminist scholar Kimberlé Crenshaw to explain the links between racism, sexism, ableism, class inequality, and other forms of oppression. Our antiracist advocacy should be inclusive of many different kinds of communities and acknowledge how racism is intertwined with other hierarchies and systems of power.

One thing to keep in mind about intersectionality is that our identities and experiences of inequality are complex. This is especially the case because most of us belong to a variety of different groups and have both social advantages and disadvantages that may shift over time. In truth, no one's experience of power can be reduced to just one aspect of their identity. There are people who have access to White privilege but experience systemic oppression as a result of being poor, queer, female, transgender, and/or disabled.

Take me, for example. As an African American woman, I experience racism and sexism. I'm also bisexual, which means that I encounter biphobia and homophobia. But because I'm cisgender, I have access to many privileges that are denied to transgender people. Today, my Ph.D. and job as a professor afford me economic and social advantages. But, because I do not come from a middle-class background, I had to overcome many odds to have access to these opportunities.

As a child, I grew up in a family without many resources and my mother had to juggle multiple jobs to provide for us. For years, we lived in a very small house in Tennessee with my grandmother. As a young Black girl from working-class roots, I certainly didn't fit the stereotype of a "genius" or a high-achieving kid. If a teacher hadn't noticed my academic potential in the second grade, I might never have been placed in the Gifted and Talented track at school—or applied to Harvard University years later. That one stroke of luck changed the course of my life. But there are countless Black and Brown students just like me whose talents are overlooked or unrecognized as a result of systemic racism and economic oppression.

Intersectionality is also important in terms of thinking about solidarity. We can't just advocate for members of our own race, ethnicity, gender, or other groups. Instead, we need to expand our hearts, our minds, and our politics to build the "beloved community" that Dr. King envisioned. To do this, we should learn from activists like Vilissa Thompson and Alice Wong who are at the forefront of bringing visibility to disability justice for Black people and people of color.[38] And we can follow the lead of Kimberlé Crenshaw herself whose project #SayHerName brings attention to the intersection of racism and sexism in the lives of Black women and girls harmed and killed by police.[39]

5. GET POLITICAL!

This final step is one that I hope you'll actually take again and again on your antiracism journey. Becoming informed about politics is key to shifting power, changing policies, and reshaping the future. What does "getting political" involve? Well, for starters, it begins with learning how politics—or power dynamics—already shape our lives.

Political education helps empower us with knowledge about our government and elections as well as the different kinds of parties and platforms supported by our representatives.

If you're under the age of eighteen, you might be wondering: "Can I even get involved in politics if I'm not able to vote?" The answer is: *Yes, you can!* You might even be more politically aware and active than some of the adults in your life! Sociologist Veronica Terriquez has spent many years studying and working with young people of color in California's Central Valley region. In her experience, youth—including undocumented immigrants—make important contributions to political advocacy:

> *They affect political change by educating and mobilizing their peers, and sometimes their teachers or fellow community members, helping to identify problems in their communities and offer solutions. They also meet with local elected officials to propose, negotiate, or even demand solutions to the problems that they are facing.*[40]

In 2018, Terriquez launched the Central Valley Freedom Summer, a project inspired by the 1964 civil rights organizing of African Americans and White allies that led to voter registrations and political mobilization throughout Mississippi. The goal was to empower youth in the Central Valley to become knowledgeable about issues facing their community and get involved in civic engagement.

Many Central Valley youth are Latinx immigrants and struggle with the intersecting crises of racism, poverty, and environmental racism. Asthma rates are high for children forced to live in polluted neighborhoods. Over the course of three months, college students worked alongside Dr. Terriquez to conduct outreach with high school students through workshops, conferences, artistic events, and voter registration drives. By the end of the summer, they built new relationships and registered thousands of people to vote.

The initiative had a major impact on Syvannah Sandoval, a high school participant who suffers from asthma and grew up feeling powerless. But getting involved in the Freedom School and organizing her own conference taught her the power young people have to uplift their community: "Our voice does matter," she said, "because when we all come together collectively, we have the ability to promote change."[41]

In addition to learning about civic engagement and voting, political education can equip us with ideas, policies, and strategies for creating the future we wish to see. You can get informed about antiracist movements in other societies across the globe. You can learn about efforts to obtain reparations for slavery and centuries of discrimination as well as the LAND BACK campaign for Indigenous people.[42] You can also read about the history of political resistance such as the Black feminist organizing of the Combahee River Collective and the Black Panthers, as well as the Puerto Rican and multiracial street activism of the Young Lords.[43]

Mariame Kaba, the educator and activist who described the discipline of hope, encourages us to learn from the political tradition of abolition. And here, we're not just talking about abolishing slavery, but also abolishing harmful systems like prisons or even policing.[44] She also teaches us about the politics of transformative justice, which is about "trying to figure out how we respond to violence and harm in a way that doesn't cause more violence and harm."[45]

From this perspective, none of us are merely victims or villains—we all can be the targets and perpetrators of harm. And any effort to change our society must also shift how we relate to one another in our everyday lives. Kaba suggests that a truly just society is one in which we change the way we respond to violence—and move beyond the need for punishment. If this sounds difficult or challenging, you're not wrong! But, then again, no one said that changing the world would be easy . . .

THE SHAPE OF OUR FUTURE

Recently, I posed this question to some of my own college students: What is the point of learning about white supremacy and facing the realities of Indigenous genocide, slavery, and centuries of legal oppression? What do they think of the idea that certain people call such topics "hateful" or "divisive"? Their answers were extraordinary.

Students spoke about the role of education in helping them understand how we are shaped by our upbringing and by ongoing histories. They described knowledge as a tool for not only making sense of society but also taking an active role in changing society for the better. Some said that becoming educated about racism and white supremacy can also help White youth who would like to speak up about racism in predominately White spaces. Others talked about the need to acknowledge the wrongs of the past in order to address present-day injustices. Many said that they never had an opportunity to learn about race or racism until university—and spoke to the need to include diverse perspectives from kindergarten through high school.

One young woman said that she felt "even more patriotic" than people who deny the history and ongoing realities of racism because she sees love of country as tied to learning from the past, addressing injustice, and creating a better society. Another expressed the view that learning the history of racism and white supremacy could actually help them build compassion and empathy for other groups. Personally, I couldn't agree more.

Our society is becoming more and more diverse every single day. And our future is full of many colors. Already, most babies and children in the United States are Black or Brown.[46] And most people on the planet are of Asian or African descent. With global challenges ranging from the COVID-19 pandemic to climate change, our collective survival depends on our ability to come together, overcome divisions, and finally see how deeply we are all connected.

Activist and organizer Fannie Lou Hamer famously said that *"Nobody's free until everybody's free."*[47]

So, what are you waiting for? Let's rise up and find our freedom!

ACKNOWLEDGMENTS

I began writing *Rise Up!* before the COVID-19 pandemic. The convergence of a global health crisis along with the racial and political traumas of 2020 made it exceptionally difficult for me to get words on the page. There's no way in the world that I could have finished this book without the love, laughter, support, and care of my partner, Kei Petersen. She read every word of every chapter—sometimes more than once!—and let me slack off a *little* bit with my chores so that I could focus on writing. Now that I'm finally done, I can get back to doing my fair share of the dishes and vacuuming! I should also thank our cat Zora for being a near constant writing companion and for stretching out across my laptop when it was time for me to take a break.

Writing a book is always a difficult thing. But writing about four hundred years of oppression and resistance for young audiences is uniquely challenging! I'm deeply grateful to Brian Geffen, my brilliant and deeply kind editor at Henry Holt for Young Readers, as well as Michael Bourret, my agent extraordinaire, for making this unexpected project a reality. Thank you both for trusting and supporting me through the process of becoming a YA author.

Friends, loved ones, and thousands of people on the internet also provided much needed community and encouragement. I thank my mom, Barbara, for being my forever champion and an early, enthusiastic reader of the manuscript. Her ideas, feedback, and questions sharpened my thinking and greatly improved the text. During the global quarantine, virtual hangouts with Zulema, Vilna, Alecia, Tracey, and many others helped me feel connected during uncertain and unsettling times. Ongoing conversations with audience members at speaking events and book signings as well as students at Stony Brook University influenced my thinking and helped me better understand the kinds of questions and topics that parents and young people grapple with when addressing racism. I'd also like to recognize the support and influence of my followers and mutuals on Twitter for engaging with my never-ending late-night threads, responding to my impromptu polls, helping me to think about issues in new ways, sharing suggestions and resources, and just generally being awesome people.

Numerous educators and colleagues contributed to this book. I thank Zulema Valdez in particular for connecting me to Veronica Terriquez, which allowed me to learn more about her work with the Central Valley Freedom Project. I'm also grateful to Alicia Whittington, Rachel Grasow, and Paula Atkeson for generously taking the time to meet with me and share insights regarding the Harvard Football Players Health Survey.

Last, though certainly not least, I'm grateful to God for literally everything.

NOTES

A NOTE ON LANGUAGE

1. I'm influenced here by multiple considerations. First, I think it's important for young people of all racial and ethnic backgrounds to feel respected. While it may make sense to use the lowercase form of *white* in some contexts, I have chosen to use the same capitalization for all groups in this book. Secondly, I agree with sociologist Eve Ewing, who eloquently explained her recent decision to capitalize the word *White* in order to foster awareness about the social and historical significance of White racial identity—and the power and resources that are associated with it. Unlike Ewing, however, I have chosen to style nouns like *blackness* and *whiteness* in lowercase because they refer not to people but rather to ideas and meanings that are attached to groups. Of course, my thinking on this could change in a future text. See Eve L. Ewing, "I'm a Black Scholar Who Studies Race. Here's Why I Capitalize 'White,'" *Zora*, July 2, 2020, https://zora.medium.com/im-a-black -scholar-who-studies-race-here-s-why -i-capitalize-white-f94883aa2dd3.

2. The Native American Journalists Association, "Reporting and Indigenous Terminology," 2018, https://najanewsroom.com /wp-content/uploads/2018/11 /NAJA_Reporting_and_Indigenous _Terminology_Guide.pdf.

3. According to the Pew Research Center, only 3 percent of people who identify as Latino or Hispanic actually use the word *Latinx*. Therefore, the words *Latino* and *Hispanic* are still used alongside Latinx throughout the book. Luis Noe-Bustamante, Lauren Mora, and Mark Hugo Popeza, "About One-in-Four U.S. Hispanics Have Heard of Latinx, but Just 3% Use It," *Pew Research Center*, August 11, 2020, https://www.pewresearch .org/hispanic/2020/08/11/about-one -in-four-u-s-hispanics-have-heard-of -latinx-but-just-3-use-it.

4. AP Stylebook, "We now write antisemitism (n.), antisemitic (adj.), without a hyphen and with no capitalization. This is a change from AP's previous style: anti-Semitism and anti-Semitic," Twitter, April 23, 2021, https://twitter.com/APStylebook /status/1385687075635204100?s = 20.

5. The *N-word* refers to the epithet *N*gger* and the *R-word* refers to R*dskin. Unfortunately, both of these harmful words have been integrated into our culture of racism and contribute to the oppression of African Americans and Indigenous people. I have chosen not to reprint them here.

INTRODUCTION

1. Tanya Golash-Boza, *Race and Racisms: A Critical Approach* (Oxford: Oxford University Press, 2015). Crystal Fleming, *How to Be Less Stupid About Race: On Racism, White Supremacy and the Racial Divide* (Boston: Beacon Press, 2018).
2. Golash-Boza, *Race and Racisms*, 106. Golash-Boza defines "structural racism" as "interinstitutional interactions across time and space that reproduce racism."
3. Hazar Kalani, "'Asthma Alley': Why Minorities Bear Burden of Pollution Inequity Caused by White People," *The Guardian*, April 4, 2019, https://www.theguardian.com/us-news/2019/apr/04/new-york-south-bronx-minorities-pollution-inequity.
4. Claudia Persico, "How Exposure to Pollution Affects Educational Outcomes and Inequality," Brookings Institution, November 20, 2019, https://www.brookings.edu/blog/brown-center-chalkboard/2019/11/20/how-exposure-to-pollution-affects-educational-outcomes-and-inequality/.
5. For a discussion of the distinction between race and ethnicity, see Golash-Boza, *Race and Racisms*, 6. "The idea of race is slightly different from the concept of ethnicity . . ."
6. George M. Fredrickson, *Racism: A Short History* (Princeton: Princeton University Press, 2015).
7. Note that Andrea Smith identifies three "pillars" of white supremacy: Slavery/Capitalism, Genocide/Capitalism, and Orientalism/War. My formulation differs somewhat from Smith's, but is also influenced her analysis. See Andrea Smith, "Heteropatriarchy and the Three Pillars of White Supremacy," in *Color of Violence: The INCITE! Anthology*, ed. Incite! Women of Color against Violence (Cambridge: South End Press, 2016) 66–78. "I call one such framework The Three Pillars of White Supremacy," p. 67.
8. Vilna Bashi Treitler, *The Ethnic Project: Transforming Racial Fiction into Ethnic Factions* (Redwood City, CA: Stanford University Press, 2013).
9. See Fredrickson, *White Supremacy: A Comparative Study of American and South African History* (New York: Oxford University Press, 1982).
10. On the transition from religiously justified oppression to racism, see Fredrickson, *White Supremacy*, Chapter 1.
11. Mariame Kaba, *We Do This 'Til We Free Us: Abolitionist Organizing and Transforming Justice* (Chicago: Haymarket Books, 2021).

CHAPTER 1

1. Dean Cristol and Belinda Gimbert, "Racial Perceptions of Young Children: A Review of Literature Post-1999," *Early Childhood Education Journal* 36.2: 201–207.

2. "'Watchmen,' which concludes its acclaimed, highly rated first season Sunday, is the first major superhero drama on TV to star an African American woman." Greg Braxton, "Regina King Has Been on the Road to 'Watchmen' for 34 years. She Has No Regrets," *Los Angeles Times*, December 15, 2019, https://www.latimes.com/entertainment-arts/tv/story/2019-12-15/regina-king-hbo-watchmen-southland-american-crime. See also: Jessica Dickerson, "'Exodus: Gods and Kings' Film Sparks Backlash For Whitewashing Characters," *Huffington Post—Black Voices*, August 5, 2014, https://www.huffpost.com/entry/exodus-gods-kings-whitewash-boycott_n_5652499. Benjamin Lee, "Gods of Egypt Posters Spark Anger with 'Whitewashed' Cast," *The Guardian*, November 13, 2015, https://www.theguardian.com/film/2015/nov/13/gods-of-egypt-posters-anger-whitewashed-cast-twitter-exodus. Dave McNary. "Marvel's First Asian-Led Superhero Movie, 'Shang-Chi,' Finds Director," March 13, 2019, *Variety*, https://variety.com/2019/film/news/shang-chi-director-destin-daniel-cretton-marvel-asian-superhero-1203162631/.

3. Sean Coughlin, "Tom and Jerry Cartoons Carry Racism Warning," *BBC*, October 1 2014, https://www.bbc.com/news/education-29427843.

CHAPTER 2

1. Ricky Lee Allen, "What About Poor White People?" in *Handbook of Social Justice in Education*, eds. William Ayers, Therese Quinn, and David Stovall (New York: Routledge, 2009), 209–230.

2. Gillian White, "In D.C., White Families Are on Average 81 Times Richer Than Black Ones," *The Atlantic*, November 26, 2016, https://www.theatlantic.com/business/archive/2016/11/racial-wealth-gap-dc/508631/.

3. See Leslie Picca and Joe Feagin, *Two-Faced Racism: Whites in the Backstage and Frontstage* (New York: Routledge, 2007), 29–30. "In the North American case, from the 1600s to the 1960s, Whites benefited greatly from 'affirmative action' programs . . . [including] the nineteenth-century and early-twentieth century provision by the federal government of hundreds of millions of acres of land for viable farm homesteads in many states. From that agricultural land many white families built up wealth that they passed to several later generations of whites, who often translated it into such things as good education, white-collar jobs, and good housing. Tens of millions of whites today are affluent because of a few large-scale federal programs of land allocation. Yet this land, for the most part, was not made available to Black Americans and other Americans of color who were present in those states during the same decades—because of widespread, sometimes violent, white opposition and discrimination."

4. For example, the Chinese Exclusion Act of 1882 ended immigration to the United States from China.

5. W.E.B. Du Bois, *Black Reconstruction in America: An Essay Toward a History of the Part Which Black Folk Played in the Attempt to Reconstruct Democracy in*

America, 1860–1880 (1935; Oxford, UK: Oxford University Press, 2007).

6. Melvin L. Oliver and Thomas M. Shapiro, *Black Wealth/White Wealth: A New Perspective on Racial Inequality*. (New York: Routledge, 2006). See also Diana Elliott, "Two American Experiences: The Racial Divide of Poverty," The Urban Institute, July 21 2016, https://www.urban.org/urban-wire/two-american-experiences-racial-divide-poverty.

7. Ira Katznelson, *When Affirmative Action Was White: An Untold History of Racial Inequality in Twentieth-Century America* (New York: W. W. Norton, 2006). See also Ta-Nehisi Coates, "The Case for Reparations," *The Atlantic*, June 2014, https://www.theatlantic.com/magazine/archive/2014/06/the-case-for-reparations/361631/.

8. Janelle Jones, "One-third of Native American and African American Children Are (Still) in Poverty," Economic Policy Institute, September 20, 2017, https://www.epi.org/publication/one-third-of-native-american-and-african-american-children-are-still-in-poverty/.

9. Darrick Hamilton,"Race, Wealth, and Intergenerational Inequality," *The American Prospect*, August 14, 2009, https://prospect.org/article/race-wealth-and-intergenerational-poverty.

10. Niall McCarthy, "Racial Wealth Inequality in the U.S. Is Rampant [Infographic]," *Forbes*, September 14, 2017, https://www.forbes.com/sites/niallmccarthy/2017/09/14/racial-wealth-inequality-in-the-u-s-is-rampant-infographic/#6c3cd20534e8. McCarthy warns that "if current trends continue, it will take 228 years for the average black family to reach the same level of wealth white families have today. For Latino families, it would take 84 years."

11. David Cooper, "Workers of Color Are Far More Likely to Be Paid Poverty-Level Wages Than White Workers," Economic Policy Institute, June 21, 2018, https://www.epi.org/blog/workers-of-color-are-far-more-likely-to-be-paid-poverty-level-wages-than-white-workers/.

12. Eric Grodsky and Devah Pager, "The Structure of Disadvantage: Individual and Occupational Determinants of the Black-White Wage Gap," *American Sociological Review* 66, no. 4 (2001): 542–567.

13. See Golash-Boza, *Race and Racisms*, 257–258.

14. Thomas Jefferson, *Notes on the State of Virginia*, 1785, https://docsouth.unc.edu/southlit/jefferson/jefferson.html. See also Nicholas E. Magnis, "Thomas Jefferson and Slavery: An Analysis of His Racist Thinking as Revealed by His Writings and Political Behavior," *Journal of Black Studies* 29, no. 4 (March 1999): 491–509.

15. On Andrew Jackson's role in advancing white supremacy through the displacement and genocide of Native peoples, see Roxanne Dunbar-Ortiz, *An Indigenous Peoples' History of the United States* (Boston: Beacon Press, 2015), chapter 6. See also Dylan Matthews, "Andrew Jackson Was a Slaver, Ethnic Cleanser, and Tyrant. He Deserves No Place on Our Money," *Vox*, April 20, 2016, https://www.vox.com/2016/4/20/11469514/andrew-jackson-indian-removal.

16. Alexa Lardieri, "Despite Diverse Demographics, Most Politicians Are Still White Men," *U.S. News and World Report*, October 24, 2017, https://www.usnews.com/news/politics/articles/2017-10-24/despite-diverse-demographics-most-politicians-are-still-white-men.

17. Richard Cohen, "Hate Crimes Rise Second Straight Year; Anti-Muslim Violence Soars Amid President Trump's Xenophobic Rhetoric," Southern Poverty Law Center, November 13, 2017, https://www.splcenter.org/news/2017/11/13/hate-crimes-rise-second-straight-year-anti-muslim-violence-soars-amid-president-trumps.

18. Eric Levitz, "GOP Congressman: Oh, So Now It's 'Offensive' to Say Whites Are the Supreme Race?," *New York Magazine*, January 10, 2019, http://nymag.com/intelligencer/2019/01/steve-king-whats-so-offensive-about-white-supremacy.html.

19. Nell I. Painter, *The History of White People* (New York: W.W. Norton, 2010) and Noel Ignatiev, *How the Irish Became White* (New York: Routledge, 1995).

20. Eric Eustace Williams, *From Columbus to Castro: The History of the Caribbean, 1492–1969* (London: Deutsch, 2003).

21. See Williams, *From Columbus to Castro*.

22. "Native American Girls Describe the REAL History Behind Thanksgiving," *Teen Vogue*, November 22, 2016, https://video.teenvogue.com/watch/the-real-history-of-thanksgiving.

23. Jackie Mansky. "P.T. Barnum Isn't the Hero the 'Greatest Showman' Wants You to Think," *Smithsonian*, December 22, 2017, https://www.smithsonianmag.com/history/true-story-pt-barnum-greatest-humbug-them-all-180967634/.

CHAPTER 3

1. Woody Guthrie, "This Land Is Your Land," https://www.woodyguthrie.org/Lyrics/This_Land.htm. For context regarding the origins and popularity of the song, see "How 'This Land Is Your Land' Roamed and Rambled into American Life," *All Things Considered*, March 14, 2019, https://www.npr.org/2019/03/14/702792467/woody-guthrie-this-land-is-your-land-american-anthem.

2. "Woody Guthrie's 'This Land Is Your Land' celebrates that the land belongs to everyone, reflecting the unconscious manifest destiny we live with." Dunbar-Ortiz, *An Indigenous Peoples' History*, 3.

3. Melissa Hogenboom, "The First People Who Populated the Americas," *BBC*, March 30, 2017, http://www.bbc.com/earth/story/20170328-the-first-people-who-populated-the-americas. See also, Tanya Basu, "There's a New Theory About Native Americans' Origins," *Time*, July 21, 2015, https://time.com/3964634/native-american-origin-theory. For a teaching guide on the origins of Native American civilizations, see "An Overview of Native American History," Scholastic, https://www.scholastic.com/teachers/articles/teaching-content/history-native-americans. Although some older estimates place Native people on the American continent only 12,000 years ago, current archaeological research and DNA

analyses point to the presence of human societies in the Americas over 20,000 years ago.

4. On the use of European language to dominate Native people throughout the southwest, see Carlos G. Vélez-Ibáñez, *Hegemonies of Language and Their Discontents: The Southwest North American Region Since 1540* (Tucson: University of Arizona Press, 2017).

5. "Turtle Island—Where's That?," https://www.cbc.ca/kidscbc2/the-feed/turtle-island-wheres-that. Note that some Indigenous people use the term "Turtle Island" to refer to the Earth—not merely North America.

6. "The American Indian and Alaska Native Population," The U.S. Census Bureau, January 2012, https://www.census.gov/prod/cen2010/briefs/c2010br-10.pdf.

7. "There are more than five hundred federally recognized Indigenous communities and nations . . ." Dunbar-Ortiz, *An Indigenous Peoples' History*, 10.

8. "Columbus's voyage was the first gold-rush in the history of the modern world." Williams, *From Columbus to Castro*, 23.

9. "The Muskogees called the squatters *ecunnaunuxulgee* . . ." Dunbar-Ortiz, *An Indigenous Peoples' History*, 90.

10. "Along with the cargo of European ships, especially the later British colonizing ventures, came the emerging concept of private property." Dunbar-Ortiz, *An Indigenous Peoples' History*, 34–36.

11. "To be a person of direct Indigenous descent in the US today is to have survived a genocide of cataclysmic proportions." Dina Gilio-Whitaker, *As Long as Grass Grows: The Indigenous Fight for Environmental Justice, From Colonization to Standing Rock* (Boston: Beacon Press, 2019), 49–52; "Settler colonialism is inherently genocidal." Dunbar-Ortiz, *An Indigenous Peoples' History*, 9–10. The term "genocide" was introduced by a Polish human rights lawyer named Raphäel Lemkin in 1944 to describe the mass killing of Jews by German Nazis during World War II. Two years later, the United Nations officially recognized genocide as a crime against humanity. See "Genocide," The United Nations Office on Genocide Prevention and the Responsibility to Protect, https://www.un.org/en/genocideprevention/genocide.shtml.

12. "In response to the decisions by five of the Iroquois Nations, General Washington . . ." Dunbar-Ortiz, *An Indigenous Peoples' History*, 77.

13. "Documented policies of genocide on the part of US administrations . . ." Dunbar-Ortiz, *An Indigenous Peoples' History*, 9–10.

14. "Those Indians who greeted him with apparent friendliness were viewed as simple children." George Fredrickson, *Racism*, 36.

15. "With these land grabs, the US government broke multiple treaties . . ." Dunbar-Ortiz, *An Indigenous Peoples' History*, 140.

16. Dylan Matthews, "Andrew Jackson Was a Slaver, Ethnic Cleanser, and Tyrant. He Deserves No Place on Our Money," *Vox*, April 20, 2016, https://www.vox.com/2016/4/20/11469514/andrew-jackson-indian-removal.

17. "The Indian Removal Act enabled the administration of President Andrew Jackson to use military power to displace at least 70,000 Native Americans . . ." Golash-Boza, *Race and Racisms*, 21. On Jackson's role in facilitating ethnic cleansing, see Howard Zinn, *A People's History of the United States* (New York: Harper Collins, 2015), chapter 7, particularly 125–130.

18. "Furthermore, Georgia went ahead with a land lottery, enacted into law in 1830, that provided for the distribution of Cherokee land to Georgia's citizens." Theda Perdue and Michael Green, *The Cherokee Removal: A Brief History with Documents (Second Edition)* (Boston: Bedford/ St. Martin's, 2005), 21.

19. "In the mid-1800s, United States troops under 'Kit' Carson burned Navajo villages . . ." Zinn, *A People's History*, 529.

20. "During the Civil War, with the southern states unrepresented, Congress at Lincoln's behest passed the Homestead Act in 1862 . . ." Dunbar-Ortiz, *An Indigenous Peoples' History*, 140.

21. "In 1878, the great Cheyenne resistance leaders Little Wolf and Dull Knife . . ." Dunbar-Ortiz, *An Indigenous Peoples' History*, 149.

22. Jaskiran Dhillon, "Thanksgiving Distorts History and Sugarcoats Continuing State Violence Against Indigenous People," *Truthout*, November 23, 2017, https://truthout .org/articles/thanksgiving-distorts -history-and-sugarcoats-continuing -state-violence-against-indigenous -people/.

23. Gilio-Whitaker, *As Long as Grass Grows*.

24. Jaskiran Dhillon, "What Standing Rock Teaches Us About Environmental Justice," December 5, 2017. Items, Social Sciences, Social Science Research Council, December 5, 2017, https:// items.ssrc.org/just-environments /what-standing-rock-teaches-us-about -environmental-justice/.

25. Alleen Brown, "Five Spills, Six Months in Operation: Dakota Access Track Record Highlights Unavoidable Reality—Pipelines Leak," *The Intercept*, January 9, 2018, https:// theintercept.com/2018/01/09/dakota -access-pipeline-leak-energy-transfer -partners/.

26. Indigenous Youth Council, "About," https://indigenousyouth.org/about/.

27. Christianna Silva, "Why Are So Many Native Americans Killed By Police?," *Newsweek*, November 11, 2017, http://www.newsweek.com/more -native-americans-are-being-killed -police-including-14-year-old-who -might-708728.

28. Rebecca Nagle, "Invisibility Is the Modern Form of Racism Against Native Americans," *Teen Vogue*, October 23, 2018, https://www .teenvogue.com/story/racism-against -native-americans.

29. Adrienne Keene, "Natives Against Redsk*ns," *Native Appropriations*, http://nativeappropriations.com /nativesagainstredskins. See also National Congress of American Indians, "Ending the Era of Harmful 'Indian' Mascots," http://www.ncai .org/proudtobe and Echo Hawk Consulting and First Nations

Development Institute, *Reclaiming Native Truth: A Project to Dispel America's Myths and Misconceptions—A Guide for Allies*, https://www.firstnations.org/publications/changing-the-narrative-about-native-americans-a-guide-for-allies/.

30. Jordan Dresser, "For Tribal Communities, Battle Over Land Is Nothing New," *Independent Lens* (blog), PBS, November 15, 2019, http://www.pbs.org/independentlens/blog/for-tribal-communities-battle-over-land-is-nothing-new/.

31. Jeremy Dennis, "On This Site— About," https://jeremynative.com/onthissite/about/.

CHAPTER 4

1. Joaquin Castro, "This is absolutely unacceptable. A @GreatHeartsTX charter school in San Antonio asked students to complete a "balanced view" assignment about slavery, requiring them to list the "positive aspects" of slave life. The teacher worked from a @pearson textbook," Twitter, April 19, 2018, https://twitter.com/JoaquinCastrotx/status/987013603424382977. See also Elyse Wanshel, "School Apologizes for Asking Students to List 'Positive Aspects' of Slavery," *Huffington Post: Black Voices*, April 20, 2018, https://www.huffpost.com/entry/school-texas-pros-cons-slavery-assignment_n_5ada30a5e4b01c279db434ca.

2. Bruce Gilley, "Was It Good Fortune to Be Enslaved by the British Empire?,"

National Association of Scholars, September 30, 2019, https://nas.org/blogs/dicta/was-it-good-fortune-of-being-enslaved-by-the-british-empire. On the misrepresentation of slavery in school and by educators, see Kate Shuster, "Teaching Hard History: American Slavery," Southern Poverty Law Center, https://www.splcenter.org/sites/default/files/tt_hard_history_american_slavery.pdf.

3. Joe Heim, "Teaching America's Truth," *The Washington Post*, August 28, 2019, https://www.washingtonpost.com/education/2019/08/28/teaching-slavery-schools/?arc404 = true. See also Joy DeGruy, who writes: "With respect to the genocide of Native Americans, and the enslavement and later oppression of those of African descent, the history we in this land learn has been greatly sanitized." DeGruy, *Post Traumatic Slave Syndrome* (Milwaukie, OR: Uptone Press, 2005), 71.

4. Rex Springston, "Happy Slaves? The Peculiar Story of Three Virginia School Textbooks," *Richmond Times-Dispatch*, April 14, 2018, https://www.richmond.com/discover-richmond/happy-slaves-the-peculiar-story-of-three-virginia-school-textbooks/article_47e79d49-eac8-575d-ac9d-1c6fce52328f.html.

5. It is important to note that the Thirteenth Amendment abolished slavery except in cases of imprisonment, which means that it is still technically legal today to enslave prisoners. See Whitney Benns, "American Slavery: Reinvented," *The Atlantic*, September 21, 2015, https://www.theatlantic.com/business/archive/2015/09/prison-labor-in-america/406177/.

6. "What makes Western racism so autonomous and conspicuous in world history has been that it developed in a context that presumed human equality of some kind." Fredrickson, *Racism*, 11.

7. Daina Ramey Berry, "Slavery in America: Why Myths and Misconceptions Persist," *Newsweek*, June 19, 2017, https://www .newsweek.com/slavery-america -popular-misconceptions-627229.

8. For a global history of slavery, see Orlando Patterson, *Slavery and Social Death: A Comparative Study* (Cambridge, MA: Harvard University Press, 1982).

9. "The very term 'slavery' derived from the word 'Slav,' because Eastern Europeans were the slaves of the medieval world." Saidiya Hartman, *Lose Your Mother: A Journey Along the Atlantic Slave Route* (New York: Farrar, Straus and Giroux, 2008), 5.

10. "England and France, in their colonies, followed the Spanish practice of enslavement of the Indians." Eric Williams, *Capitalism and Slavery* (Chapel Hill: University of North Carolina Press, 1994), 8–9. See also Andrés Reséndez, "Native Americans Were Kept as Slaves, Too," *Newsweek*, April 30, 2016, https://www. newsweek.com/native-americans -were-kept-slaves-too-454023.

11. "With the limited population of Europe in the sixteenth century, the free laborers necessary to cultivate the staple crops of sugar, tobacco and cotton in the New World could not have been supplied in quantities adequate to permit large-scale production. Slavery was necessary for this, and to get slaves the Europeans turned first to the aborigines and then to Africa." Williams, *Capitalism and Slavery*, 6. See also Marissa Fessenden, "Colonial America Depended on the Enslavement of Indigenous People," *Smithsonian*, January 29, 2016, https://www .smithsonianmag.com/smart -news/colonial-america-depended -enslavement-indigenous-people -180957900/#joX03i27y7m4z4oc.99.

12. "In 1526, enslaved Africans were part of a Spanish expedition to establish an outpost on the North American coast in present-day South Carolina." Michael Guasco, "The Misguided Focus on 1619 as the Beginning of Slavery in the U.S. Damages Our Understanding of American History," *Smithsonian*, September 13, 2017, https://www.smithsonianmag .com/history/misguided-focus-1619 -beginning-slavery-us-damages -our-understanding-american -history-180964873. See also Matthew Restall, "Black Conquistadors: Armed Africans in Early Spanish America," *Americas* 57.2 (2000): 171–205, and Olivia Waxman, "The First Africans in Virginia Landed in 1619. It Was a Turning Point for Slavery in American History—but Not the Beginning," *Time*, August 20, 2019, https://time .com/5653369/august-1619 -jamestown-history/.

13. "The first non-Native American settler on Manhattan Island, Jan Rodrigues, was of African and possibly Afro-European descent, a free man and a sailor . . ." Leslie M. Harris, *In*

the *Shadow of Slavery: African Americans in New York City, 1626–1863* (Chicago: University of Chicago Press, 2003), 12–13. See also Sam Roberts, "Honoring a Very Early New Yorker," *The New York Times,* October 2, 2012, https://cityroom.blogs.nytimes.com/2012/10/02/honoring-a-very-early-new-yorker. Note that Juan Rodrigues was also referred to as "Jan."

14. For an image depicting the triangular route of the trade, see "The Slave Route," UNESCO, http://www.unesco.org/new/fileadmin/MULTIMEDIA/HQ/CLT/pdf/MapSlaveRoute.pdf.

15. For historical perspective on the involvement of African traders in transatlantic slavery, see Barbara Ransby, "Henry Louis Gates' Dangerously Wrong Slave History," *Colorlines*, May 3, 2010, https://www.colorlines.com/articles/henry-louis-gates-dangerously-wrong-slave-history.

16. Scholarly estimates of the number of Africans deported in the transatlantic slave trade range from 12 million to as many as 30 million. See "The African American Migration Story—The African Americans: Many Rivers to Cross," PBS, http://www.pbs.org/wnet/african-americans-many-rivers-to-cross/history/on-african-american-migrations. See also "Transatlantic Slave Trade," UNESCO, http://www.unesco.org/new/en/social-and-human-sciences/themes/slave-route/transatlantic-slave-trade.

17. Henry Louis Gates, Jr., "How Many Slaves Landed in the US?," *The Root*, January 6, 2014, https://www.theroot.com/how-many-slaves-landed-in-the-us-1790873989.

18. "In December 1865, the American states ratified the Thirteenth Amendment to the U.S. Constitution, formally emancipating over 4 million blacks . . ." Martin Ruef and Ben Fletcher, "Legacies of American Slavery: Status Attainment Among Southern Blacks After Emancipation," *Social Forces* 82.2 (2003): 445.

19. For a gripping and heartbreaking account of an African girl who was tortured and murdered by a slave ship captain, see Hartman, *Lose Your Mother*, 136–153.

20. On the history and practice of chattel slavery during the transatlantic trade, see Molefi Kete Asante, "Slavery Remembrance Day Memorial Lecture: The Ideological Origins of Chattel Slavery in the British World," International Slavery Museum, August 21, 2017, https://www.liverpoolmuseums.org.uk/ism/resources/origins_chattel_slavery.aspx. Asante provides the following definition of chattel slavery: "The word 'chattel' is akin to the word 'cattle' and in fact both words share a common origin in Medieval Latin and Old French. The word capital comes from the same root. Chattel slavery means that one person has total ownership of another."

21. "A racial twist has thereby been given to what is basically an economic phenomenon. Slavery was not born of racism . . ." Williams, *Capitalism and Slavery*, 7.

22. See James Loewen, who writes that "the slavery started by Europeans in the fifteenth century was different, because it became the enslavement of one *race* by another. Increasingly,

whites viewed the enslavement of whites as illegitimate, while the enslavement of Africans became acceptable." James W. Loewen, *Lies My Teacher Told Me: Everything Your American History Textbook Got Wrong* (New York: Touchstone, 2007), 143.

23. For an overview of anti-Black racism in the United States, see Treitler, *The Ethnic Project*.

24. *Scott vs. Sanford*, Cornell Legal Information Institute, https://www.law.cornell.edu/supremecourt/text/60/393.

25. Harriet Jacobs, *Incidents in the Life of a Slave Girl* (Mineola, NY: Dover Publications, 2001 [1861]), 17.

26. Jacobs, *Incidents*, 11.

27. Olivia Waxman, "'What to the Slave Is the Fourth of July?': The History of Frederick Douglass' Searing Independence Day Oration," *Time*, July 3, 2019, https://time.com/5614930/frederick-douglass-fourth-of-july.

28. "Nat Turner's rebellion in Southampton County, Virginia, in the summer of 1831, threw the slaveholding South into a panic . . ." Howard Zinn, *A People's History of the United States*, (New York: HarperPerennial, 2015), 174.

29. "It compactly describes Brown's Harpers Ferry raid: On October 16, 1859, the former Kansas raider John Brown and a small group of men attacked a federal arsenal . . ." Loewen, *Lies*, 175.

30. Williams, *Capitalism and Slavery*, 202.

31. Isabel Macdonald, "France's Debt of Dishonour to Haiti," *The Guardian*, August 16, 2010, https://www.theguardian.com/commentisfree/cifamerica/2010/aug/16/haiti-france.

On the legacies of slavery in France, see Crystal M. Fleming, *Resurrecting Slavery: Racial Legacies and White Supremacy in France* (Philadelphia, PA: Temple University Press, 2017).

32. Tera W. Hunter, "When Slave Owners Got Reparations," *The New York Times*, April 16, 2019, https://www.nytimes.com/2019/04/16/opinion/when-slaveowners-got-reparations.html.

33. "This is the afterlife of slavery—skewed life changes, limited access to health and education, premature death, incarceration, and impoverishment." Hartman, *Lose Your Mother*, 6.

34. DeGruy, *Post Traumatic Slave Syndrome*.

35. "Post Traumatic Slave Syndrome is a condition that exists when a population has experienced multigenerational trauma resulting from centuries of slavery and continues to experience oppression and institutionalized racism today." DeGruy, *Post Traumatic Slave Syndrome*, 121.

36. "Slavery's twin legacies to the present are the social and economic inferiority conferred upon blacks and the cultural racism it instilled in whites." Loewen, *Lies My Teacher Told Me*, 143.

37. Kate Shuster, "Teaching Hard History: American Slavery," Southern Poverty Law Center, 2018, https://www.splcenter.org/sites/default/files/tt_hard_history_american_slavery.pdf.

38. According to Guinness World Records, Qarawiyyin University (also referred to as "Karueein" University) is the oldest continually existing institution

of higher education in the world. See Guinness World Records. "Oldest higher-learning institution, oldest university." Available online: https://www.guinnessworldrecords.com/world-records/oldest-university. See also Kareem Shaheen, "World's oldest library reopens in Fez: 'You can hurt us, but you can't hurt the books,'" *The Guardian*, September 19, 2016, https://www.theguardian.com/cities/2016/sep/19/books-world-oldest-library-fez-morocco.

39. Jim Downs, "Dying for Freedom," *The New York Times*, January 5, 2013, https://opinionator.blogs.nytimes.com/2013/01/05/dying-for-freedom/.

40. "Empathy is the ability to understand and share the feelings of others . . ." Golash-Boza, *Race and Racisms*, 430.

41. William Darity Jr., "How Barack Obama Failed Black Americans," *The Atlantic*, December 22, 2016, https://www.theatlantic.com/politics/archive/2016/12/how-barack-obama-failed-black-americans/511358/.

42. Hartman, *Lose Your Mother*, 170.

CHAPTER 5

1. Transcription by the author, "Looking Like the Enemy," *Densho*, April 9, 2015, https://youtu.be/sUEXSNBVdGY. See also: Nancy Matsumoto, "Aki Kurose," *Densho Encyclopedia*, January 18, 2016, https://encyclopedia.densho.org/Aki%20Kurose.

2. "Just three years after rejecting Holocaust refugees, FDR signed Executive Order 9066 in February 1942, thereby initiating the racist policy euphemistically known as the 'internment' of Japanese Americans." Fleming, *How to Be Less Stupid*, 111. On the number of Japanese Americans interned in concentration camps in the United States during World War II, see "Japanese Relocation During World War II," The National Archives, https://www.archives.gov/education/lessons/japanese-relocation: "Roosevelt's order affected 117,000 people of Japanese descent, two-thirds of whom were native-born citizens of the United States." Note that Japanese Americans were incarcerated in Arkansas, Arizona, California, Colorado, Idaho, Utah, Washington, and Wyoming. See also, *A People's History*, p. 416, and T.A. Frail, "The Injustice of Japanese-American Internment Camps Resonates Strongly to This Day," *Smithsonian*, January/February 2017, https://www.smithsonianmag.com/history/injustice-japanese-americans-internment-camps-resonates-strongly-180961422.

3. Estimates of the number of minors held in internment camps vary. While many sources estimate that half of those interned were children, Densho, a nonprofit dedicated to memorializing the internment of Japanese Americans, reports that one third of the internment population was age nineteen or younger. See Brian Niiya, "Common Myths of WW II Incarceration: 'More Than Half Were Children,'" *Densho Blog*, June 21, 2016, https://densho.org/common-myths-wwii-incarceration-half-children. See also "Children in Internment Camps: A Japanese

American's Reflection," *Smithsonian Channel*, June 21, 2018, https://www.youtube.com/watch?v = IiZxBHGA4Ds.

4. Louis Fiset, "Puyallup (detention facility)," *Densho Encyclopedia*, July 1, 2020, https://encyclopedia.densho.org/Puyallup%20(detention%20facility)/.

5. Nancy Matsumoto, "Aki Kurose," *Densho Encyclopedia*, January 18, 2016, https://encyclopedia.densho.org/Aki%20Kurose.

6. See Commission on Wartime Relocation and Internment of Civilians, "Personal Justice Denied," The National Archives, December 1982, https://www.archives.gov/research/japanese-americans/justice-denied, Summary, 6.

7. Golash-Boza, *Race and Racisms*, 378.

8. Fredrickson defines xenophobia as "a reflexive feeling of hostility to the stranger or Other." See Fredrickson, *Racism*, 6.

9. Linda K. Kerber, "The Meanings of Citizenship," *The Journal of American History* 84, no. 3 (1997): 836. See also Golash-Boza, *Race and Racisms*, 382. "The first group of Mexicans to enter the United States were not immigrants . . ." See also Tom Gray and The National Archives, n.d., "Educator Resources: The Treaty of Hidalgo," https://www.archives.gov/education/lessons/guadalupe-hidalgo. "By its terms, Mexico ceded 55 percent of its territory, including parts of present-day Arizona, California, New Mexico, Texas, Colorado, Nevada, and Utah, to the United States. Mexico relinquished all claims to Texas, and recognized the Rio Grande as the southern boundary with the United States."

10. See Golash-Boza, *Race and Racisms*, 46.

11. Kerber, "The Meanings of Citizenship," 837. "I tell my students that the phrase 'race, class, gender' is a cliché and I challenge them to avoid it. But the strands of the braided narrative of citizenship as experienced historically in the United States are . . . woven into the three ropes of race, class, and gender—the categories I have tried to avoid but find impossible to ignore."

12. Dana Hedgpeth, "'Jim Crow, Indian style': How Native Americans were denied the right to vote for decades," *The Washington Post*, November 1, 2020, https://www.washingtonpost.com/history/2020/11/01/native-americans-right-to-vote-history.

13. Kerber, "The Meanings of Citizenship," 836. "The meanings of citizenship have been inconsistent from the beginning . . ." See also Fredrickson, *Racism*, 81. "The Fourteenth Amendment, ratified in 1868, wrote equal citizenship for all people born in the United States (except "Indians not taxed") into the Constitution. But the federal effort to enforce civic and political equality for blacks during Reconstruction failed because the government proved unwilling or unable to overcome the violent White resistance to black equality that erupted in the South."

14. Fredrickson, *Racism*, 81.

15. Kerber, "The Meanings of Citizenship," 836. ". . . voluntary immigrants from Europe, all of whom were eligible for naturalization and citizenship . . ."

16. Treitler, *The Ethnic Project*, 45. "Racial systems rank groups into racial categories, forcing them to vie for unequal positions of power . . ."

17. Treitler, *The Ethnic Project*, 169. "The problem of African Americans is their placement in the bottom racial category . . ."

18. Ida B. Wells, "The Red Record: Tabulated Statistics and Alleged Causes of Lynching in the United States," 1895, https://www.gutenberg .org/files/14977/14977-h/14977-h .htm. See also Paula Giddings, *Ida: A Sword Among Lions*. (New York: Amistad/HarperCollins, 2009), 182–184. "At about 2:30 A.M. on March 9, seventy-five men wearing black masks surrounded the Shelby County Jail."

19. Rosalind S. Chou and Joe R. Feagin, *The Myth of the Model Minority: Asian Americans Facing Racism—Second Edition* (New York: Routledge, 2015), 6.

20. Gordon H. Chang, "Op-Ed: Remember the Chinese Immigrants Who Built America's First Transcontinental Railroad," *Los Angeles Times*, May 10, 2019, https://www.latimes .com/opinion/op-ed/la-oe-chang -transcontinental-railroad-anniversary -chinese-workers-20190510-story.html.

21. Golash-Boza, *Race and Racisms*, 43. "The Chinese Exclusion Act (1882) was overtly racist . . ." Mari Uyehara, "The Roots of the Atlanta Shooting Go Back to the First Law Restricting Immigration," *The Nation*, March 22, 2021, https://www.thenation.com /article/society/atlanta-shooting -history.

22. On the colonization of the Philippines, see Ch. 2 in Anthony Christian Ocampo, *The Latinos of Asia: How Filipino Americans Break the Rules of Race* (Stanford, CA: Stanford University Press, 2016). On the 1893 overthrow of Hawaiian Queen Liliʻuokalani, see *The Learning Network*. "Jan. 17, 1893 | Hawaiian Monarchy Overthrown by America-Backed Businessmen," *The New York Times*, January 17, 2012, https://learning.blogs.nytimes .com/2012/01/17/jan-17-1893 -hawaiian-monarchy-overthrown -by-america-backed-businessmen. For a timeline of the history of colonization in Hawaii, see *Facing History and Ourselves*, "Hawaii's Legacy of Colonialism," https://www .facinghistory.org/sites/default/files /Hawaiis_Legacy_of_Colonialism.pdf.

23. Gregory H. Robinson, *By Order of the President: FDR and the Internment of Japanese Americans* (Cambridge, MA: Harvard University Press, 2001), 38.

24. Golash-Boza, *Race and Racisms*, 48–49. "Two of the prerequisite cases that reached the Supreme Court were *Takao Ozawa vs. United States* and *United States vs. Bhagat Singh Thind . . .*"

25. Pamela Oliver, "What the Treaty of Guadalupe Hidalgo Actually Says," *Race, Politics, Justice*, June 12, 2017, https://www.ssc.wisc.edu/soc /racepoliticsjustice/2017/07/12/what -the-treaty-of-guadalupe-actually-says. See also Enrique Krauze, "Will Mexico Get Half of Its Territory Back?," *The New York Times*, April 6, 2017, https://www.google.com/amp/s /www.nytimes.com/2017/04/06 /opinion/will-mexico-get-half-of-its -territory-back.amp.html.

26. For example, between 1942 and 1964, the United States government maintained the *Bracero* Program, a policy that underpaid and exploited Mexicans as temporary workers. Golash-Boza, *Race and Racisms*, 383. "The second wave of Mexican immigration came during the bracero program . . ."

27. Frances Negrón-Muntaner, "The Latino Media Gap: A Report on the State of Latinos in U.S. Media," 2014, https://media-alliance.org/wp-content/uploads/2016/05/Latino_Media_Gap_Report.pdf, pp. 16–17: "Not only does the media significantly underrepresent Latinos and other groups, but also, in the few instances when Latinos appear, they tend to embody many of the same stereotypes first visualized in cinema over a century ago: criminals, cheap labor, and sexual objects." See also Golash-Boza, *Race and Racisms*, 152. "Table 5-2. Prominent Gendered Stereotypes by Racial/Ethnic Group"

28. William D. Carrigan and Clive Webb, "When Americans Lynched Mexicans," *The New York Times*, February 20, 2015, https://www.nytimes.com/2015/02/20/opinion/when-americans-lynched-mexicans.html.

29. Alexia Fernández Campbell, "The El Paso Shooter Told Police That He Was Targeting Mexicans," *Vox*, August 9, 2019, https://www.vox.com/2019/8/6/20756750/el-paso-shooter-targeted-latinx-walmart.

30. Christine Bolaños, "A US-Born Teen Was in Border Custody for 23 days. Now He's Suing the Government," *The Guardian*, July 27, 2019, https://www.theguardian.com/us-news/2019/jul/26/francisco-galicia-us-mexico-immigration-border.

31. Ben Zimmer, "Where Does Trump's 'Invasion' Rhetoric Come From?," *The Atlantic*, August 6, 2019, https://www.theatlantic.com/entertainment/archive/2019/08/trump-immigrant-invasion-language-origins/595579.

32. Matsumoto. "Aki Kurose."

33. "Fred T. Korematsu—Abbreviated Biography." Fred T. Korematsu Institute, https://korematsuinstitute.org/freds-story/. See also: *Of Civil Wrongs and Rights: The Fred Korematsu Story* (film, 2006).

34. "Fred Korematsu Presidential Medal of Freedom," *C-SPAN*, January 15, 1998, https://www.c-span.org/video/?c4549633/fred-korematsu-presidential-medal-freedom.

35. "Long Road to Redress," History, Art & Archives—United States House of Representatives, https://history.house.gov/Exhibitions-and-Publications/APA/Historical-Essays/Exclusion-to-Inclusion/Redress/.

36. "About UWD," United We Dream. https://unitedwedream.org/about.

37. "Our Vision," Power California, https://powercalifornia.org/history.

CHAPTER 6

1. Evan MacDonald, "911 Caller Was Frightened Tamir Rice Might Shoot Him," *Cleveland.com*, June 13, 2015, https://www.cleveland.com/metro/2015/06/911_caller_was_frightened_tami.html. Joey Morona,

"The Tamir Rice Shooting: A Timeline of Events," *Cleveland.com*, November 28, 2014, https://www.cleveland .com/metro/2014/11/the_tamir _rice_shooting_a_time.html. See also eyewitness video of Tajai Rice reacting to the officer's attack: "Tamir Rice's Sister: They Killed My Baby Brother," *NBC News*, November 24, 2014, https://www.nbcnews.com/video /tamir-rices-sister-they-killed-my-baby-brother-363230787609.

2. Cory Shaffer, "Extended Tamir Rice Shooting Video Shows Officers Restrained Sister," *Cleveland.com*, January 8, 2015, https://www .cleveland.com/metro/2015/01 /extended_tamir_rice_shooting_v.html. Associated Press. "Police Pushed, Cuffed Tamir Rice's Sister After Boy's Shooting, Video Shows," *Los Angeles Times*, January 8, 2015, https://www .latimes.com/nation /nationnow/la-na-nn-tamir-rice-video -20150108-story.html.

3. Minyvonne Burke, "Officer Who Fatally Shot Tamir Rice Quits Ohio Police Department Days After He Was Hired," *NBC News*, October 11, 2018, https:// www.nbcnews.com/news/us-news /officer-who-fatally-shot-tamir-rice-quits -ohio-police-department-n919046. See also Matthew Haag, "Cleveland Officer Who Killed Tamir Rice Is Hired by an Ohio Police Department," *The New York Times*, October 2, 2018, https://www .nytimes.com/2018/10/08/us /timothy-loehmann-tamir-rice-shooting. html. Jon Swaine, Oliver Laughland, and Afi Scruggs, "Cleveland Agrees to Pay Tamir Rice Family $6m Over Police Shooting," *The Guardian*, April 25, 2016, https://www.theguardian .com/us-news/2016/apr/25/cleveland -tamir-rice-family-lawsuit-settlement. Cory Shaffer, "Tamir Rice's Sister Says Cleveland Police Lacked 'Decency' and 'Respect' in Detaining Her After Shooting," *Cleveland.com*, January 12, 2019, https://www.cleveland.com /metro/2015/02/tamir_rices_sister_says _clevel.html. James Hill, "Cleveland Cop in Toy Gun Killing Resigned from Previous Job After 'Dismal' Handgun Performance, According to Files," *ABC News*, December 4, 2014, https:// abcnews.go.com/US/cleveland-cop-toy -gun-killing-resigned-previous-job /story?id = 27352626.

4. Amina Khan, "Getting Killed by Police Is a Leading Cause of Death for Young Black Men in America." *Los Angeles Times*, August 16, 2019, https://www.latimes.com/science /story/2019-08-15/police-shootings -are-a-leading-cause-of-death-for -black-men. See also Frank Edwards, Hedwig Lee, and Michael Esposito, "Risk of Being Killed by Police Use of Force in the United States by Age, Race-Ethnicity, and Sex," *Proceedings of the National Academy of Sciences of the United States of America* 16, no. 34 (2019): 16793–16798. https://doi .org/10.1073/pnas.1821204116: "Among all groups, black men and boys face the highest lifetime risk of being killed by police. Our models predict that about 1 in 1,000 black men and boys will be killed by police over the life course (96 [77, 120] per 100,000). We predict that between 36 and 81 American Indian/ Alaska Native men and boys per 100,000 will be killed by police over the

life course. Latino men and boys have an estimated risk of being killed by police of about 53 per 100,000 [41, 67]. Asian/Pacific Islander men and boys face a lifetime risk of between 9 and 23 per 100,000, while White men and boys face a lifetime risk of about 39 [31, 48] per 100,000" (16794-16795).

5. Samuel Walker, *Popular Justice: A History of American Criminal Justice.* (New York: Oxford University Press, 1998), 8.

6. Radley Balko, "There's Overwhelming Evidence That the Criminal-Justice System Is Racist. Here's the Proof," *The Washington Post*, September 18, 2018, https://www.washingtonpost.com/news/opinions/wp/2018/09/18/theres-overwhelming-evidence-that-the-criminal-justice-system-is-racist-heres-the-proof/.

7. Adam Malka, "Why Law Enforcement Has a Blind Spot for White Male Violence," *The Washington Post*, August 12, 2019, https://www.washingtonpost.com/outlook/2019/08/12/why-law-enforcement-has-blind-spot-white-male-violence/.

8. Note that most of the statistics in this chapter on racism and the criminal justice system focus on Latinx Americans, African Americans, and Indigenous Americans. This is due to the unfortunate fact that Asian Americans and Pacific Islanders (AAPI) are often excluded from research on the criminal justice system. However, Asian Americans have also suffered from harsh policing and mass incarceration. Consider, for example, the fact that "[d]uring the prison boom of the 1990s, the AAPI prisoner population grew by 250%. During this time, Asian juveniles in California were more than twice as likely to be tried as adults, as compared to White juveniles who committed similar crimes." Paul Jung, Gregory Cendana, William Chiang, Ben Wang, Eddy Zheng, Monica Thammarath, Quyen Dinh, and Katrina Dizon Mariategue, "Asian Americans & Pacific Islanders Behind Bars: Exposing the School to Prison to Deportation Pipeline," National Education Association, 2015, https://www.advancingjustice-la.org/sites/default/files/18877%20AAPIs%20Behind%20Bars.pdf, p. 1.

9. Martin Luther King Jr., "Letter from a Birmingham Jail," 1963, https://www.africa.upenn.edu/Articles_Gen/Letter_Birmingham.html.

10. "The FBI investigated Bamn for potential 'conspiracy' against the 'rights' of the 'Ku Klux Klan' and white supremacists. The FBI considered the KKK as victims and the leftist protesters as potential terror threats, and downplayed the threats of the Klan, writing: 'The KKK consisted of members that some perceived to be supportive of a white supremacist agenda.'" Sam Levin, "Revealed: FBI Investigated Civil Rights Group as 'Terrorism' Threat and Viewed KKK as Victims," *The Guardian*, February 1, 2019, https://www.theguardian.com/us-news/2019/feb/01/sacramento-rally-fbi-kkk-domestic-terrorism-california. See also Jeanne Theoharis, "Comey Says FBI's Surveillance of MLK Was 'Shameful'—but Comey's FBI Targeted Black Activities and Muslim Communities Anyway," *The*

Intercept, April 24, 2018, https:// theintercept.com/2018/04/24 /james-comey-mlk-martin-luther-king -surveillance-muslims.

11. The Oxford Dictionary defines the criminal justice system as the "system of law enforcement that is directly involved in apprehending, prosecuting, defending, sentencing, and punishing those who are suspected or convicted of criminal offences," See: "Criminal Justice System," Lexico, https://www .lexico.com/en/definition /criminal_justice_system.

12. "Non-Hispanic White Americans account for 77% of voting members in the new Congress, considerably larger than their 60% share of the U.S. population overall." Katherine Schaeffer, "Racial, Ethnic Diversity Increases Yet Again with the 117th Congress," Pew Research Center, January 28, 2021, https://www.pewresearch.org /fact-tank/2021/01/28/racial-ethnic -diversity-increases-yet-again-with -the-117th-congress. According to data published by the Bureau of Justice Statistics, 71.5% of all police officers are non-Hispanic Whites. See Dan Keating and Kevin Uhrmacher, "In Urban Areas, Police Are Consistently Much Whiter Than the People They Serve," *The Washington Post*, June 4, 2020, https://www.washingtonpost .com/nation/2020/06/04/urban-areas -police-are-consistently-much-whiter -than-people-they-serve. See also Emily Baxter and Jamie Keane, "The Excessive Political Power of White Men in the United States, in One Chart," ThinkProgress, October 10, 2014, https://archive.thinkprogress .org/the-excessive-political-power-of -white-men-in-the-united-states-in -one-chart-bbc11d4f52b7/.

13. Baxter and Keane. "The Excessive Political Power of White Men," "State courts handle more than 95 percent of America's court cases, and they continue to be run primarily by White male judges. A recent report on racial and gender diversity from the American Constitution Society found that White men comprise 58 percent of state court judges, even though they make up less than one-third of the population." Michele L. Jawando and Allie Anderson, "Racial and Gender Diversity Sorely Lacking in America's Courts," Center for American Progress, September 15, 2016, https://www .americanprogress.org/issues /courts/news/2016/09/15/144287 /racial-and-gender-diversity-sorely -lacking-in-americas-courts/. "Nearly three-quarters of all police officers are White, while the U.S. population is about 63% White, U.S. Census data show." Yamiche Alcindor and Nick Penzenstadler, "Police Redouble Efforts to Recruit Diverse Officers," *USA Today*, January 21, 2015, https://www.usatoday.com /story/news/2015/01/21/police -redoubling-efforts-to-recruit-diverse -officers/21574081.

14. "Justice for All? A Project of the Reflective Democracy Campaign," Women's Donors Network, https://wholeads.us/wp-content /uploads/2019/03/Justice-For-All -Report_31319.pdf. See also: David Graham, "Most States Elect No Black

Prosecutors," *The Atlantic*, July 7, 2015, https://www.theatlantic.com /politics/archive/2015/07/american -prosecutors-are-incredible-Whitedoes -it-matter/397847.

15. "Women of Color in the United States: Quick Take," *Catalyst*, November 7, 2018, https://www.catalyst.org /research/women-of-color-in-the -united-states/.

16. German Lopez, "This Is the Most Diverse Congress Ever. But It's Still Pretty White," *Vox*, February 8, 2019, https://www.vox.com/policy-and -politics/2019/2/8/18217076/congress -racial-diversity-White.

17. "But officials say that having a diverse force is only one way of moving forward. In fact, they point out, research is mixed as to whether diversity helps reduce tensions. Other strategies, they say, help as much or more, such as hiring officers who know and understand the community, asking officers to build better relationships with neighborhoods they serve, reducing officers' use of aggressive arrest tactics and increasing officer training." Jen Fifield, "Can Diverse Police Departments Ease Community Tension?," *PBS News Hour*, August 22, 2016, https:// www.pbs.org/newshour/nation /can-diverse-police-departments-ease -community-tension.

18. "The first modern police agencies in the U.S. appeared roughly in the 1830s, and from the very beginning were dominated by local politics with no commitment to public service or to the rule of law . . . First, during the time of chattel slavery and then from Reconstruction to the civil rights era (ending roughly in 1964), the police and the entire criminal justice system were devoted to upholding the racial status quo . . . the police have traditionally served the will of the dominant White majority." Samuel Walker, "Governing the American Police: Wrestling with the Problems of Democracy," *The University of Chicago Legal Forum* 1 (2016): 626.

19. Ashley Nellis, "The Color of Justice: Racial and Ethnic Disparity in State Prisons," *The Sentencing Project*, June 4, 2016, https://www .sentencingproject.org/publications /color-of-justice-racial-and-ethnic -disparity-in-state-prisons.

20. Julia Cass and Connie Curry, *America's Cradle to Prison Pipeline, A Report of the Children's Defense Fund*, 2007, https://www.childrensdefense .org/wp-content/uploads/2018/08 /cradle-prison-pipeline-report-2007-full -lowres.pdf.

21. Regarding the case of Aiyana Stanley Jones as well as other Black women and girls killed by police, see Kimberlé Crenshaw et al., *Say Her Name: Resisting Police Brutality Against Black Women*. African American Policy Forum, 2015, http://www.aapf.org/s /merged_document_2-1.pdf.

22. Crenshaw et al., *Say Her Name*, 20. "Detroit police officer Joseph Weekley shot and killed seven-year-old Aiyana Stanley-Jones in her sleep during a raid on her grandmother's home . . . Weekley was tried twice and cleared of all charges, most recently in January 2015. He returned to work in April 2015."

23. Associated Press, "Body Cam Captures 6-Year-Old's Tearful Pleas During Arrest," *ABC News*, February 25, 2020, https://abcnews.go.com/US /wireStory/body-cam-captures-year -olds-tearful-pleas-arrest-69207390.

24. Monique W. Morris, *Pushout: The Criminalization of Black Girls in Schools* (New York: The New Press, 2016), 57. See also Phillip A. Goff, Matthew C. Jackson, Brooke A. L. Di Leone, Carmen M. Culotta, and Natalie A. DiTomasso, "The Essence of Innocence: Consequences of Dehumanizing Black Children," *Journal of Personality and Social Psychology* 106, no. 4 (2014): 526–545.

25. "Although most teachers have good intentions, the reality is that teachers are members of our society and, like all of us, they are inundated with media images that reinforce stereotypes. The prevalence of stereotypes about Blacks and criminality . . . influences how teachers respond to Black boys who misbehave." Golash-Boza, *Race and Racisms*, 240.

26. "American Indian youth are grossly over-represented in state and federal juvenile justice systems and secure confinement. Incarcerated Indian youth . . . AI/AN youth are 50% more likely than Whites to receive the most punitive measures. Pepper spray, restraint and isolation appear to be grossly and disproportionately applied to Indian youth, who have no recourse, no alternatives and few advocates." Terry L. Cross. "Native Americans and Juvenile Justice: A Hidden Tragedy," *Poverty & Race Journal*, November–December 2008, https://prrac.org/native-americans -and-juvenile-justice-a-hidden-tragedy/.

27. On the ineffectiveness of the D.A.R.E. program, see Christopher Ingraham. "A Brief History of DARE, the Anti-Drug Program Jeff Sessions Wants to Revive," *The Washington Post*, July 12, 2017, https://www.washingtonpost .com/news/wonk/wp/2017/07/12/a -brief-history-of-d-a-r-e-the-anti-drug -program-jeff-sessions-wants-to-revive.

28. "Timeline: America's War on Drugs," *NPR*, April 2, 2007, https://www .npr.org/templates/story/story .php?storyId = 9252490. See also Emily Dufton, "The War on Drugs: How President Nixon Tied Addiction to Crime," *The Atlantic*, March 26, 2012, https://www.theatlantic.com/health /archive/2012/03/the-war-on-drugs -how-president-nixon-tied-addiction -to-crime/254319.

29. "At the federal level, three major laws were passed . . ." Golash-Boza, *Race and Racisms*, 322.

30. "Zealous enforcement of drug laws disproportionately affects people of color, even though Whites are more likely to use and sell drugs." Golash-Boza, *Race and Racisms*, 321.

31. "In 1986, before the enactment of federal mandatory minimum sentencing for crack cocaine offenses, the average federal drug sentence for African Americans was 11% higher than for Whites. Four years later, the average federal drug sentence for African Americans was 49% higher." Deborah J. Vagins and Jesselyn McCurdy, "Cracks in the System: 20 Years of the Unjust Federal Crack Cocaine Law,"

ACLU, 2016, https://www.aclu.org
/other/cracks-system-20-years-unjust
-federal-crack-cocaine-law.

32. "The U.S. incarceration rate was about
1 per 1,000 residents for almost the
entire twentieth century until the
1970s. That rate doubled between
1972 and 1984 and again between
1984 and 1994 . . . In 2016, the rate
was more than 7 per 1,000 . . ."
Golash-Boza, *Race and Racisms*, 313.

33. "According to the manifesto, Roof
allegedly typed 'black on White crime'
in a Google search to make sense of
the news reporting on Trayvon Martin,
a young African American teenager
who was killed and whose killer,
George Zimmerman, was acquitted
of murder." Safiya Umoja Noble,
*Algorithms of Oppression: How Search
Engines Reinforce Racism* (New York:
New York University Press, 2018), 111.
See also: "Never was Klan violence
or the lynching of black people by
White people ascribed to an inherent
White trait." Southern Poverty Law
Center, "The Biggest Lie in the White
Supremacist Propaganda Playbook:
Unraveling the Truth About 'Black-on-
White Crime,'" June 14, 2018, https://
www.splcenter.org/20180614/biggest
-lie-White-supremacist-propaganda
-playbook-unraveling-truth-about
-'black-White-crime.

34. Devah Pager, "The Mark of a Criminal
Record," *American Journal of
Sociology* 108, no. 5 (2003): 937–975.
"In fact, even Whites *with* criminal
records received more favorable
treatment (17%) than blacks *without*
criminal records (14%). The rank
ordering of groups in this graph
is painfully revealing of employer
preferences: race continues to play a
dominant role in shaping employment
opportunities, equal to or greater than
the impact of a criminal record" (958).

35. Redditt Hudson. "I'm a Black
Ex-Cop, and This Is the Real Truth
About Race and Policing," *Vox*,
July 7, 2016, https://www.vox
.com/2015/5/28/8661977/race-police
-officer. See also German Lopez,
"How Systemic Racism Entangles All
Police Officers—Even Black Cops,"
Vox, August 15, 2016, https://www
.vox.com/2015/5/7/8562077/police
-racism-implicit-bias.

36. "Regardless of the race of the victim,
the rate of violent crime was higher
for intraracial victimizations than
for interracial victimizations during
2012–15. The rate of violent crime
committed against a White victim
by a White offender was 12.0
victimizations per 1,000 persons,
compared to 3.1 per 1,000 for those
committed by a black offender . . .
The rate of violent crime committed
against a black victim by a black
offender was 16.5 victimizations
per 1,000 persons, compared to 2.8
per 1,000 for those committed by a
White offender. The rate of violent
crime committed against a Hispanic
victim by a Hispanic offender was
8.3 victimizations per 1,000 persons,
compared to 4.1 per 1,000 for those
committed by a White offender and
4.2 per 1,000 for those committed
by a black offender." Rachel E.
Morgan, "Race and Hispanic Origin
of Victims and Offenders, 2012–15,"
U.S. Department of Justice: Bureau

of *Justice Statistics*, October 2017, https://www.bjs.gov/content/pub/pdf/rhovo1215.pdf, p. 4.

37. See Figure 8, page 13: "Poverty Rate and Percentage Point Change by Selected Characteristics: People." Jessica Semega, Melissa Kollar, John Creamer, and Abinash Mohanty, "Income and Poverty in the United States: 2018—Current Population Reports," U.S. Census Bureau, September 2019, https://www.census.gov/content/dam/Census/library/publications/2019/demo/p60-266.pdf.

38. "Overall, a third of Cleveland's residents live in poverty. Worse yet, poverty is the life for more than half the city's children." Rich Exner, "Poverty in Cleveland and Cuyahoga Suburbs Remains Above Pre-Recession Levels, New Census Estimates Say," *Cleveland.com*, September 26, 2019, https://www.cleveland.com/datacentral/2019/09/poverty-in-cleveland-and-cuyahoga-suburbs-remains-above-pre-recession-levels-new-census-estimates-say.html.

39. "A 2014 Bureau of Justice Statistics study showed that persons from poor households experienced the highest rates of violent victimization, and that rates were consistent for both blacks and Whites. When sociologists asked 'Is Poverty's Detrimental Effect Race-Specific?' they found the answer was no: policies aimed at reducing poverty effectively reduced violent crime and the crime reduction rates were similar in both black and White neighborhoods, meaning it was poverty—rather than race—that contributed to the violent crime rate in the first place." Southern Poverty Law Center, "The Biggest Lie in the White Supremacist Propaganda Playbook." See also Lance Hannon and Robert DeFina, "Violent Crime in African American and White Neighborhoods: Is Poverty's Detrimental Effect Race-Specific?," *Journal of Poverty* 9 (2005): 49–67.

40. See Kaba, *We Do This 'Til We Free Us*.

41. See "The Tamir Rice Afrocentric Cultural Center: Vision," https://www.tamiricefoundation.org/vision.

42. See "The Tamir Rice Afrocentric Cultural Center: Mission," https://www.tamiricefoundation.org.

CHAPTER 7

1. Before Miles Morales made his Hollywood debut, he first swung into action on the pages of Marvel's *Ultimate Fallout* in 2011. See "Marvel. Character Closeup—Spider-Man: Miles Morales," https://www.marvel.com/comics/discover/993/spider-man-miles-morales.

2. Color of Change, "Not to Be Trusted: Dangerous Levels of Inaccuracy in TV Crime Reporting in NYC," 8.

3. Stacy L. Smith, Marc Choueiti, Ariana Case, Katherine Pieper, Hannah Clark, Karla Hernandez, Jacqueline Martinez, Benjamin Lopez, and Mauricio Mota, "Latinos in Film: Erasure on Screen and Behind the Camera Across 1,200 Popular Movies," USC Annenberg Inclusion Initiative, 2019, http://assets.uscannenberg.org/docs

/aii-study-latinos-in-film-2019.pdf. See page 2: "Just under a quarter (24%) of all of Latino speaking characters and 28% of top billed Latino talent were depicted as law breakers across a range of violent and non-violent crimes. Over half (61.9%) of all characters shown engaged in illegal activity were part of an organized crime group such as gang members or drug dealers. Thirty-eight percent of criminals were depicted committing fraud, thievery, murder, or having previously been in prison for reasons not made clear in the film." See also Eva Recinos, "Why Are Half of Latino Immigrant TV Characters Portrayed As Criminals?," *The Guardian*, November 14, 2017, https://www.theguardian.com/tv-and-radio/2017/nov/14/why-are-half-of-latino-immigrant-tv-characters-portrayed-as-criminals.

4. Golash-Boza, *Race and Racisms*, 129: "Representations of blacks and Latinos as poor and lawbreaking, for example, reinforce popular notions about black and Latino cultural deficiencies."

5. Peggy McIntosh, *On Privilege, Fraudulence, and Teaching as Learning: Selected Essays 1981–2019* (New York: Routledge, 2020), 19.

6. McIntosh, *On Privilege*, 42.

7. Leah Donnella, "Is Beauty in the Eye of the Colonizer?," *NPR Code Sw!tch*, February 6, 2019, https://www.npr.org/sections/codeswitch/2019/02/06/685506578/is-beauty-in-the-eyes-of-the-colonizer.

8. Nell Irvin Painter, "Why Are White People Called 'Caucasian'?," Proceedings of the Fifth Annual Gilder Lehrman Center International Conference at Yale University, November 7–8, 2003, https://glc.yale.edu/sites/default/files/files/events/race/Painter.pdf. "More than a century after Blumenbach, 'Caucasian' and beauty still went together. The classic (1910–1911) eleventh edition of the *Encyclopedia Britannica* even singled out the most beautiful of the beautiful" (27).

9. Cordelia Tai, "Here's One Good Thing About 2016: Magazine Covers Were More Diverse Than Ever (Report)," *The Fashion Spot,* December 14, 2016. "In 2016, 29 percent of cover models were women of color . . ." See also Nancy Wang Yuen, *Reel Inequality: Hollywood Actors and Racism* (New Brunswick, NJ: Rutgers University Press, 2017).

10. Sociologist Tanya Golash-Boza points out that Latinos are "both underrepresented and misrepresented." *Race and Racisms*, 136.

11. Safiya Umoja Noble, *Algorithms of Oppression: How Search Engines Reinforce Racism,* (New York: New York University Press, 2018).

12. Golash-Boza, *Race and Racisms*, 66: "The media also perpetuate stereotypes—widely held but fixed and oversimplified images or ideas of types of people or things."

13. Popular images and discourses in our society have often described Whiteness as "free, civilized, and superior against blackness, which was defined as savage, inferior, and destined to be enslaved." Erica Chito Childs, *Fade to Black and White* (Lanham, MD: Rowman & Littlefield, 2009), 18.

14. Kimberlé Crenshaw, "Demarginalizing the Intersection of Race and Sex: A Black Feminist Critique of Antidiscrimination Doctrine, Feminist Theory and Antiracist Politics," *The University of Chicago Legal Forum* 1, no. 8 (1989): 149. Kimberlé Crenshaw, "Mapping the Margins: Intersectionality, Identity Politics, and Violence Against Women of Color," *Stanford Law Review*, 43, no. 6 (1991): 1241–1299. Crenshaw notes that the idea of intersectionality has its roots in the work of other scholars and activists working in the Black feminist tradition. On the impact of the Combahee River Collective and Black lesbian organizing, see also "Chapter 3: Listen to Black Women" in Fleming, *How to Be Less Stupid About Race*.

15. "Portrayals of people of color on television are raced, gendered and classed—meaning that the representations vary by race, class and gender, and that they influence how we think about various racial groups . . ." Golash-Boza, *Race and Racisms*, 150. See also Patricia Hill Collins, "Learning from the Outsider Within: The Sociological Significance of Black Feminist Thought," *Social Problems* 33, no. 6 (1986): S17. ". . . Black women have been assaulted with a variety of externally-defined negative images designed to control assertive Black female behavior."

16. Karen K. Ho, "Crazy Rich Asians Is Going to Change Hollywood. It's About Time," *Time*, August 15, 2018, https://time.com/longform/crazy -rich-asians.

17. Golash-Boza, *Race and Racisms*, 142: "In the early years of the United States, when White settlers were endeavoring to take over Indian lands in the newly formed nation, Native Americans were most popularly depicted as savages . . ."

18. Golash-Boza, *Race and Racisms*, 151: "Raced and Classed Categories of Black Representations on Television" and p. 152: "Prominent Gendered Stereotypes by Racial/Ethnic Group"

19. Golash-Boza, *Race and Racisms*, 40: "One of the main proponents of eugenics was Madison Grant (1865–1937), a lawyer, historian, and physical anthropologist. In much of his work, including the 1916 book *The Passing of the Great Race*, Grant put forward the idea that Europe could be divided into three races: 'Nordics,' 'Alpines,' and 'Mediterraneans.' He forcefully argued that Nordics were the most fit of the three and that measures should be taken to ensure their racial purity and survival."

20. "'Head of Christ,' created in 1940, was reproduced more than 500 million times, appearing on church bulletins, calendars, posters, bookmarks, prayer cards, tracts, buttons, stickers and stationery." William Grimes, "The Man Who Rendered Jesus For the Age of Duplication," *The New York Times*, October 12, 1994, https://www .nytimes.com/1994/10/12/arts/the -man-who-rendered-jesus-for-the-age -of-duplication.html. See also Edward J. Blum and Paul Harvey, *The Color of Christ: The Son of God and the Saga of Race in America* (Chapel Hill: The

University of North Carolina Press, 2012), 208–209.

21. Mike Fillon, "The Real Face of Jesus," *Popular Science*, December 2002, https://www.popularmechanics.com /science/health/a234/1282186/.

22. "The practice of White actors playing characters of color came from minstrel shows, popularized in the United States in the 1830s and 1840s. The early performers were mainly Irish and Jewish . . ." Yuen, *Reel Inequality*, 9.

23. "American theater production embraced these productions and practices of yellowface casting as well; Voltaire's *L'Orphelin de la Chine* (1755) was adapted by Irish playwright Arthur Murphy into the *Orphan of China* (1759), first performed in New York in 1768." Josephine Lee, "Yellowface Performance: Historical and Contemporary Contexts," *Oxford Research Encyclopedias: Literature*, 2019, https://oxfordre.com /literature/view/10.1093 /acrefore/9780190201098.001.0001 /acrefore-9780190201098-e-834.

24. National Museum of African American History and Culture, "Blackface: The Birth of an American Stereotype," https://nmaahc.si.edu/blog-post /blackface-birth-american-stereotype.

25. "They took the opportunity they saw to vie for Whiteness in the United States and made use of the chance to register themselves as superior to the blacks to which they were once compared . . ." Treitler, *The Ethnic Project*, 73. "By distorting the features and culture of African Americans—including their looks, language, dance, deportment, and character—White Americans were able to codify *Whiteness* across class and geopolitical lines as its antithesis." National Museum of African American History and Culture, "Blackface: The Birth of An American Stereotype," n.d., https://nmaahc.si.edu/blog-post /blackface-birth-american-stereotype.

26. Becky Little, "Who Was Jim Crow?," *National Geographic*, August 6, 2015, https://www.nationalgeographic.com /news/2015/08/150806-voting-rights -act-anniversary-jim-crow-segregation -discrimination-racism-history/.

27. "In each instance, those facing scrutiny for blackface performances insist no malice or racial hatred was intended." National Museum of African American History and Culture, "Blackface: The Birth of An American Stereotype," https:// nmaahc.si.edu/blog-post/blackface -birth-american-stereotype. See also: Jennifer C. Mueller, Danielle Dirks, and Leslie Houts Picca, "Unmasking Racism: Halloween Costuming and Engagement of the Racial Other," *Qualitative Sociology* 30, no. 3 (2007): 315–335.

28. Historian Vincent Brown as quoted in *The Birth of a Movement: The Battle Against America's First Blockbuster*. Directed by Susan Gray and Bestor Cram. *PBS Independent Lens*, 2017. Note that Brown also describes *Birth of a Nation* as "the single most important American film in early cinema."

29. Rachel Janik, "'Writing History With Lightning': *The Birth of a Nation* at

100," *Time*. February 8, 2015, https://time.com/3699084/100-years-birth-of-a-nation.

30. "There was a reason, for instance, that *The Birth of a Nation* was originally released as *The Clansman* . . ." Kerri Greenidge, *Black Radical: The Life and Times of William Monroe Trotter* (New York: Liveright, 2020), 209.

31. Historian David Blight as quoted in *The Birth of a Movement*.

32. NPR. "Revisiting 'Birth of a Nation' in Today's America," *All Things Considered*, May 2, 2006, https://www.npr.org/transcripts/5377305. ". . . There is a sequence . . . during the reconstruction era and black men have overtaken this southern community, and one is eating chicken. Another takes off his shoe and props his barefoot onto a table. Another complains about the odor. I mean it's, for us today, we can't quite believe that this movie actually was actually made."

33. Thomas Doherty, "'The Birth of a Nation' at 100: 'Important, Innovative and Despicable,'" *The Hollywood Reporter*, February 7, 2015, https://www.hollywoodreporter.com/race/birth-a-nation-at-100-770620.

34. Historian Kerri Greenidge points out that *Birth of a Nation* "incited both angry boycotts and resurgence of the modern Ku Klux Klan." Greenidge, *Black Radical*, 207.

35. "Trotter and his supporters fomented a disturbance outside Tremont Theater, which resulted in ten arrests, including his own . . ." Greenidge, *Black Radical*, 212.

36. Greenidge, *Black Radical*, 212. See also Richard Brody, "The Black Activist Who Fought Against D.W. Griffith's 'The Birth of a Nation,'" *The New Yorker*, February 6, 2017, https://www.newyorker.com/culture/richard-brody/the-black-activist-who-fought-against-d-w-griffiths-the-birth-of-a-nation.

37. Roy Rosenzweig Center for History and New Media, "The Birth of a Nation and Black Protest," https://chnm.gmu.edu/episodes/the-birth-of-a-nation-and-black-protest. On Mary Childs Nerney and other White activists within the NAACP, see also Adam Fairclough, *Better Day Coming: Blacks and Equality, 1890–2000* (New York: Penguin, 2002), 72. "Thus during the NAACP's first two decades, a handful of Whites dominated the organization . . ."

38. American Social History Project/Center for Media and Learning (Graduate Center, CUNY) and the Roy Rosenzweig Center for History and New Media (George Mason University), "Reformer Jane Addams Critiques The Birth of a Nation," http://historymatters.gmu.edu/d/4994.

39. "Actors of color fare worse in lead roles . . ." Yuen, *Reel Inequality*, 21.

40. Yuen, *Reel Inequality*, 25.

41. Yuen, *Reel Inequality*, 71.

42. Brian Young, "Why I Won't Wear War Paint and Feathers in a Movie Again," *Time*, June 11, 2015, https://time.com/3916680/native-american-hollywood-film.

43. Ruha Benjamin, *Race After Technology* (Cambridge, UK: Polity Press. 2019) 9: "In a now classic study, computer scientist Latanya Sweeney examined how online search results associated

Black names with arrest records at a much higher rate than White names." See also Safiya Umoja Noble, *Algorithms of Oppression: How Search Engines Reinforce Racism* (New York: New York University Press, 2018).

44. Joy Buolamwini and Timnit Gebru, "Gender Shades: Intersectional Accuracy Disparities in Commercial Gender Classification," *Proceedings of Machine Learning Research* 81 (2018): 1–15.

45. André Brock, "'When Keeping It Real Goes Wrong': Resident Evil 5, Racial Representation, and Gamers," *Games and Culture* 6, no. 5 (2011): 429–452. For more resources on racism in gaming, see the following tweet thread where scholars and gamers generously replied to my request for research and writing on the subject: Crystal Fleming (@alwaystheself), "What's the best writing and analysis on racism within video games?," Twitter, July 13, 2020, https://twitter.com/alwaystheself /status/1282766201412780033?s = 20. I'm grateful to my former student Michael Mazza, who first brought racism in video games to my attention during my course on Racism and Ethnic Relations at Stony Brook.

46. Sandy Ong, "The Video Game Industry's Problem with Racial Diversity," *Newsweek*, October 13, 2016, https://www.newsweek .com/2016/10/21/video-games-race -black-protagonists-509328.html. Derek Manns, a developer, describes video game caricatures this way: "Like she's from this broken home. Or he's a rapper guy. Or he's poor, and his mom is on drugs, and his daddy's gone."

47. Kishonna L. Gray and David K. Leonard, "Introduction," in eds. Kishonna L. Gray and David K. Leonard, *Woke Gaming: Digital Challenges to Oppression and Social Injustice,* (Seattle: University of Washington Press, 2018), 9.

48. International Game Developers Association, "Developer Satisfaction Survey: Summary Report," 2019, https://s3-us-east-2.amazonaws .com/igda-website/wp-content /uploads/2020/01/29093706/IGDA -DSS-2019_Summary-Report_Nov-20 -2019.pdf 13.

49. Mark Muro, Alan Berube, and Jacob Whiton, "Black and Hispanic Underrepresentation in Tech: It's Time to Change the Equation," Brookings Institution, March 28, 2018, https:// www.brookings.edu/research/black -and-hispanic-underrepresentation-in -tech-its-time-to-change-the-equation.

50. Meg Anderson, "Where's the Color in Kids' Lit? Ask the Girl With 1,000 Books (and Counting)," *NPR: Morning Edition,* February 26, 2016, https://www.npr.org/sections /ed/2016/02/26/467969663/wheres -the-color-in-kids-lit-ask-the-girl -with-1-000-books-and-counting. See also Trey Mangum, *Shadow and Act,* August 25, 2020, https:// shadowandact.com/netflixs -bookmarks-celebrating-black-voices -with-marley-dias-drops-first-trailer.

51. "Abercrombie & Fitch removes 'Racist' T-shirts," *Chicago Tribune,* April 24, 2002, https://www.chicagotribune .com/news/ct-xpm-2002-04-24 -0204240012-story.html. See also: "Abercrombie & Fitch in Trouble,"

Vogue, April 23, 2002, https://www
.vogue.co.uk/article/abercrombie-and
-fitch-in-trouble.

52. Lauren Thomas, "H&M Slammed
as Racist for 'Monkey in the Jungle'
Hoodie," CNBC, January 8, 2018,
https://www.cnbc.com/2018/01/08
/hm-slammed-for-racist-monkey-in
-the-jungle-hoodie.html.

53. *The Problem with Apu,* directed by
Michael Melamedoff, truTV, 2017.

54. "In 'The Problem With Apu,'
Hari Kondabolu Discusses South
Asian Representation," *All
Things Considered*, November
17, 2017, https://www.npr
.org/2017/11/17/564936511/in-the
-problem-with-apu-hari-kondabolu
-discusses-south-asian-representation.

55. Dave Itzkoff, "Why Hank Azaria
Won't Play Apu on 'The Simpsons'
Anymore," *The New York Times,*
February 25, 2020, https://www
.nytimes.com/2020/02/25/arts
/hank-azaria-simpsons-apu.html.
See also: Sharareh Drury, "As 'The
Simpsons' Silences Apu, South
Asian Creatives Hope for Character's
Authentic Revival," *The Hollywood
Reporter,* February 26, 2020, https://
www.hollywoodreporter.com/news
/as-simpsons-silences-apu-south
-asian-creatives-hope-characters
-authentic-revival-1272222.

56. Vincent Schilling, "Native Actors Walk
Off Set of Adam Sandler Movie After
Insults to Women, Elders," *Indian
Country Today,* April 23, 2015, https://
indiancountrytoday.com/archive
/native-actors-walk-off-set-of-adam
-sandler-movie-after-insults-to-women
-elders-ow8Q1448EUenijZ2JV5alA.

See also Yuen, *Reel Inequality*, 129,
and Justin Wm. Moyer, "Adam
Sandler's 'Ridiculous 6' Insulted Some
Native Americans. Now It's Netflix's
'No. 1' Movie," *The Washington
Post*, January 7, 2016, https://www
.washingtonpost.com/news
/morning-mix/wp/2016/01/07/adam
-sandlers-ridiculous-6-insulted-some
-native-americans-now-its-netflixs-no
-1-movie.

57. "Outside of the Hollywood system,
Native American artists continually
wrote, produced, directed and acted
in their own short film productions.
In 1909, James Young Deer, of the
Nanticoke tribe, began his directing
career with *The Falling Arrow*. In
1966, several Navajos near Pine
Springs, Arizona, participated in an
anthropological study that produced
several short films known collectively
as *Navajos Film Themselves.* Victor
Masayesva, Jr., directed *Weaving* in
1981." Young, "Why I Won't Wear
War Paint."

58. Ho, "Crazy Rich Asians."

59. Abraham Riesman, "Is Miles Morales
Finally Getting His Due as Spider-
Man?," *Vulture*, December 14, 2018,
https://www.vulture.com/2018/12
/miles-morales-of-into-the-spider
-verse-the-race-problem.html. See
also *Shadow and Act*, February 24,
2019: "With 'Spider-Man: Into The
Spider-Verse' Peter Ramsey Is the
First Black Oscar Winner for
Animated Film," https://
shadowandact.com/with-spider-man
-into-the-spider-verse-peter-ramsey
-is-the-first-black-oscar-winner-for
-animated-film.

CHAPTER 8

1. Matt Ellentuck, "4 Minneapolis Cops Leave Minnesota Lynx Security Posts After Players Call for Justice and Peace," *SB Nation*, July 12, 2016, https://www.sbnation.com/2016/7/12/12160566/minneapolis-police-minnesota-lynx-wnba-protest.

2. Catherine E. Shoichet and Jill Martin, "Off-duty Cops Walk Out Over WNBA Players' Black Lives Matter Shirts," *CNN*, July 12, 2016, https://www.cnn.com/2016/07/12/us/wnba-minnesota-lynx-black-lives-matter-shirts.

3. Tim Hill, "Colin Kaepernick on Death Threats: If I'm Killed 'You've Proved My Point,'" *The Guardian*, September 21, 2016, https://www.theguardian.com/sport/2016/sep/20/colin-kaepernick-death-threats-national-anthem-protest-nfl.

4. Peter Dreier, "Half a Century Before Colin Kaepernick, Jackie Robinson Said, 'I Cannot Stand and Sing the Anthem,'" *The Nation*, July 18, 2019, https://www.thenation.com/article/archive/huac-jackie-robinson-paul-robeson/.

5. Harry Edwards, "Perspectives on Olympic Sport Politics: 1968–1984," *National Black Law Journal*, 9, no. 1 (1984): 38–50. Quote cited from page 38.

6. Dave Zirin, "Debunking the Myth that Sports and Politics Don't Overlap," *YouTube/The Nation*, August 1, 2011, https://www.youtube.com/watch?v=Fpd_4luxc0o.

7. Tyler Conway, "LeBron James Says He Will Not 'Shut Up and Dribble' in Response to Fox News Host," *Bleacher Report*, February 17, 2018, https://bleacherreport.com/articles/2760029-lebron-james-says-he-will-not-shut-up-and-dribble-in-response-to-fox-news-host.

8. See Harry Edwards, *The Revolt of the Black Athlete—50th Anniversary Edition* (Champaign, IL: University of Illinois Press, 2017), xxix: "And there was also this: since the onset of Jackie Robinson's tenure with the Brooklyn Dodgers, the media, both Negro and White, had propagated the notion that sport in America was evolving as an 'institution apart,' as an institution on a trajectory of racial equality and justice that contrasted starkly with the racist traditions of the society at large."

9. Dave Zirin, "Shut Up and Play? Patriotism, Jock Culture and the Limits of Free Speech," *The Nation*, May 4, 2011, https://www.thenation.com/article/archive/shut-and-play-patriotism-jock-culture-and-limits-free-speech.

10. Norman Gelb, "Francis Scott Key, the Reluctant Patriot," *Smithsonian Magazine*, September 2004, https://www.smithsonianmag.com/history/francis-scott-key-the-reluctant-patriot-180937178/.

11. Tom Goldman, "How Sports Met 'The Star-Spangled Banner,'" NPR, September 6, 2018, https://www.npr.org/2018/09/06/644991357/how-sports-met-the-star-spangled-banner.

12. Gillian Brockell, "The Ugly Reason 'The Star-Spangled Banner' Didn't Become Our National Anthem for a Century," *The Washington*

Post, October 18, 2020, https://
www.washingtonpost.com
/history/2020/10/18/star-spangled
-banner-racist-national-anthem.

13. Brockell, "The Ugly Reason."

14. The lyrics in question read: *"No refuge
could save the hireling and slave / From
the terror of flight or the gloom of the
grave, / And the star-spangled banner
in triumph doth wave /O'er the land
of the free and the home of the brave."*
See Brockell (2020) and Jon Schwarz,
"Colin Kapernick Is Righter Than
You Know: The National Anthem Is a
Celebration of Slavery." *The Intercept*,
August 28, 2016, https://theintercept
.com/2016/08/28/colin-kaepernick-is
-righter-than-you-know-the-national
-anthem-is-a-celebration-of-slavery.

15. Brockell, "The Ugly Reason."

16. Jefferson Morley and Jon Schwarz,
"More Proof the U.S. National Anthem
Has Always Been Tainted with
Racism," *The Intercept*, September
13, 2016, https://theintercept
.com/2016/09/13/more-proof-the-u
-s-national-anthem-has-always-been
-tainted-with-racism/.

17. Dave Zirin, *A People's History of Sports
in the United States: 250 Years of
Politics, Protest, People and Play*. (New
York: The New Press, 2008), 5.

18. Edwards, *The Revolt of the Black
Athlete*, 22: "Blacks were excluded
from White athletic clubs, so they
established their own. The reasons
given for the exclusion were the
same tired rationalizations and racist
cover-ups that are so prevalent today
in athletic circles. Some coaches felt
that their 'racially pure' White players
would not play beside a black man."

19. Note that before Walker, one other
mixed-race player is known to have
competed in major league baseball.
William Edward White played one
game in the major league in 1879.
However, unlike Walker, White hid his
African ancestry and identified himself
as White. See Andrew Lawrence,
"Moses Fleetwood Walker: Editor,
Author and Major League Baseball's
First Black Star," *The Guardian*,
February 26, 2021, https://www
.theguardian.com/sport/2021/feb/26
/moses-fleetwood-walker-baseball-first
-black-player-in-majors.

20. John Harris, "Moses Fleetwood Walker
Was the First African American to
Play Pro Baseball, Six Decades Before
Jackie Robinson," *The Undefeated*,
February 22, 2017, https://
theundefeated.com/features
/moses-fleetwood-walker-was-the-first
-african-american-to-play-pro-baseball
-six-decades-before-jackie-robinson.

21. John R. Husman, "Weldy Walker,"
Society for American Baseball
Research, n.d., https://sabr.org
/bioproj/person/weldy-walker.

22. Harris, "Moses Fleetwood Walker."

23. Benjamin Hill, "Walker's Interests
Were Far and Wide," *MiLB.com*,
February 18, 2008, https://www
.milb.com/news/moses-fleetwood
-walker-was-baseball-renaissance
-man-303457114.

24. Major Taylor Association, Inc., "Who
Was Major Taylor?," n.d., http://
majortaylorassociation.org/who.shtml;
See also: Lesa Cline-Ransome, *Major
Taylor: Champion Cyclist* (New York:
Atheneum Books for Young Readers,
2012); Michael Kranish, *The World's*

Fastest Man: The Extraordinary Life of Cyclist Major Taylor (New York: Scribner, 2019); NPR/Morning Edition, "Life of Black Cyclist Major Taylor Chronicled in New Book 'The World's Fastest Man,'" July 26, 2019, https://www.npr.org/2019/07/26/745521148/life-of-black-cyclist-major-taylor-chronicled-in-new-book-the-worlds-fastest-man.

25. "Shortly after I had won my very first race, that ten-mile event on the Indianapolis highways as a boy of thirteen . . ." Marshall W. Taylor, *The Fastest Bicycle Rider in the World: The Story of a Colored Boy's Indomitable Courage and Success Against Great Odds* (Worcester, MA: Wormley, 1928), 163. https://babel.hathitrust.org/cgi/pt?id=mdp.390150-10834771&view=1up&seq=11.

26. On his friendships with and support from Whites, Taylor wrote: "I wish to say that while I was sorely beset by a number of White riders in my racing days, I have also enjoyed the friendship of countless thousands of White men whom I class as among my closest friends. I made them in this country and all the foreign countries in which I competed. My personal observation and experiences indicate to me that while the majority of White people are considerate of my people, the minority are so bitter in their race prejudice that they actually overshadow the goodwill entertained for us by the majority." Taylor, *The Fastest Bicycle Rider*, 449.

27. "'We soon became the best of friends . . .'" Kranish, *The World's Fastest Man*, 24.

28. "One of the judges . . . used his official position of trust and honor in order to take an unfair advantage of me, simply because nature had decreed that the color of my skin should be black." Taylor, *The Fastest Bicycle Rider*, 156.

29. Major Taylor, "The Other Side," *The Bearings,* February 9, 1894, http://archive.org/details/bearings91894cycl/page/n82/mode/1up?view=theater.

30. Avery Yang, "Black History Month: Marshall 'Major' Taylor Made History as the World's Fastest Cyclist," *Sports Illustrated*, February 11, 2020, https://www.si.com/cycling/2020/02/11/black-history-month-major-taylor.

31. Taylor, *The Fastest Bicycle Rider*, 140.

32. John Bloom, *To Show What an Indian Can Do: Sports at Native American Boarding Schools* (Minneapolis: University of Minnesota Press, 2000), 7.

33. Nick Estes, "The U.S. Stole Generations of Indigenous Children to Open the West," *HighCountry News*, October 14, 2019, https://www.hcn.org/issues/51.17/indigenous-affairs-the-us-stole-generations-of-indigenous-children-to-open-the-west. See also Bloom: "They also saw their own optimism as symbolic of a benevolence they claimed to feel toward Indigenous people . . ." (xv) and Mary Annette Pember, "Death by Civilization," *The Atlantic*, March 8, 2019, https://www.theatlantic.com/education/archive/2019/03/traumatic-legacy-indian-boarding-schools/584293/.

34. Graham Lee Brewer, "Stickball: Indigenous Women Show Who's Got Game," *HighCountry News*,

September 10, 2019, https://www
.hcn.org/articles/tribal-affairs-stickball
-indigenous-women-show-whos-got
-game.

35. Bloom, *To Show What an Indian Can Do*, xii.

36. "Football and track teams that competed successfully allowed boarding school advocates to show that Indians could be successfully 'Americanized.'" Bloom, *To Show What an Indian Can Do*, 65.

37. "In subarctic and circumpolar cultures, the active involvement of Indian women in community life also extended to games and sporting activities . . ." Fabrice Delsahut and Thierry Terret, "First Nations Women, Games, and Sport in Pre- and Post-Colonial North America," *Women's History Review* 23, no. 6 (2014): 977.

38. Delsahut and Terret, "First Nations Women, Games, and Sport," 985.

39. Sally Jenkins, "Why Are Jim Thorpe's Olympic Records Still Not Recognized?," *Smithsonian Magazine*, July 2012, https://www.smithsonianmag.com /history/why-are-jim-thorpes-olympic -records-still-not-recognized-130986336. Emphasis added.

40. Note that Thorpe was later unjustly stripped of his medals due to accusations that he broke Olympic rules by playing semi-professional baseball. The decision has been characterized as motivated by racial discrimination and a campaign to restore his name resulted in the International Olympic Committee reinstating his medals. See Victor Mather, "The 100-Year Dispute for Jim Thorpe's Olympic Golds," *The New York Times*, December 9, 2020, https://www.nytimes .com/2020/12/09 /sports/olympics/jim-thorpe-olympic -golds.html: "A key piece of evidence in Thorpe's case, in the 1980s and today, is the regulations of the 1912 Games. Despite being told that there were no written rules, Florence Ridlon, an advocate for Thorpe, searched the Library of Congress in 1982 and eventually discovered them between two bookcases. They revealed that protests against gold medalists had to be made within 30 days; Thorpe's brief professional baseball career was not uncovered until six months after the Games." See also Jenkins, "Why Are Jim Thorpe's Olympic Records Still Not Recognized?"

41. Jesse Washington, "Jack Johnson, Still Unforgivable?," *The Undefeated*, December 29, 2016, https:// theundefeated.com/features/will -obama-pardon-heavyweight-boxing -champ-jack-johnson.

42. Washington, "Jack Johnson, Still Unforgivable?"

43. Kevin Mitchell, "Jack Johnson Was a Pioneer Who Gave Hope to Black Boxers Everywhere," *The Guardian*, July 3, 2010, https://www .theguardian.com /sport/blog/2010/jul/04/jack-johnson -pioneer-black-boxer.

44. Washington. "Jack Johnson, Still Unforgivable?"

45. Jeremy Schaap, "An Olympic Boycott That Almost Worked," *ESPN*, August 13, 2009, https://www.espn.com /olympics/news/story?id = 4396362.

46. Schaap, "An Olympic Boycott." See also Zirin, *A People's History of Sports*, 74–76.

47. For an overview of the atrocities of the Holocaust, see Yad Vashem. "What Was the Holocaust?," https://www.yadvashem.org/holocaust/about.html#learnmore. See also: United States Holocaust Memorial Museum, "The Nazi Olympics: African-American Athletes (Part 1)," *YouTube*, August 14, 2008, https://www.youtube.com/watch?v=56wEF2E_1SU.

48. Lonnae O'Neal, "Harry Edwards, a Giant of Sports Activism, Still Has People Shook," *The Undefeated*, October 15, 2018, https://theundefeated.com/features/harry-edwards-mexico-city-olympics-sports-activism-john-carlos-tommie-smith-1968. See also Michael Shapiro, "How Tommie Smith's 'Cry for Freedom' Sparked a Legacy of Athlete Activism," *Sports Illustrated*, August 12, 2020, https://www.si.com/olympics/2020/08/12/tommie-smith-john-carlos-1968-olympics-protest-athlete-activism, and Douglas Hartmann, "The Politics of Race and Sport: Resistance and Domination in the 1968 African American Olympic Protest Movement," *Ethnic and Racial Studies* 19, no. 3 (1996): 548–566.

49. Andrew Maraniss, "The Mexico City Olympics Protest and the Media," *The Undefeated*, October 15, 2018, https://theundefeated.com/features/mexico-city-olympics-protest-media-john-carlos-tommie-smith.

50. As sportswriter Dave Zirin notes: "Many see the iconic image and assume Norman was just a bystander to history, or as he would joke, 'the White guy.' But he was standing in full solidarity with Smith and Carlos, wearing a patch on his chest that reads, "Olympic Project for Human Rights." As Norman recalled to sportswriter Mike Wise, when he heard what Carlos and Smith were going to do he had to show his support. 'I couldn't see why a Black man wasn't allowed to drink out of the same water fountain or sit in the same bus or go to the same schools as a White guy. That was just social injustice that I couldn't do anything about from where I was, but I certainly abhorred it.'" See Dave Zirin, "Australian Government Will Issue Overdue Apology to 1968 Olympic Hero Peter Norman," *The Nation*, August 19, 2012, https://www.thenation.com/article/archive/australian-government-will-issue-overdue-apology-1968-olympic-hero-peter-norman/. The apartheid system known as "White Australia Policy" was legally established from 1901 through the 1960s. It began to be challenged and overturned beginning in 1966. See National Museum Australia, "End of White Australia Policy," https://www.nma.gov.au/defining-moments/resources/end-of-white-australia-policy. On Peter Norman's role in the protest, see Ted Widmer, "Why Two Black Athletes Raised Their Fists During the Anthem," *The New York Times*, October 16, 2018, https://www.nytimes.com/2018/10/16/opinion/why-smith-and-carlos-raised-their

-fists.html and John Carlos with Dave Zirin, *The John Carlos Story* (Chicago: Haymarket Books, 2011), 116–118. For a brief overview of the protest, see this Twitter thread (October 16, 2020) from the African American Policy Forum: https://twitter.com /AAPolicyForum/status /1317131482176040960?s = 20.

51. The boycott effort also targeted the African state of Rhodesia.

52. On the OPHR athletes' demands, see Carlos, *The John Carlos Story*, xii and 83.

53. "The Olympics: Boycotting South Africa," *Time*, March 8, 1968, http:// content.time.com/time/subscriber /article/0,33009,900012,00.html.

54. Youssef M. Ibrahim, "OLYMPICS; Olympics Committee Ends Its Ban On Participation by South Africa," *The New York Times*, July 10, 1991, https://www.nytimes .com/1991/07/10/sports/olympics -olympics-committee-ends-its-ban-on -participation-by-south-africa.html.

55. Carlos, *The John Carlos Story*, 121.

56. David Davis, "Olympic Athletes Who Took a Stand," *Smithsonian Magazine*, August 2008, https:// www.smithsonianmag.com/articles /olympic-athletes-who-took-a -stand-593920/. According to Davis, "Smith and Carlos returned home to a wave of opprobrium—they were 'black-skinned storm troopers,' in the words of Brent Musburger, who would gain fame as a TV sportscaster but was then a columnist for the *Chicago American* newspaper—and anonymous death threats."

57. As of 2020, Tommie Smith was *still* receiving death threats and racist hate speech—over 50 years after the protest! Paul Kasabian, "Tommie Smith Says He Still Receives Death Threats over 1968 Olympics Protest," *Bleacher Report*, July 1, 2020, https://bleacherreport .com/articles/2898535-tommie-smith -says-he-still-receives-death-threats -over-1968-olympics-protest.

58. Carlos, *The John Carlos Story*, 123.

59. Dave Zirin, "Australian Government Will Issue Overdue Apology to 1968 Olympic Hero Peter Norman," *The Nation*, August 19, 2012, https:// www.thenation.com/article/archive /australian-government-will-issue -overdue-apology-1968-olympic-hero -peter-norman/.

60. Rupert Cornwell, "Great Olympic Friendships: John Carlos, Peter Norman and Tommie Smith—Divided by Their Colour, United by the Cause," *The Independent*, August 5, 2016, https://www.independent.co.uk /sport/olympics/rio-2016-olympic -friendships-john-carlos-peter-norman -tommie-smith-mexico-city-1968 -black-power-salute-7166771.html.

61. Cary Chow, "Wataru Misaka Helped Break Pro Basketball's Color Barrier; You Should Know His Name," *The Undefeated*, November 29, 2019, https://theundefeated.com/features /wataru-misaka-broke-pro-basketballs -color-barrier-you-should-know-his -name. Note this caveat regarding Misaka's integration of professional basketball: "This does not include the accomplishments of the Professional Basketball League, established in 1937, which merged with the BAA

to form the NBA in 1949. The NBA recognizes BAA statistics in its history, but limited PBL, which featured African American players like Dolly King."

62. Ohm Youngmisuk, "Jeremy Lin Says Racist Remarks He Heard from Opponents Were Worse in NCAA than NBA," *ESPN*, May 10, 2017, https://www.espn.com/nba/story /_/id/19353394/jeremy-lin-brooklyn -nets-says-heard-racist-remarks-more -frequently-college-nba.

63. Cynthia Silva, "Basketball Player Who Called Jeremy Lin 'Coronavirus' Identified," *NBC News*, March 16, 2021, https://www.nbcnews.com /news/asian-america/basketball -player-called-jeremy-lin-coronavirus -identified-rcna421. See also AJ Willingham, "Toronto Raptors' Jeremy Lin Is Now the First Asian American to Be Crowned an NBA Champ," *CNN*, June 14, 2019, https://www .cnn.com/2019/06/14/sport/toronto -raptors-nba-jeremy-lin-finals-asian -american-trnd/index.html.

64. Richard Lapchick, "Racism Reported in Sports Decreasing but Still Prevalent," *ESPN*, February 19, 2020, https://www.espn.com/espn/story /_/id/28738336/racism-reported -sports-decreasing-prevalent.

65. Bryan Armen Graham, "High School Announcer Caught by Hot Mic Blames Racist Outburst on High Blood Sugar," *The Guardian*, March 12, 2021, https://www.theguardian.com /sport/2021/mar/12/oklahoma-high -school-basketball-racial-slur.

66. These examples are direct quotes. Bob Cook, "What's Behind All the Racism at Youth Sports Events?," *Forbes*, February 9, 2018, https://www.forbes .com/sites/bobcook/2018/02/09 /whats-behind-all-the-racism-at-youth -sports-events/?sh=212527d82b85.

67. Kalen Goodluck, "Native American Athletes and Fans Face Ongoing Racism," *High Country News*, April 10, 2019, https://www.hcn.org /issues/51.7/tribal-affairs-native -american-athletes-and-fans-face -ongoing-racism. According to Goodluck, "[from] 2008 to 2018, there have been at least 52 reported incidents across the U.S. of racial harassment directed at Native American athletes, coaches and fans, according to data compiled from news articles, federal reports and court documents . . ."

68. Perry Bacon Jr. and Neil Paine, "A 5-Part Plan To Fix the NFL's Coaching Diversity Problem," *FiveThirtyEight*, January 29, 2020, https://fivethirtyeight.com /features/a-5-part-plan-to-fix-the -nfls-coaching-diversity-problem. For an overview of diversity statistics in the NFL, see Richard E. Lapchick, "Making Waves of Change—The 2020 Racial and Gender Report Card—National Football League," The Institute for Diversity and Ethics in Sports, https://43530132-36e9-4f52 -811a-182c7a91933b.filesusr.com /ugd/326b62_b84c731ad8dc4e62 ba330772b283c9e3.pdf.

69. In *The Revolt of the Black Athlete*, Harry Edwards writes that: "At most White schools, certain positions are reserved exclusively for Whites. Take the position of quarterback. You could count the number of quarterbacks

who have played intercollegiate football for predominantly White colleges without taking off your shoes . . . Many coaches and athletic establishment members feel that Blacks lack the necessary intellectual equipment to become quarterbacks, that they will be unable to remember plays or formations and pick apart a defense . . ." Edwards, *The Revolt of the Black Athlete*, 27.

70. There are some African Americans—including Venus and Serena Williams—who own a minority share of an NFL team, but none that own a majority stake. Associated Press. "Williams sisters buy into Dolphins group," *ESPN*, August 25, 2009, https://www.espn.com/nfl/news/story?id = 4422313.

71. For a summary of the study, see The Football Players Health Study at Harvard University, "Study Points to Health Disparities Among Former NFL Players," August 11, 2020, https://footballplayershealth.harvard.edu/about/news/study-points-to-health-disparities-among-former-nfl-players, and HMS Communications, "After the Game Is Over," *Harvard Gazette*, August 12, 2020, https://news.harvard.edu/gazette/story/2020/08/study-points-to-health-disparities-among-former-nfl-players. Andrea L. Roberts, Herman A. Taylor, Alicia J. Whittington, Ross D. Zafonte, Frank E. Speizer, Alvaro Pascual-Leone, Aaron Baggish, and Marc G. Weisskopf, "Race in Association with Physical and Mental Health Among Former Professional American-Style Football Players: Findings from the Football Players Health Study," *Annals of Epidemiology* 51 (2020): 48–52.

72. Jackie Mansky and Maya Wei-Haas, "The Rise of the Modern Sportswoman," *Smithsonian Magazine*, August 18, 2016, https://www.smithsonianmag.com/science-nature/rise-modern-sportswoman-180960174.

73. Bonnie D. Ford and Alyssa Roenigk, "How Dianne Durham, Bela Karolyi's First National Champion, Paved the Way for Black Gymnasts," *ESPN*, July 18, 2020, https://www.espn.com/olympics/story/_/id/29469312/how-dianne-durham-bela-karolyi-first-national-champion-paved-way-black-gymnasts.

74. "Throughline: On the Shoulders of Giants," February 14, 2019, *NPR*, https://www.npr.org/transcripts/693878396. See also: Arlisha R. Norwood, "Wilma Rudolph (1940–1994)," National Women's History Museum, n.d., https://www.womenshistory.org/education-resources/biographies/wilma-rudolph.

75. Scott N. Brooks and Aram Goudsouzian, "Remembering Wilma Rudolph, the 'Queen of the Olympics,'" *Black Perspectives*, October 2, 2020, https://www.aaihs.org/remembering-wilma-rudolph-the-queen-of-the-olympics.

76. Andrea Canales, "Latinas Are Embracing Softball," *ESPN*, March 28, 2017, https://www.espn.com/blog/onenacion/post/_/id/7216/latinas-are-embracing-softball.

77. Graham Hays, "Aleshia Ocasio Uses Athletes Unlimited Platform to Make a

Difference in the World Around Her," *ESPN*, September 26, 2020, https://www.espn.com/olympics/story/_/id/29962670/aleshia-ocasio-uses-athletes-unlimited-platform-make-difference-world-her.

78. André Wheeler, "WNBA Star Natasha Cloud Is the Latest Celeb to Have a Secret Wedding," *Them*, March 12, 2021, https://www.them.us/story/wnba-star-natasha-cloud-latest-celeb-have-secret-gay-wedding.

79. Nick Selbe, "Jonathan Irons, Man Helped by Maya Moore After Wrongful Conviction, Freed From Prison," *Sports Illustrated*, July 2, 2020, https://www.si.com/wnba/2020/07/02/maya-moore-jonathan-irons-released-from-prison-wrongful-conviction.

80. Sean Gregory, "Maya Moore Was One of the WNBA's Biggest Stars. Then She Stepped Away to Fight for Justice," *Time*, March 5, 2020, https://time.com/5793243/maya-moore-basketball-justice. See also Blayne Alexander and Katie Wall, "WNBA Legend Maya Moore Leaves Basketball to Fight Prisoner's Conviction," *NBC News*, September 30, 2019, https://www.nbcnews.com/news/us-news/wnba-legend-maya-moore-leaves-basketball-fight-prisoner-s-conviction-n1060156.

CHAPTER 9

1. Sophie Lewis, "Billions of People Are Under Coronavirus Lockdowns—and Now the Upper Crust of the Earth Is Shaking Less," *CBS News*, April 3, 2020, https://www.cbsnews.com/news/coronavirus-lockdowns-earth-shaking-less-seismic-noise.

2. Nina Lakhani, "Exclusive: Indigenous Americans Dying from Covid at Twice the Rate of White Americans," *The Guardian*, February 4, 2021, https://www.theguardian.com/us-news/2021/feb/04/native-americans-coronavirus-covid-death-rate. See also Rashawn Ray, Jane Fran Morgan, Lydia Wileden, Samantha Elizondo, and Destiny Wiley-Yancy, "Examining and Addressing COVID-19 Racial Disparities in Detroit," Brookings Institution, March 2, 2021, https://www.brookings.edu/research/examining-and-addressing-covid-19-racial-disparities-in-detroit.

3. Maria Caspani and Jonathan Allen, "Coronavirus Deadliest in New York City's Black and Latino Neighborhoods, Data Shows," *Reuters*, May 18, 2020, https://www.reuters.com/article/us-health-coronavirus-new-york-deaths/coronavirus-deadliest-in-new-york-citys-black-and-latino-neighborhoods-data-shows-idUSKBN22U32A.

4. "Imagine if every single day a jumbo jet loaded with 230 African American passengers took off into the sky, reached a cruising altitude, then crashed to the ground . . ." Dorothy Roberts, *Fatal Invention: How Science, Politics and Big Business Re-Create Race in the Twenty-first Century* (New York: The New Press, 2011), 81.

5. "American Indians, African Americans and Hispanics are about twice as likely as Whites to be diagnosed with diabetes." Golash-Boza, *Race and Racisms*, 352. See also Golash-Boza,

p. 350: "African-Americans do not experience the same health gains as Whites do by virtue of an increase in socioeconomic status . . ."

6. "The previously cited incidents involving R. W. and Cho raise the issue of Asian American mental health in a dramatic way . . ." Rosalind S. Chou and Joe R. Feagin, *The Myth of the Model Minority: Asian Americans Facing Racism* (New York: Routledge, 2016), 21.

7. Elise Gould and Valerie Wilson, "Black Workers Face Two of the Most Lethal Preexisting Conditions for Coronavirus—Racism and Economic Inequality," Economic Policy Institute, June 1, 2020, https://www.epi.org/publication/black-workers-covid.

8. Whitney Laster Pirtle, "Racial Capitalism: A Fundamental Cause of Novel Coronavirus (COVID-19) Pandemic Inequities in the United States," *Health Education & Behavior.* 47, no. 4 (2020): 504–508. https://journals.sagepub.com/doi/full/10.1177/1090198120922942. See also Camara P. Jones, "Systems of Power, Axes of Inequity Parallels, Intersections, Braiding the Strands," *Medical Care* 52, no. 10, Suppl. 3: S71–S75.

9. American Society for Microbiology, "Biographies: Kizzmekia S. Corbett, Ph.D.," n.d., https://asm.org/Biographies/Kizzmekia-S-Corbett,-Ph-D.

10. Nidhi Subbaraman, "This COVID-Vaccine Designer Is Tackling Vaccine Hesitancy—in Churches and on Twitter," *Nature*, February 11, 2021, https://www.nature.com/articles/d41586-021-00338-y.

11. Masood Farivar, "Anti-Asian Hate Crime Crosses Racial and Ethnic Lines," *VOA News*, March 24, 2021.

12. Riché Richardson, "Can We Please, Finally, Get Rid of 'Aunt Jemima'?," *The New York Times*, June 24, 2015, https://www.nytimes.com/roomfordebate/2015/06/24/besides-the-confederate-flag-what-other-symbols-should-go/can-we-please-finally-get-rid-of-aunt-jemima. See also Elisabeth Buchwald, "Aunt Jemima, Uncle Ben's, Cream of Wheat, Mrs. Butterworth's Reveal Plans to Rebrand: A Look Back at Their Racist Origins," *MarketWatch*, June 21, 2020, https://www.marketwatch.com/story/with-aunt-jemima-and-uncle-ben-poised-to-disappear-from-american-kitchens-a-look-back-at-their-racist-origins-2020-06-17. Buchwald writes: "'The Aunt Jemima caricature was a product of the White imagination and the minstrel shows of 19th-Century America,' said Gregory Smithers, a history professor at Virginia Commonwealth University. "'Aunt Jemima was also part of the 'blackface' tradition that, in the decades after the Civil War, harkened back to a simpler time of plantations and 'happy slaves.'"

13. "Hope Is a Discipline: Mariame Kaba on Dismantling the Carceral State," *Intercepted*, March 17, 2021, https://theintercept.com/2021/03/17/intercepted-mariame-kaba-abolitionist-organizing.

14. According to Cook and Hegtvedt, "equity is typically defined as the equivalence of the outcome" (218).

See Karen S. Cook and Karen A. Hegtvedt, "Distributive Justice, Equity, and Equality," *Annual Review of Sociology* 9, no. 1 (1983): 217–241. Race equity, more specifically, can also be defined as "a state in which all children have the same opportunity to reach the potential we know they have." See The Annie E. Casey Foundation, "Embracing Equity. Race Equity and Inclusion Action Guide," http://www.aecf.org/resources/race-equity-and-inclusion-action-guide.

15. Amy Sun, "Equality Is Not Enough: What the Classroom Has Taught Me About Justice," *Everyday Feminism*, September 16, 2014, https://everydayfeminism.com/2014/09/equality-is-not-enough/.

16. "Program Transcript—RACE: The Power of an Illusion, Episode 3," PBS, https://www.pbs.org/race/000_About/002_04-about-03-01.htm. Emphasis added.

17. Dr. Martin Luther King Jr., *A Gift of Love: Sermons from Strength to Love and Other Preachings* (Boston: Beacon Press, 2012), 40.

18. Martin Luther King Jr., and Cornel West, *The Radical King* (Boston: Beacon Press, 2014), 50.

19. Alisha Haridasani Gupta, "A Teacher Held a Famous Racism Exercise in 1968. She's Still at It," *The New York Times*, July 4, 2020, https://www.nytimes.com/2020/07/04/us/jane-elliott-anti-racism-blue-eyes-brown-eyes.html.

20. ". . . I learned that only Blacks' presence in a sport could be explained by biological characteristics, and even their absence from certain sports could be attributed to their physical capacities (e.g., lack of body fat to swim). When Whites or other groups were at issue, however, culture replaced biology entirely as the most plausible explanation for the racial makeup of professional sports leagues. In contrast, fewer than half of the students thought cultural traditions could explain Blacks' football participation." Ann Morning, *The Nature of Race: How Scientists Think and Teach About Human Difference* (Berkeley: University of California Press, 2011), 169.

21. Ben Carrington, a scholar of race, argues that sports "played a central role in popularizing notions of absolute biological difference." Ben Carrington, *Race, Sport and Politics: The Sporting Black Diaspora* (London: SAGE, 2010).

22. Sociologist Harry Edwards points out that African Americans are a mixed population. "The fact of the matter is that our best sociological, genetic, and demographical knowledge indicates that the genetic makeup of blacks in America is at least 35% White, not counting genetic influences from various other so-called racial groupings." Harry Edwards, "The Sources of the Black Athlete's Superiority," *The Black Scholar* 3, no. 3 (1971): 32–41 (38). In *The Nature of Race*, Ann Morning makes a similar point: "In my college interviews, blacks figured as an anomaly, uniquely designated by students as physically a group apart—a perception that is quite striking given African Americans' mixed ancestry as well

as the common African origins of our entire species" (170).

23. In his protest speech against the Vietnam War, Dr. King said: ". . . I was increasingly compelled to see the war as an enemy of the poor and to attack it as such." Martin Luther King Jr. 1964. "Beyond Vietnam: A Time to Break Silence," *King Encyclopedia*. n.d., http://kingencyclopedia.stanford .edu/encyclopedia/encyclopedia/enc _beyond_vietnam_4_april_1967.

24. Li Cohen, "'We're Not Just Relics of the Past': How #NativeTikTok Is Preserving Indigenous Cultures and Inspiring a Younger Generation," *CBS News*, January 28, 2021, https://www .cbsnews.com/news/nativetiktok -is-preserving-and-showcasing -indigenous-culture. See also: @the_land, November 29, 2020, TikTok: https://www.tiktok.com/@the_land /video/6900688035743108354.

25. Michael Williams, "How Ray Hal-britter's Rise Helped the Fight Against Native American Mascots in Sports," *The Undefeated*, January 8, 2021, https://theundefeated.com/features /ray-halbritter-helped-fight-against -native-american-mascots-in-sports/.

26. Sean Kirst, "Retire 'Redskins'? An Upstate High School Student Searched Her Heart, and Said 'Yes,'" Syracuse .com, October 8, 2013, https://www .syracuse.com/kirst/2013/10/dump _redskins_an_upstate_high.html. See also: Mike Freeman, "Why Dan Snyder Won't Relent on 'Redskins,' and Why I Did," *Bleacher Report*, June 10, 2014, https://bleacherreport.com /articles/2088756-why-dan-snyder-wont -relent-on-redskins-and-why-i-did.

27. Leeanne Root, "Oneida Nation Donates $10,000 to Cooperstown School for Mascot Change," *Indian Country Today*, September 13, 2018, https://indiancountrytoday.com /archive/oneida-nation-donates -10000-to-cooperstown-school-for -mascot-change. Oneida Indian Nation, Change the Mascot Symposium Remarks by Cooperstown School, *YouTube*, October 15, 2013, https://www.youtube.com /watch?v = rB3ThdMq0k4

28. Anthony Castrovince, "Cleveland Indians to Change Team Name," *MLB .com*, December 14, 2020, https:// www.mlb.com/news/cleveland -indians-team-name-change.

29. Hayley Munguia, "The 2,128 Native American Mascots People Aren't Talking About," September 5, 2014, https://fivethirtyeight.com /features/the-2128-native-american -mascots-people-arent-talking -about/. See also Hope Allchin, "Hundreds of Schools Are Still Using Native Americans as Team Mascots," *FiveThirtyEight*, October 12, 2020, https://fivethirtyeight.com /features/hundreds-of-schools-are -still-using-native-americans-as-team -mascots/.

30. Research suggests that most Native people who are involved with their tribal nations oppose the use of these mascots. IllumiNative, an advocacy group, explains that racist mascots contribute to the oppression of Indigenous people. IllumiNative, "IllumiNative & Not in Our Honor. Super Bowl LV Change the Name Social Media Toolkit,"

https://illuminatives.org/wp-content
/uploads/2018/04/Super-Bowl
-LV-Social-Media-Kit.pdf?x18008.
Stephanie A. Fryberg, Arianne E.
Eason, Laura M. Brady, Nadia Jessop,
and Julisa J. Lopez, "Unpacking the
Mascot Debate: Native American
Identification Predicts Opposition to
Native Mascots," *Social Psychological
and Personality Science* 12, no. 1
(2021): 3–13. See also Jared Wadley,
"Study Shows Much Opposition to
Native American Mascots, Names,"
*University of Michigan—The University
Record*, February 6, 2020, https://
record.umich.edu/articles/study
-opposition-high-to-native-american
-mascots-names.

31. Fryberg et. al.: "Exposure to American
Indian mascot images has a negative
impact on American Indian high
school and college students' feelings of
personal and community worth, and
achievement-related possible selves."
American Psychological Association.
"Stephanie Fryberg, Ph.D.—Featured
Psychologist," n.d., https://www
.apa.org/pi/oema/resources/ethnicity
-health/psychologists/stephanie
-fryberg. "American Indian students
also reported lower personal and
community worth when they
are exposed to other common
characterizations of American Indians
(i.e., Disney's *Pocahontas* and negative
stereotypes such as high alcoholism,
school dropout, and suicide rates)
. . ." (215–216). Stephanie A. Fryberg,
Hazel R. Markus, Daphna Oyserman,
and Joseph M. Stone, "Of Warrior
Chiefs and Indian Princesses: The
Psychological Consequences of

American Indian Mascots," *Basic
and Applied Social Psychology*
30, no. 3 (2008): 208–218. Anna
Purna Kambhampaty, "The Deep
History—and Troubling Impact—of
Sports Teams Using Native American
Mascots," *Time*, July 14, 2020,
https://time.com/5866481
/native-american-mascots. American
Psychological Association, "APA
Resolution Recommending the
Immediate Retirement of American
Indian Mascots, Symbols, Images, and
Personalities by Schools, Colleges,
Universities, Athletic Teams, and
Organizations," 2005, https://www
.apa.org/about/policy/mascots
.pdf. "Can a Mascot Really Cause
Psychological Harm?," *Tell Me More*,
November 12, 2013, https://www.npr
.org/transcripts/244767646.

32. Many people have compared social
justice and equity work to a relay
race—and for good reason! The basic
idea is that the work of building a
more just society is collective and
ongoing. For example, in describing
the impact of her book, *The New
Jim Crow*, Michelle Alexander states:
"To see others take it and run with
it in their own way and carry the
work forward, it's almost like a relay
race handing off so that this work
can continue." See June Christian,
"A Conversation with Michelle
Alexander," *Learning for Justice*,
no. 48, Fall 2014. https://www
.learningforjustice.org/magazine/fall
-2014/a-conversation-with-michelle
-alexander.

33. Christopher Ingraham, "Three-
Quarters of Whites Don't Have Any

Non-White Friends," *The Washington Post*, August 25, 2014, https://www .washingtonpost.com/news/wonk /wp/2014/08/25/three-quarters-of -whites-dont-have-any-non-white -friends.

34. Brittany Wong, "Why We Need More Close Interracial Friendships (and Why We're Bad at Them)," September 4, 2020, https://www.huffpost.com /entry/close-interraacial-friendships _l_5f5122c8c5b6946f3eaed704.

35. For suggestions on how to recognize and combat racial stereotypes in the media, see: Amanda Sharples and Elizabeth Page-Gould, "How to Avoid Picking Up Prejudice from the Media," *Greater Good Magazine*, September 7, 2016, https://greatergood.berkeley .edu/article/item/how_to_avoid _picking_up_prejudice_from_media.

36. See Leslie Picca and Joe Feagin, *Two-Faced Racism: Whites in the Backstage and Frontstage* (London: Routledge, 2007), 70.

37. For resources on bystander training, check out HollaBack! "Bystander Intervention Training," https://www .ihollaback.org/bystander-resources.

38. "Confronting the Whitewashing of Disability: Interview with #DisabilityTooWhite Creator Vilissa Thompson," *Huff Post*, June 28, 2016, https://www.huffpost .com/entry/confronting-the -Whitewash_b_10574994. See also: "Disability Visibility Project—About," https://disabilityvisibilityproject.com /about.

39. Homa Khaleeli, "#SayHerName: why Kimberlé Crenshaw Is Fighting for Forgotten Women," *The Guardian*, May 30, 2016, https://www .theguardian.com/lifeandstyle/2016 /may/30/sayhername-why-kimberle -crenshaw-is-fighting-for-forgotten -women.

40. John Rogers, "Energizing the Civic Engagement of Youth from Immigrant Families: Veronica Terriquez," UCLA Center X, June 22, 2017, https:// centerx.gseis.ucla.edu/energizing -the-civic-engagement-of-youth -from-immigrant-families-veronica -terriquez.

41. Aria Zapata, "Voices from the Valley," September 27, 2018. Vimeo. https:// vimeo.com/292235794. See also: "Youth Perspectives: The Youth Are Engaged and Ready to Vote," *Kern Sol News*, October 15, 2018, https://southkernsol .org/2018/10/15/youth-perspectives-the -youth-are-engaged-and-ready-to-vote.

42. The National Coalition of Blacks for Reparations in America, "About N'COBRA," https://www .ncobraonline.org/about-ncobra. NDN Collective, "LAND BACK Update: From Launch to Looking Forward," October 28, 2020, https:// ndncollective.org/landback-updates -from-launch-to-looking-forward.

43. On the Combahee River Collective, see Keeanga-Yamahtta Taylor, ed., *How We Get Free: Black Feminism and the Combahee River Collective* (Chicago: Haymarket Books, 2016). On the community health programs created by the Black Panthers, see Olivia Waxman, "With Free Medical Clinics and Patient Advocacy, the Black Panthers Created a Legacy in Community Health That Still Exists Amid COVID-19," *Time*, February 25,

2021, https://time.com/5937647/black-panther-medical-clinics-history-school-covid-19. On the Young Lords' activism and violent decline, see Ed Morales, "The Roots of Organizing," *The Nation*, March 24, 2020, https://www.thenation.com/article/culture/young-lords-radical-history-johanna-fernandez-review.

44. Mariame Kaba, "Yes, We Mean Literally Abolish the Police," *The New York Times*, June 12, 2020, https://www.nytimes.com/2020/06/12/opinion/sunday/floyd-abolish-defund-police.html.

45. Kaba, *We Do This 'Til We Free Us*, 149–150.

46. Kendra Yoshinaga, "Babies of Color Are Now the Majority, Census Says," *NPR*, July 1, 2016, https://www.npr.org/sections/ed/2016/07/01/484325664/babies-of-color-are-now-the-majority-census-says. William H. Frey, "Less Than Half of US Children Under 15 Are White, Census Shows," Brookings Institution, June 24, 2019, https://www.brookings.edu/research/less-than-half-of-us-children-under-15-are-White-census-shows.

47. Eileen Shanahan, "Women Organize for Political Power," *The New York Times*, July 11, 1971, https://www.nytimes.com/1971/07/11/archives/women-organize-for-political-power-200-women-organize-for-political.html.

INDEX

E

economy
  slavery and, 49, 51–52
  structural racism and, 17, 21–24
education, 24, 62
  learning and, 175–76
  racism in, 91–92
Edwards, Harry, 127, 142
Elliott, Jane, 11
employment, 24, 117
Enlightenment, xi, xvi
environmental racism, xii
equity, 159–60
ethnicity
  racial identity and, xiii–xvi, 26–27
  religion and, xiv
European ethnicity, 26–27
extremism, 13–14, 94–95

F

family, 2
Floyd, George, 156, *156*
founding fathers, 24–25
Fredrickson, George, 48, 70
freedom, 24–25, 48, 56–60, 62–63
Fryberg, Stephanie, 166

G

Galicia, Francisco, 77
Gebru, Timnit, 116
gender, 103–5, 116, 137, 171–72
genocide, 37. *See also* Indigenous genocide
Geronimo, 41–42
GI Bill, 22
Goodman, Alan, 161
Gray, Kishonna, 116

The Greatest Showman (film), 29–31
Griffith, D. W., 110, 112

H

Haitian Revolution, 59–60
Hamer, Fannie Lou, 176
Hartman, Saidiya, 60, 64
health, 148–49, 152–56
hero portrayals, *3*, 3–5, 27, 98–101, 116
Heth, Joice, 30–31
Holocaust, xv, *xv*, 139–41
Homestead Act (1862), 17–18, 41
hope, 157–58
housing, xii, 18, 20–23

I

immigration
  activism, 79–80, 173–74
  citizenship and, 68–71, 73–80
  Dreamers and, 79–80, *80*
  exclusion, deportation, and, 75–77,
    80
  politics and, 76–80
  racism and, 70–71, 73–80
  violence and, 76–77
Immigration Act (1917), 74
Incidents in the Life of a Slave Girl
    (Jacobs), 55–56
Independence Day, 56–58
Indian Americans, 119–20
Indian Removal Act (1830), 25, 40–41
Indigenous genocide
  colonization and, 33–45
  politics and, 39–42
  religion and, 28, 38
  white supremacy and, xvi–xvii, 25,
    27–29, 34–45

racism in, 3–7, 77, 99–102
social, 117–18, 164
white supremacy in, 29–31
Mexico, 68, 75–77
Middle Passage, 51–53
minstrel shows, 107–9, *109*
Misaka, Wataru, 145
Moore, Maya, 123, 151
moral beliefs, 84
Morning, Ann, 162–63

N

national anthem, 129–31, 141–43
National Association for the Advance-
    ment of Colored People (NAACP),
    112–13, 140
Naturalization Act (1790), 69–70
Nazis, xv, 13–14, 26, 139–41, 143
Nixon, Richard, 92–93
Norman, Peter, 141–44

O

Obama, Barack, 13, 23, 25
Ocasio, Aleshia, 151
Oliver, Melvin, 161
Olympics, 140–44, 149–50
On This Site (Dennis), 45
Ozawa, Takao, 74–75

P

Page Act (1875), 74
Persico, Claudia, xii
police brutality, 44, 81–84, 87–88, 90–91,
    96–97, 122–23, 156–57
politics
    antiracism and, xxv, 172–75

immigration and, 76–80
Indigenous genocide and, 39–42
wealth and, 22
white supremacy and, 19–22, 24–26
post-traumatic slave syndrome, 61
poverty, 15–16, 20–23
Power California, 80
power relations
    racial images and, 102–5
    systemic racism and, xii–xvi
    white supremacy and, 14–16

R

racial gaps, 16–24
    in criminal justice system, 90–92
    in health, 148–49, 152–56
racial identity, xx–xxi
    ethnicity and, xiii–xvi, 26–27
    religion and, xiv–xv
    representation and, 113–21
racial images
    antiracism and reimagining, 110–11,
        113–21
    of Asian people, 104–5, 107–8, *108*
    beauty and, 100–101
    of Black women, *5*, 5–6, 103–4
    cartoons and caricatures, 5, 6, 107–9,
        118–20
    hero portrayals and, *3*, 3–5, 27,
        98–101, 116
    Latinx portrayals and, 77, 99–100, 104
    power and representations in, 102–5
    racial stereotypes and, 102–6, 113–16,
        119–20
    racist cinema and, 5–6, 99–102,
        110–14, 119–21
    religion and, 105–7
    throughout history, 105–7
    of today, 113–21
racial labels, x–xii, xvi, 8–10, 15, 26